DATE DUE

			Printed in USA.

Dialogue and History

Constructing South India, 1795–1895

Eugene F. Irschick

UNIVERSITY OF CALIFORNIA PRESS
Berkeley · Los Angeles · London

University of California Press
Berkeley and Los Angeles, California

University of California Press, Ltd.
London, England

© 1994 by
The Regents of the University of California

Library of Congress Cataloging-in-Publication Data

Irschick, Eugene F.
    Dialogue and history : constructing South
India, 1795–1895 / Eugene F. Irschick.
        p.   cm.
    Includes bibliographical references and index.
    ISBN 0-520-08404-7 (alk. paper). —
    ISBN 0-520-08405-5 (pbk. : alk. paper)
    1. India, South—History.   I. Title.
DS484.7.I77 1994
954',8031—dc20   93-10238
                                                          CIP

Printed in the United States of America
9 8 7 6 5 4 3 2 1

Contents

Maps and Tables

Preface

This book is largely based on colonial archives located either in Madras or in London. Since the evidence I used was filtered through a series of colonial lenses, even the petitions of ordinary people were transcribed for inclusion in what ultimately became part of revenue and other records of the English East India Company. Moreover, the presentation here seeks to show how structures of meaning and institutions are cultural products negotiated by a large number of persons from every level of society in a given place and time. It therefore presumes that a single individual cannot produce meaning, a cultural development, or an institution by herself or himself. Nonetheless, the documents used here have perforce focused on individuals and my presentation, therefore, despite my efforts to the contrary, seems to center itself on the accomplishments of particular persons, especially men. As cultural historians, we have to work with the materials that are available and my discussion is no exception. Readers will therefore find that whole chapters are seemingly devoted to the activities of a single person. My presentation simply seeks to employ the activities of these individuals to illustrate the way in which culture is constructed from a wide variety of materials.

Acknowledgments

In the course of writing this book, I have benefited from the assistance of many people. I would like first of all to express my thanks to the American Institute of Indian Studies and the Council for the International Exchange of Scholars who funded my work in Madras. I was aided in my work by the staffs of the Tamil Nad State Archives, the Madras Oriental Manuscripts Library, the India Office Library and Records, the National Library of Scotland, the Archives d'Outre Mer, and the Frankesche Stiftungen.

Many people have provided me with materials and have helped me with translations of difficult material. I would like particularly to thank Mrs. Kausalya Hart for her time in working on translations and to Dr. Emmanuel Divien for helping me get photocopies of valuable materials.

Many colleagues and students have read all or part of the manuscript, sometimes in multiple versions. Others have listened to presentations of the materials that have formed the basis of this book. I gave an account of the Conclusion at the annual meeting of the Association of Asian Studies in Washington, D.C., in the spring of 1992 and derived much advantage from comments on that and other presentations. I would like to thank Stuart Blackburn, Katharine Flemming, Thomas Brady, David Hollinger, Martin Jay, Thomas Metcalf, James Gregory, Douglas Haynes, Stephen Dale, Susan Neild Basu, William Meehan, David Kuchta, Jeffery Ravel, Dane Kennedy, Nasser Hussain, Sumathi Ramaswami, Michael Katten, Natalie Pickering, Aloka Parasher Sen, and

Jeanne-Marie Stumpf-Carome for their comments and ideas. My students in my seminars over the last decade have commented on my notions and I am most grateful to them: they and my colleagues have helped to make me what I am. Both Anand Yang and Mattison Mines wrote long and detailed criticisms of the manuscript that enabled me to enhance the force of the argument in many ways. I am grateful to two organizations who helped germinate the ideas that appear in this book, the French History Group and the WIRTH group. In both cases, members of these groups have provided me useful perspectives. David Gilmartin read the manuscript two times and enabled me to make the argument more precise. Ines Županov read the manuscript in three different versions. At the time, she was herself writing her dissertation and I profited enormously from her insights. Sandria Freitag helped me to clarify further the argument and develop an intelligible text. I would also like to thank Cherie Semens, who drew the maps, and Lynne Withey, who assisted me through the process of publication.

Transliteration and Other Conventions

I have tried to reduce the amount of transcription in the text to aid readability. However, I have indicated the correct transliteration (usually from Tamil) the first time a word is used. Often, I have put the correct transliteration in parentheses and have adopted the Madras Lexicon style of transliteration. I use diacritics for a word when it first appears in the text and in the Bibliography.

The large number of functional terms in the text side by side with caste names has posed some problems of intelligibility. In the interests of clarity, I have put all caste names in lowercase (i.e., paraiyar, vellala, palli, agamudaiyar). However, in the instance of Kondaikatti vellala, I have indicated the subcaste name with uppercase. I have also decided to put functional names in uppercase. By far the most confusing terms are Pannaiyal (bonded laborers) and Padiyal (laborers employed by years or shorter periods). The reader will therefore be confronted on several occasions with phrases that place paraiyar or palli—both caste names—alongside Pannaiyal or Padiyal. In these cases, it means that these bonded or employed laborers are from either the paraiyar or the palli caste.

Introduction

This book is about how people created knowledge regarding agricultural space and cultural identity. In the process, a population became fixed in a resacralized land—an outcome ultimately useful in different ways to British administrators, Tamil nationalists, and local agriculturalists of various classes. This study, therefore, looks at the way both the British and local people in the area around Madras, in what came to be South India, formulated answers to urgent questions concerning the relation of culture to villages as part of that newly consecrated geography. These problems and the answers the people generated were attempts to resolve tensions implicit in the development of a new society.

Fixed population and resacralized land stand out as the two most important changes we can identify in this critical period. Even before the arrival of the Europeans in the seventeenth and eighteenth centuries, individuals in Tamil society moved around a great deal. The society was divided into two varieties of subcastes, each of whom had specific spatial orientations. The "right" castes oriented themselves to local areas, had local temples, and looked on these local zones as areas to which they "belonged." The "left" castes, by contrast, had a conception of belonging to a space that was expansive, occupying many hundreds of villages. Their temples were separated far from one another. Since many of them were artisans and weavers, they had a tradition of mobility. Membership in "right" and "left" caste divisions was under dispute and "switching" prompted contestation on spatial questions as well.

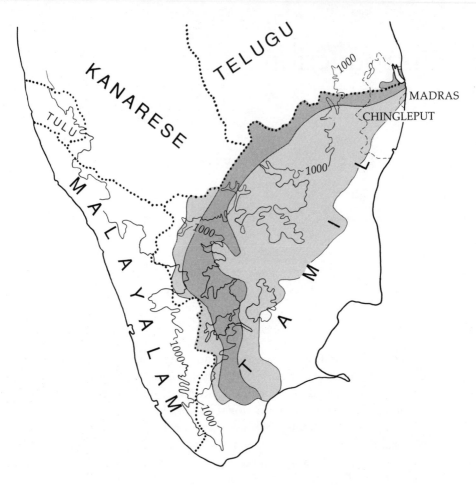

- - - -   District boundaries
••••••••   Major language boundary
-1000-   1000' elevation contour
Telugu mother tongue in Tamil districts:

> 15%
10–15%
< 10%

Map 1.   Relationship between elevation and distribution of Telugus in Tamil districts, 1931. Based on maps in M. W. M. Yeatts, Madras Report, vol. 14 of *Census of India* (Madras: Superintendent, Government Press, 1932), opposite 286, and Eugene F. Irschick, *Politics and Social Conflict in South India* (Berkeley: University of California Press, 1969), 2.

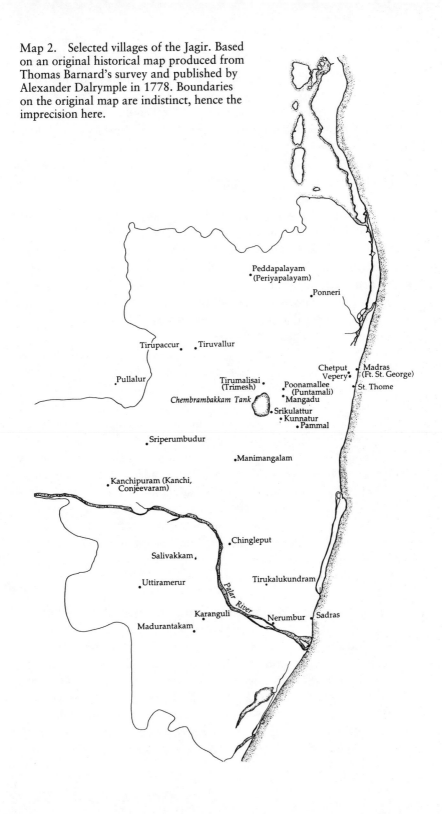

Map 2.   Selected villages of the Jagir. Based on an original historical map produced from Thomas Barnard's survey and published by Alexander Dalrymple in 1778. Boundaries on the original map are indistinct, hence the imprecision here.

Between 1795 and 1895, these spatial orientations were altered by the project to identify for each village outside Madras a corporate life stretching back almost two millennia into the Tamil past. Such a project connected not only the present with the past but also each village with what came to be "the Tamil country." In this way, the spatial orientations of both left and right subcastes were harnessed and reshaped in a dialogic way to help create the nodules around which the Tamil country was based. Tamil culture came to be identified with territory.

During the intervening century, both local people and the British sought to formulate not only ideas about each other but also ideas about each other's pasts. This book seeks to look at the way in which that preoccupation with pasts was used to create the future. In particular, it seeks to understand how rural society around Madras town transformed itself from one of great spatial mobility into one in which inhabitants remained in their villages and, from these fixed points, formulated a cultural entity recognized as distinctly Tamil.

The interaction through which new formulations of territory and identity were forged was dialogic and heteroglot in nature. Cultural negotiations regarding contested meanings involved many voices in a dialogue with unexpected outcomes. Certainly, the purposes inspiring these myriad voices were often contradictory or focused on entirely different problems and proposed solutions. The history that emerged from this set of dialogues, then, created discursive structures that have served several ends at once and over time: British administrators sought to create a fixed and productive society; Tamil nationalists defined a place and identifiable culture for that homeland; disputants struggling to retain control over land and human resources established competing claims. The forms taken by these cultural negotiations changed over time; the dialogues described here were historically contingent and thus need to be delineated with some care.

During the early 1780s, the agriculturalists largely deserted the area outside Madras, on the southeast coast of the Indian subcontinent. Between 1780 and 1782, Hyder Ali, a warrior-prince from the upland area called Mysore to the southwest of Madras, burnt many of the villages around the town. In his attempt to isolate the British, Hyder—often pictured at the time and later as an Asiatic despot—forced most villagers out of this area. Almost two decades later, Lionel Place, an English East India Company employee, described the situation he had never actually seen in a highly colored style. There were, he said, "hardly any other signs . . . left of the country having been once inhabited by human beings than the bones of their bodies that had been massacred, or the naked walls of their houses that had been burnt."[1] In his description, Place construed both the villagers and the huts in the villages as beings who were murdered. To this image must be added that created several years later by Mark Wilks, the historian of Mysore who wrote that the "minute traits in the manners and habits" of a people "break the force of despotism, or partially compensate, by a spirit of rude but manly independence, for the evils that spirit must encounter."[2] Thus, Wilks helped to create the image of a despot by describing those elements in ordinary people that could serve as a foil to him.

The style and formulations of Place and Wilks resulted from a long historical process. From the mid-1780s, employees of the English East India Company were no longer permitted to participate in commerce. Instead, they focused on an administrative preoccupation with reforming decayed societies by freeing them from despotism and internecine conflict. To envision this state of affairs meant describing the previous environment as totally disorderly. The most direct strategy, employed by individuals in the generation after the direct assumption of the Jagir in 1782, was to depict local culture, particularly village culture, as being in a state of moral disarray. This degenerate society, many British and local individuals believed, was permeated by suspicion, opulence, and corruption. Place, who exemplified this tendency, believed that "we should judge Hindu institutions not by the fallen natives of the present day, but by the reliques of antient tranquillity, happiness, agriculture and wealth of the country. . . . Where else do we hear of peace being undisturbed by any commotion, whatsoever, for thousands of years?"[3] This reasoning presented the individuals encountered near Madras in the 1790s as fallen examples of a much more tranquil and wealthy society, a society that had persisted for many, many years.

Not only did many individuals reconstitute their ideas of local society but also, in the process, they redefined themselves entirely. Not least of those who redefined themselves were British administrators. During the nineteenth century, officers of the English East India Company distanced themselves more and more from activities they considered to be "indigenous." They no longer used hunger strikes against local individuals, which they had done earlier in the century, or themselves sought to confine people to retrieve money or supplies.[4] As we will see in Chapter 2, Place sought to act like a local king to revive what he perceived as a degraded culture. This taking of the role of the other by one individual was a momentary and experimental strategy to renew local society, an attempt to accelerate the kind of cultural change occurring everywhere at the time. It was perhaps the last in a series of transitional attempts to try to copy what were considered to be "essential" and "indigenous" symbolic expressions.

Since this process formed part of a large-scale interaction over many years, even preceding the arrival of the Europeans, it naturally involved many local participants, who used the context to create new answers to new existential problems. Given the change underway, it is impossible to refer to a pure, unalloyed indigenous system with values untouched by other elements.[5] Rather, the British entered society through a long, continuing process already in motion that could not be called "indigenous" because it cannot be defined as existing in contradistinction to a foreign (British) alternative. The British and all other forces from the West or from other localities were immediately incorporated into a single analytical field that emerged from dialogic processes.

British and local interpreters participated equally in constructing new institutions with a new way of thinking to produce a new kind of knowledge. One writer who called himself a "native revenue officer" of Madras presidency, in the 1858 document *On Bribery as Practiced in the Revenue administration of the Madras Presidency,* wrote that "there was indeed a time not far back when universal content, concord and mutual sympathy reigned amongst the landholders and their labourers, when the cultivation was arranged amongst themselves, when their rights were mutually respected and violations of them amicably adjusted in the village without the interference of Government."[6] According to this construction, the decay of trust among villagers themselves and between villagers and outsiders was recent, producing an increase in amorality, deception, and mistrust. As we will see, during the 1790s the production of meaning and institutions for the villages of the region came to include an idea that the entire tax system was corrupt. Amorality came to be seen as a product of a culture born of cities, invading kings, and colonial powers who lived ostentatiously either in the present or in the immediate past. According to this thinking, the ubiquitous wealth and morality of the distant past was destroyed by an effete colonizing culture, either British or Muslim. In the construction of ideas about local cultural decay, both the Company employees and local participants sought to carry forward urgent cultural imperatives. Therefore, the social description of local society was an interactive product of these new historical necessities. One of the presumptions of this analysis is that all new ways of thinking resulted from contingent circumstances.

According to these perceptions, whether shaped by European or local perspectives, society in the Jagir outside Madras and elsewhere in South India needed restoration. This necessitated a reordering of society to fix and essentialize it, to "get to the bottom of it." This revivalist movement emerging from within both the British bureaucracy and local society to retrieve the "original" institutions of the society, this effort to characterize a former time, resulted in interactively constructed perceptions of the previous land system and the social hierarchy on which it was based. In other words, what was described resulted from attempts to create a new land system and social hierarchy. In effect, this was a dialogic production of a negotiated system of rules and institutions that included an equally mediated cultural system of juridical power.[7] Thus, the construction of what both British and local participants conceived of as the values of a former age formed an attempt to interactively generate answers to solve current pressing cultural problems. These answers had to be expressed in new significations, of which "prior decay" and the "restoration" of an "indigenous system" were but three.

As we will see in Chapter 1, categorizing a rural dispute by local land controllers as an "insurrection" in 1795–96 became another device to create a new signification for village society. This holds similarities to the production of meaning in sixteenth-century Mexico between Cortés and Montezuma, or between Captain Cook and the Hawaiians in 1779, that provided "new" signification for "old" activities. In the same manner, Place and his superiors conceived of the "insurrection" in the Jagir outside Madras in 1795–96 in a very different way from that ascribed to it by the local villagers.

Because there was a difference in interpretation about these behaviors, the experience jeopardized the views of both local individuals and Company employees. That is to say, a "crisis in truth" had been created about the meaning of rural relations in the Jagir at this time. This crisis in meaning was illustrated, as we will see, by Place's desire to try to bring in more taxes, to "get to the bottom of things," to find out what was the "true" motivation of the villagers. Because of his persistence, Place proceeded much further than had any previous European in his attempt to understand the structure of local social and political relations.

Nonetheless, the villagers did not behave as the British expected. British expectations operated in an intellectual and institutional environment already tension-filled with alien concepts and value judgments, in which things were already agitated and contested. These alien concepts formed active subjects in the continuing production of meaning. For their part, villagers employed negotiated behaviors that were only partly based on activities they had pursued on previous occasions. They already actively anticipated the equally alien expectations of the British: the villagers' attempt to "understand" British expectations was itself a dynamic behavior. However, Company employees—because they operated under new rules—also did not react as the villagers would have predicted that rulers would, not least because the British were also energetically preparing to "understand" local individuals.

The pragmatic context, the goals, the signifiers, the historic requirements had all changed dramatically for all participants. Everything seemed open to dispute and charged with value. As a result, the meanings placed on these activities both by the British and by the local population were being altered continuously. As products of this cultural negotiation emerged over the next century, new institutions and new kinds of knowledge were created to capture the nature of society and polity in this colonial environment and elsewhere. Moreover, as we shall see, dialogic activities carry with them internal contradictions inherent in heteroglossia.

What this process suggests is that we can no longer presume that the view of local or what later became Indian society was a product of an "imposition" by the hegemonic colonial power onto a mindless and subordinate colonized society. Writers like Edward Said have argued that the construction of meaning was a "willed activity" by white European colonizers of the Middle East and South Asia. "My contention is," Said writes, "that Orientalism is fundamentally a political doctrine willed over the Orient because the Orient was weaker than the West, which elided the Orient's difference with its weakness."[8] The research presented here questions this claim that knowledge is constructed by willed activity of a stronger over a weaker group. It suggests, instead, that changed significations are the heteroglot and dialogic production of all members of any historical situation, though not always in equal measure; this is so whether they have a Weberian monopoly on violence or not.

This characterization of the process nevertheless presumes that in the colonial situation both domination and exploitation occurred on a constant basis. The colonial environment was used by imperial actors to derive political, economic, and social advantages for themselves. Constant efforts by these actors excluded the colonized from areas of formal juridical and economic power. Domination involved constant violence or threats of violence, and inequality. Exploitation and victimization were more than mere perception; they happened constantly in all colonial environments.

But in the Jagir in the late eighteenth and early nineteenth centuries, many British employees of the Company felt their control over their territories to be very shaky. Lionel Place confronted violent raids into the Jagir from the territories of the Nawab (or Nabob) of Arcot, a local prince ruling to the west of Madras, and attempts by Company employees of the newly founded police committee from Madras town to impose their authority. Referring to these challenges, Place said to his superiors at the Board of Revenue in Madras, "The Board know, by what a tender thread, the Collector's authority hangs, and from past experience, how necessary to the administration of the Revenue, that it should be respected."[9] As we will see from the account that follows, the precariousness of British authority over many groups not only in this local area but on the subcontinent as a whole continued for many years.[10] Moreover, the attempt of the British to impose their ideas on the proprietary system of the Jagir was continually used by local inhabitants to conjure up something else. Indeed, the shaping of the proprietary system became an activity mediated by many other local individuals. It would therefore be hard to say that in this realm the British were dominant. If anything, nineteenth-century evidence shows that in the area the local Mirasidars exercised greater dominance than did the British.

Moreover, the segmentary organization of local polity enabled the population to develop significant arenas of juridical power not subject to formal British authority for many years. In the nineteenth century, after the British evolved their bureaucratic structure and a system of living in specific spatial areas set apart from the local population, there were hundreds of domains on the subcontinent where British authority was altogether lacking or uncertain. The shakiness of British dominance enabled these regions to serve throughout the period as critical sites for productive epistemological projects.

The discussion here begins with a sense that previous characterizations have been incomplete. It does not see the British presence in India as a "limited" or a repressive state.[11] Nor does this study look on the creation of culture as part of what Ashis Nandy has called the "intimate enemy," a view in which he characterized this creative and dialogic pro-

cess as an "oppressive structure."[12] Nor does it look on colonialism as
something that involves "cultural damage."[13] The argument here focuses
less on the willed or repressive aspect of a colonial state as part of the
construction of knowledge than on the dialogic, heteroglot productive
process through which culture is formed. The result is a necessary cor-
rective to what has been an unbalanced picture of a complex process.

This is not to say that there was no resistance to the meanings that
were created by these interactions. Recent work by scholars suggests
that as individuals or historical forces operated in local areas of South
Asia, the significations granted to those forces or to those individuals'
actions were in many ways "subaltern" or "local." These meanings com-
peted with each other in the conflict that precedes the centripetal movement toward a unitary and scientific discourse.[14] To put it in another
way, the centripetal movement to create a unitary structure of meaning
both at this time and later operated in the midst of an equally powerful
centrifugal movement to create local meaning from many different
voices and epochs. In the long term, therefore, scientific discourse and
the institutions that represent it create a negotiated, heteroglot construction shaped by both the weak and the strong, the colonized and the
colonizer, from the present and the past. Thus, it is not possible to find
a single, definite origin to these meanings and institutions. They are
neither "European" nor "indigenous." We must not essentialize any of
the positions held by those involved in the dialogue. Equally important,
we must recognize that the voices speaking at any given moment are
tied to that specific historic instant.

Moreover, the process by which these knowledges and institutions
compete with each other and the mechanism by which centripetal, scientific discourse is formed are something quite different from simple
repression. If anything, repression helps to create new knowledge. Instead, discourse was also constructed through what Bakhtin called Rabelaisian laughter.[15] Laughter, according to Bakhtin, represents a positive, regenerating and creative epistemic force. Rabelaisian laughter
suggests a process of becoming that is open, unfulfilled, and ambivalent.
It is a way the present and the past are buried in the process of looking
at the future. It also proposes the creativity and radicalism of the people's unofficial truth. What Place, a Company employee, had to say
about the chaos and decay of contemporary Tamil society constituted a
kind of Rabelaisian laughter in the bazaar. Laughter, according to this
formulation, is new meaning not directed at anybody in particular and
not intended to threaten anybody. These new meanings—Bakhtinian

laughter or Durkheimian religious electricity—drew on a wide variety of voices from many social classes and many epochs in time. But this laughter and religious electricity, this competition between local knowledges and voices, was itself connected with meanings from other epochs. Bakhtin's formulation of laughter therefore demonstrates the way in which discourse develops to deal with new historical requirements. Laughter and bazaar voices can usefully be made part of a centrifugal and nonvaluative projection of new competing formulations. In this system, there is no attempt to enclose. Often this process can be thought of as an emptying, a deforming, and a naturalizing mechanism in order to accomplish a major change in signification, to realize a new project.

The dynamic of this process is much more important than the attribution of authorship on which we usually rely. It was part of an emptying process. It formed a statement that came out of a crowd and was addressed to a crowd of competing local, "subaltern," or bazaar voices. If we say that a certain person (such as Place) is an author of any given set of views, this is simply an illusion that is socially accepted. All authorized products are the product of a work group that includes those who agree and those who disagree with each set of ideas.[16] Place simply played a part in a worldwide crowd of competing voices, a large intellectual work group. However, no single individual can determine meaning.

The methodological implications for a historian of this production process are necessarily complicated. Historians traditionally deal with documentary evidence, and documents are—mechanically though not intellectually—produced by a single author. One way of balancing out the weight of this form of primary evidence is to treat a range of behavioral evidence also as "primary" documentation, and this effort is made repeatedly in the pages that follow. Nevertheless, the overall weightage in a study like this one unintentionally privileges the written word proffered by elite actors, many of them British. Only by reminding ourselves continually that this evidence is but the tip of a much larger iceberg of dialogic interaction can we resist a single, straight-line interpretation connected to elite concerns.

We remind ourselves, then, that the project to describe society around Madras in the 1790s as needing reconstruction involved local individuals—Europeans and many others. Though it was a project of domination, it was an intensely collaborative, if not harmonious, project. The dialogue of which this history is made emerges from connected processes of negotiation and mediation, as these developed throughout the nine-

teenth century. All these persons participated in it with compelling excitement and interest. Interactions in constructing local culture and its
institutions involved many special pleasures. The imperatives associated
with this historical task in a new historical era provoked an equally
compelling stimulus to create "truth" about themselves. Many local individuals, for example, sought to "discover the truth" about the Tamil
past. Their goal was to speak about this history of the Tamil area to
prepare for the future. Their enthusiastic participation helped to induce
a large-scale centripetal codification of knowledge about the Tamil past
and involved great and persistent pleasure for all who took part, both
colonizer and colonized.

Therefore, contrary to the argument proffered by Edward Said, the
production of categories or juridical institutions was not a production
simply of unmediated willed activities imposed by the western colonial
state from the top. Active voices came from all segments of society (those
who dominated and those who were being dominated) and from all
epochs. This study focuses on key epistemological moments to elucidate
that process for a particular part of South India in the late eighteenth
and nineteenth centuries. Through these key moments, we may examine
the interactive aspects of the process for creating meaning.

The production of meaning could be studied in many ways. One of
the most important ways is the focus here: the organization of rural
space and society to settle an agrarian population. This process resulted
in an embedded society, with concomitant implications for alternative
actions available to participants in dialogic processes. "Embedded" refers to a society in which individuals are enmeshed by ties of restraint.

I have divided this study into four chapters. The first sets the historical
stage for the investigations of Place and many other individuals. These
investigations formed part of a general historical project not confined
to the Jagir or to South India. This project, in its attempt to find out
"what was going on," brought together unlikely elements of knowledge
regarding culture, religion, social relations, and economic productivity
of the land. By seeking to understand how proprietary relations operated, Place provoked a rural disturbance that Company officials called
an "insurrection." The crisis of this disturbance, in turn, offered an opportunity to redefine the way in which village culture was conceived. It
also offered an opportunity to define local society as one characterized
by immorality and deceit, a society that needed reconstruction.

Chapters 2 and 3 represent respectively the theoretical and practical working out of these conceptions of spatializing, reconstructing, and resacralizing rural society in the late eighteenth and early nineteenth centuries. They propose that the future society of the area was projected from a constructed past dialogically produced by both British officials and local individuals.

Chapter 4 is concerned to show that this "production of the past" involved "finding the original settlers" of the territory not only to grant them antiquity but also to fix them in specific villages and homes. The general historical project on which all these activities focused gave the entire population a reason not to wander about the countryside, to fix them in place. The implications of this sedentarization process continue to be played out in the late twentieth century and thus have great import for those wishing to understand the major aspects of change in the modern postcolonial world.

CHAPTER I

To Fix the People to Their Respective Villages

The Transformation of the East India Company

Between the 1780 war fought by the English East India Company and Hyder Ali and the takeover of the Carnatic by the Company in 1801, many social practices and cultural repertoires came to be questioned. The negotiations and mediations arising from this questioning may be used as the first key epistemological moment. In part, the moment emerged from the new juridical dominance exercised by the British in South India. Even more important was the fact that Company employees transformed themselves from traders into bureaucrats. Moreover, the invasion and depredations of Hyder Ali's army in the war of 1780 concentrated largely on the areas surrounding the town of Madras.

About seventy-five miles to the west of Madras lay Arcot and Vellore, the heart of the territory of the local prince, the Nawab of Arcot. In between lay the northern part of what the British called the Arcot province. Madras faced the Bay of Bengal but also occupied the edge of an agrarian area called the Jagir stretching to the north, south, and west of it. Between 1780 and 1782, Hyder Ali tried to denude the Jagir of its population. Aware that the Jagir was a source of food, fodder, labor, and even betel leaves for the inhabitants of Madras, Hyder burned villages and either killed or scattered their local populations to intimidate the British.[1]

In the 1780 war, Hyder made a largely successful attempt to destroy the villages of the area within a radius of thirty to fifty-five miles from the seacoast. He also either destroyed or dispersed the population in this region.[2] Even more important, in the parts of the Arcot area to the west and south of the Jagir, Hyder also sought to extract land taxes to support his military operations.[3] During the early months of the war of 1780, almost all of Arcot province except for two or three forts fell into the hands of Hyder Ali.

Between 1780 and 1792, the Company was confronted with two wars, first with Hyder Ali and then with his son, Tipu Sultan. During this time, the Company supported another prince, Muhammad Ali, the Nawab of Arcot, who allowed some of his territories to be taxed by the Company to help pay for the wars with Hyder and Tipu. However, the interaction was important less for these military maneuvers than for the epistemic space that it offered to create knowledge about what was termed an "Oriental" or "Asiatic despot."

In these and other activities, the goal was to formulate the idea that these Muslim princes were wanton, profligate, and inefficient. For instance, the Company employees alternately complained bitterly about "the barbarous policy of Hyder [that] had early stript . . . [the Arcot province] of its most useful inhabitants" and about Muhammad Ali's tax collection charges, which consisted of "irregular sepoys, horsemen, sibandies [foot soldiers] . . . and those offices employed in the collection of the revenues [taxes]."[4] Later, when the Company got access to the taxes of what was called the Carnatic—the coastal area to the east of the hills in the Tamil areas and part of the coastal Telugu area of South India—by displacing the tax collectors of Muhammad Ali, Company employees wrote that the area had been "disburthened of an intolerable weight." The "intolerable weight" was, according to this assessment, just "sinecures under the government of the Nabob."[5] "Knowledge" in this context, however, was constructed as much as it was gathered. The process of construction was in turn shaped more by the purpose to which such knowledge would be put than by any "facts" discovered on the ground.

The construction of knowledge was shaped not only by the need to see local princes as unsatisfactory but also by the need to justify greater extractive policies by the Company itself. The Company had little direct information about this area and its villages and found itself in desperate financial straits as well. During the war of 1780, the English Company funded their army very poorly. Often the pay of the troops was eleven or twelve months in arrears. When they were paid, the soldiers were unable to change the currency in which they were paid (gold coins called "star pagodas") without paying a huge discount to money changers. If the British authorities tried to force the money changers to give fair exchange for the gold coins, the changers simply left town.[6] After the war, as arrears were paid off with promissory notes to soldiers and officers, considerable unhappiness resulted. At that time, the credit of the Company was so poor that officers could not raise any loans on the basis of the promissory notes issued by the Company without having 40 percent of their value discounted. Though this markdown was reduced to 30 percent in 1786 when the Madras Company authorities received funds from Bengal, money changers considered the discount quite moderate given the desperate state of the Company's finances. The Company was therefore less financially and politically credible than were local rulers. To excavate the purposes to which these new constructions were put, we will briefly examine several events and the source materials they generated. They include a wide range of very different experiences—a battle, a revenue survey, idol protection, temple and agrarian conflicts—that nevertheless together underscore the ways in which knowledge was constructed.

The Battle of Pullalur and the Naturalization of the British on the Subcontinent

After the treaty of Paris in 1763, the only serious political threats to the British in the Madras area came from Hyder Ali and his son Tipu Sultan. During the war of 1780, the prowess of Hyder Ali and his cavalry sometimes greatly intimidated the British. In no situation was this more apparent than during the battle of Pullalur, an area about ten miles north of Kanchipuram to the west of Madras. This battle was fought by a British force under the command of Colonel John Baillie against those of Hyder Ali and Tipu on 10 September 1780, shortly after the beginning of the war. Various mistakes made by the British commander-in-chief Sir Hector Munro and by Baillie himself resulted in the isolation of Baillie's force. Hyder Ali and Tipu, aided by the French, soundly defeated Baillie's forces: of the eighty-six officers in Baillie's force who participated, thirty-six were killed or died of their wounds, thirty-four were wounded and taken prisoner, and sixteen were unwounded but taken prisoner.[7]

Though the military encounter was brief, it had great consequences for the fortunes and self-esteem of the British at the time and long afterwards. Moreover, because the defeat placed in doubt the British ability to defend Madras, Hyder's rout of Baillie greatly decreased British political and economic credibility. Writing in January 1781, the governor of Madras, Charles Smith, noted: "The consternation occasioned by this defeat, in which we lost the flower of our army, was universal. The inhabitants of the country and villages fled. The wealthiest merchants resident even at the Presidency [i.e., Madras town] sent away their [families]; and out of the vast number who have houses and property in the black town, not above one half of them remained."[8] Another indication of the way in which this battle affected local British fortunes is that in 1780 the authorities of the three temples in Kanchipuram or Kanchi (forty-five miles west of Madras)—Varadarajaswami (Vaishnava), Ekambarantha (Saiva), and Kamatciyamman—decided that they had to find ways to protect the idols from Hyder Ali's armies. According to C. S. Crole, author of the *Chingleput, late Madras, District* (hereafter the *Chingleput Manual*), they took them away disguised as corpses.[9]

Beyond these indicators of lack of confidence by both British and Indian observers, many other elements combined to construct the ideas connected with this battle. For instance, one of the participants in combat was a British cadet also by chance named Baillie. Cadet John Baillie wrote an account of the experience of the battle and his later imprisonment by Tipu and Hyder in Seringapatam on the tableland now called Karnataka. This account enjoyed some popularity as the cadet asked his father to correct his spelling and grammar mistakes and to circulate it to other people to read. This letter and many others like it spoke to a British audience in much the same way as had the Jesuit letters of the seventeenth and the eighteenth centuries. They provided material to a particular community who sought to construct knowledge about this encounter as well as political behavior on the subcontinent.[10]

Another important contributor to the construction of knowledge about the battle was C. S. Crole, writing in the 1870s. In his *Chingleput Manual*—Chingleput was the name for the area originally called the Jagir—Crole remarked that the village of Pullalur was

> remarkable as the scene of the most grievous disaster which has yet befallen British arms in India. On the 10th September 1780, Colonel Baillie, who was marching from Madras to effect a junction with Sir Hector Munro at Conjeevaram [Kanchipuram], was here totally routed and his whole force either cut to pieces or captured by the united armies of Hyder Ali and his

son, Tipu Sultan. The palmyrah [palm] trees still bear unmistakable evidence of the fierceness of the cannonade.[11]

Thus, marks on the trees ninety years after the battle near Pullalur could be used by Crole to argue that the ferociousness of Hyder's cannon had been responsible for the British defeat. Crole's account seeks also to indicate the extent to which the British had become part of the natural scenery of the area. He naturalized them to the area by picturing Colonel Baillie coming from Madras when in fact he was coming from the north. This reworking of events formed part of a creative activity.

We know that Hyder Ali and Tipu Sultan collaborated in the creation of ideas about this battle. After the encounter, Tipu had a large mural of the scene commissioned for his palace in Seringapatam. He later feared that it might prompt the British to be vindictive, however, and ordered it whitewashed over in 1792 as British troops approached Seringapatam. It was restored by the British in the 1830s and 1840s. Indeed, the process of creating knowledge about the battle of Pullalur has continued into our own day, as a painted cloth version of this scene was exhibited in London in 1990.[12]

Mapping the Jagir as a Form of Self-Deception

Following the 1780 war (also known as the second Anglo-Mysore war), the employees of the Company were gradually converted into public servants. Shortly after the British surrendered the "assigned" areas to the Nawab, and after the Madras authorities received large sums of money from Bengal to pay off their commitments to the army, the Company issued orders on 17 July 1786 prohibiting army officers from engaging in any kind of monetary transaction and from interfering with tax matters in the Nawab's territories.[13] At the end of 1785, the Company Court of Directors in London also prohibited any members of the Madras council from engaging in mercantile activity. At the same moment, the Company raised the salaries of the governor, the commander-in-chief, and the members of the council.[14] Therefore, despite the Company's vulnerable financial position, its employees experienced a bureaucratic revolution that suddenly defined public life in a new way.

British possessions in the Carnatic in the 1780s consisted of the villages around the town of Madras, the town itself, the northern circars or territories on the Telugu coast to the north of Madras, and the agrarian area known as the Jagir. It is worth noting how this territory grew.

In 1749, Muhammad Ali, a contender to the throne of Arcot, had granted Poonamallee, a part of the Jagir, to the Company.[15] Poonamallee consisted of 330 square miles and contained 231 villages south and west of the town of Madras. Later in 1763, Muhammad Ali, who had by then achieved his position as Nawab through British armed support, gave the British the Jagir, an area consisting of more than two thousand villages and 2,284 square miles located north, south, and west of Madras.[16]

Soon after the Jagir came into the hands of the British, a Company employee named Thomas Barnard surveyed it to indicate its total value as a tax-producing property. His survey, carried out with the help of Indian assistants, was considered at the time of its completion to be one of the finest pieces of mapping of any region in India.[17] Without the help of Indian assistants, the entire project would have been impossible. The dialogic implications of a collaborative enterprise such as this survey are readily apparent. The outcome necessarily reflected not only Barnard's assumptions about agrarian practices and even land tenure rights but also the very different ones possessed by his assistants, as well as those held by the inhabitants of the area surveyed.

That these views shifted becomes apparent when we see how the survey was judged in later years. The enormous dependence placed by Barnard on these assistants was later characterized by the Company's collector of the Jagir, Lionel Place:

> That Mr. Barnard should have been deceived in this [understanding of the correct distribution of shares of the harvest between the inhabitants and the state], and every other respect touching the interest of the inhabitants, can be no wonder, since unarmed with any authority, his references on the subject could only be to themselves [the villagers], who, unless there existed two opposite parties, [which was] sometimes the case, one of which could be prevailed upon to produce the authentic documents of the village, [the inhabitants] were always able to obscure the truth, from him. Even in those matters which seemed perfectly open to his enquiries he was misled.[18]

Thus, this first survey and mapping exercise by the Company yielded what was viewed as a confusing picture, a confusion that became a part of the way in which the British interaction with others in this enterprise fitted them into the rural landscape. The bewilderment surrounding Baillie's defeat, the description of it by Crole, and Barnard's map give the impression of precision but in fact they all represented "confusions" and new knowledge. This new epistemic production emptied the old meanings about the British presence and naturalized the British anew in the

Jagir. In the end, Barnard could not provide sufficient reliable information to enable an appraisal of the tax-producing potential of the
area.[19]

Temple Conflicts

When the British first took over direct control of the Jagir in January
1782, all but a few villages were uninhabited and their fields largely
uncultivated. Without cultivation it was impossible to collect land taxes.
In 1782, however, the last of the horsemen of Hyder Ali departed from
the Jagir and, as the effects of the war began to fade, villagers returned
gradually to the area. The confusion of the war and its aftermath also
allowed many families to establish themselves in villages in more dominant positions than they had previously enjoyed.

As part of the strategy of establishing a hold on the region, the governor of Madras and the council agreed that, in addition to regulating
the villages, the reestablishment and repair of religious centers would
greatly contribute toward "restoring the country to its former flourishing state, by drawing together its dispersed inhabitants."[20] British attempts to protect the transport of temple images were at least partly a
result of the feeling that temple images were critical to maintaining civil
order. This attitude incorporated knowledge of a famous episode concerning an earlier attack by the Kallars on a British armed force when
a Colonel Heron had taken the temple images of the Kallar from Kovilkudi in 1755.[21] Thus, for the British the protection of temple images
apparently became a way to establish political legitimacy.

Crole in the *Chingleput Manual* had sought to connect the battle of
Pullalur with the retrieval of the images by the Kanchipuram brahmans.
He wrote:

> It evidently took a long time to reestablish the confidence of the natives
> of the Jaghire in British ascendancy after Colonel Baillie's defeat and Sir
> Hector Munro's precipitate retreat from Conjeevaram, for we find that it
> was not till 1799, that is, after the taking of Seringapatam had finally extin-
> guished Hyder's hated dynasty that it was deemed prudent to bring back the
> sacred images from their exile.[22]

Refurbishing temples and reintroducing temple worship thus required
the protection of a strong and ascendant British presence. Accordingly,
in 1785 the governor of Madras wrote to the commander of a Company
detachment in Chandragiri that the brahmans of the "little" or Varadarajaswami (Vaishnava) temple in Kanchipuram were about to bring

a number of idols from the sacred center of Tirupati to Kanchipuram. The governor of Madras, considering it appropriate that the temple brahmans be protected on their journey, requested a military guard.[23] Like Barnard's maps and Crole's account of the battle of Pullalur, government protection of brahmans and idols became another way in which the British were inscribed and naturalized into the environment. The use of an armed detachment served as another active attempt to "understand" and to "fit in." It helped to produce new knowledge. In a similar way in 1785, the Jaghire Committee of the Company in Madras wrote to the British superintendent of the Jagir (an individual later called the collector) that, since the main celebration of the Vaishnava Varadarajaswami temple in Kanchipuram was about to start, he should make every attempt to assist the brahmans so that it would proceed "with the usual pomp and ceremony."[24]

The construction of events surrounding establishment of British control over territory thus linked military prowess, local knowledge, and protection of the cultural expressions of civil society. That each of these aspects could be shaped by local actors as well as British ones suggests the complexity of the interaction necessary to produce knowledge of these events. Nor did the simple relocation of the images conclude British involvement. Indeed, as soon as Company employees became involved in the supervision of the temples of the Jagir, they discovered that many temple disputes had to be resolved. In the process, these disputes led both local individuals and British Company employees to argue that society was totally degenerate.

One of these conflicts, reported in 1786, took place between two Hindu groups associated with two major temples in Kanchi. The first of these brahman sects, the Smarthas, was associated with the larger of the two temples in the northeast part of Periya, or Big Kanchi. This temple was dedicated to Ekambaranatha or Lord Shiva. The other sect was Vaishnava and was associated with the temple in Chinna, or Little Kanchi, dedicated to the deity Varadarajaswami or Lord Vishnu. According to the British report, this dispute involved enmity between the "long [Vaishnava] and cross-marked [Smartha] Bramins" and concerned the rights connected to taking the patron deity in procession through the streets of Kanchi. The conflict related to a number of local issues that need not concern us here. For our purposes, we may merely note that the conflict that emerged from the interaction of local competitors and the new British authorities required the British to act on the basis of new knowledge, and in new ways. The Jaghire Committee decided to permit the procession of Varadarajaswami, the Vaishnava deity. To forestall any difficulties, however, the superintendent decided to advertise this decision by a drum known in Tamil as a "tamukku" (called a "tom tom" by the British).[25] This followed a practice established by Tamil kings to announce state policy; it was adopted by the Company to communicate "a strict injunction to the Inhabitants to pay due respect and obedience to the orders of the Government."[26] Thus, even in the mode of communication used, the British interpretation of events was shaped in part by presumptions about local precedents and understandings.

Village Disputes

Many other disputes arose as well in the Jagir after the war of 1780, a fact reflected by the 1787 comment of Richard Dighton, superintendent of the Jagir, that the local population was unhappy about the delay in introducing a judicial system. Furthermore, he said, "their dispositions are so prone to litigation that disputes accumulate daily, which cannot but affect the state of the country."[27] Moreover, "the usurpation of property before and during the late war and a variety of other causes has given rise to so many disputes" that much land remained uncultivated. In particular, he pointed to a conflict between reddis and agamudaiyār (two peasant castes, the first Telugu, the second Tamil) and brahmans over rights to a proprietary system called mirasi in the village of Sriperumbudur west of Madras. He continued, "Contested claims of this nature prevail in many villages in the Jaghire and are from the loss or suppression of former records in almost inextricable confusion to adjust their disputes between the natives, to enquire into the various tenures." This dispute in Sriperumbudur "originated from religious jealousy which has been increased by the Agamoodies who being people of property, are desirous of decorating the Pagoda [temple]. This gives great offense to the Brahmans of the other sect." As a result, the disputants deserted the village and no cultivation took place.[28] He had tried, he said, to associate local individuals known as Nāṭṭārs with the Company judicial decisions over land in the Jagir.[29] However, he found that many litigants appealed the decisions of the Nattars, doubtless because these individuals had formerly been "the instruments of oppression." Moreover, Dighton noted that the disputes over property were so intricate that the Nattars complained that the pursuit of Company tasks did not allow them to attend to their own affairs. Then, said Dighton, he tried to use the arbitration process of the caste kaccēris or caste councils. He found this also to be impracticable "owing to the intrigues and jealousies subsisting among the members of each tribe respecting the privilege of being head of a tribe." He found it very difficult to deal with disputes concerned with accounts, partnerships, and contested bargains. This was, he said, because "the party who was conscious of being in the wrong would never willingly submit the matter to arbitration which totally . . . destroyed the intent of arbitration."[30]

Social scientists would say that it was precisely these kinds of village and temple contestations that had formed the basis of the previous system. They could identify elements of a system in which no single group could dispense with any other group. In this structure, consensus and balance were realized through conflict; everyone knew that there were others who would enter the contest.[31] Given the kind of knowledge being constituted in the late eighteenth century, however, this conflict was perceived by many local individuals as well as Company employees to be a recent, effete development. Taken together, the conflicts were seen as emerging from a degenerate society that needed reformation.

The Company as Tax Collector in the Jagir

In 1792, as a result of the concessions granted after the third Anglo-Mysore war with Tipu, the Company acquired among other territories the Baramahal, which later became the Salem district to the southwest of Madras. In 1801, the Company took over the remaining areas of the Carnatic not already in their hands because the Nawab of Arcot had been corresponding with Tipu Sultan, a Company enemy. Captain Alexander Read, an army officer, was appointed collector of the Baramahal shortly afterward. The sheer amount of money produced by Read's tax collections in the Baramahal convinced the Madras Board of Revenue that the same strategy could be usefully followed in other areas of the Carnatic under their control, particularly the Jagir. Indeed, the data and money provided by Read and his assistants changed the entire nature of Company expectations of the taxation possibilities of the South Indian region. At the same time, his mode of operation and self-presentation changed British notions about their purpose and place in South India. What may we discern from Read's revenue collection that illuminates this significant transformation?

Read, for the first time, did not use "tax farmers" as intermediaries. Instead, he dealt with Company tax employees who in turn worked with villagers without the mediation of a local rent farmer. Read also represented himself to the Board of Revenue as dealing openly with the individual cultivators in a fair way. In 1793, Read wrote:

> My first object is the setting on foot the new [tax] settlements, on principles perfectly understood and approved of. My next is to give my sentiments fully on the proposed mode of administering justice in those Districts [of Baramahal]. Though the last is necessarily postponed, your Board [of revenue] may rely upon it that it is of no loss or prejudice to the inhabitants, my best endeavours being employed in partially hearing and redressing such complaints as are brought before me, for all my evenings are entirely dedicated to this very necessary function, and the open street is my place of audience that the meanest may not meet with any difficulty of access.[32]

Read's behavior suggests that he was adopting local behavior and presenting it as British policy. He was seeking to be personal and in this way was using a local formulation of accessibility to political authority to make his own British administration more understandable and useful. In this way, Read's behavior was being transformed by the historical requirements of the time. We cannot construe this construction as either British or local. It was something new. We will see that accessibility to all elements of the population as self-presentation becomes an important theme not only for Place but also for Puckle, the head of the Madras Board of Revenue later in the nineteenth century, to legitimize revenue enhancement. Though the Company increasingly emphasized impersonal bureaucratic inaccessibility, in fact the tendency was to invoke local understandings of accessibility. The Company authorities in Madras also relied on this kind of tax collecting to protect the weak. Later, the Board of Revenue wrote, "We have frequently had the satisfaction to acknowledge the exertions of this gentleman [Read] and the realization of so considerable a [tax] revenue as Star Pagodas 441,308-10-3 ⅛ will reflect additional credit on his management."[33] Referring to his work in another context, C. N. White, a member of the Madras Board of Revenue, said, "Nothing could be so desirable however to this Board, as to find others emulating his [Read's] example in endeavouring to effect similar public benefits [i.e., bring in more taxes], and to render the condition of the lower classes more comfortable."[34]

Read produced the most substantial amount of tax revenue in any one assessment by a single British servant of the Company up to that time in the Madras area.[35] Therefore, in their desperate financial state, the Company authorities raised the stakes on taxable capacities of all Company territory while at the same time invoking new moral requirements for behavior among its employees. Naturally, however, the impact of Read's income-producing strategies electrified many of those individuals whose job it was to collect taxes. The news of the substantial tax revenues produced by Read from the Baramahal circulated among other members of what then was referred to as the "revenue line" of Company employees (until then recruited entirely from civilians). Those already in the Company's revenue line resented Read's success and were angered by the precedence being given to personnel from the army.[36] Thus, the transformation to an aggressively extractive authority, legitimized by a self-presentation of upright administrative values to be used in the protection of its subjects, collided with existing tensions in the bureaucratic structure. The economic constraints faced by this bureaucracy, however, tilted the contest in favor of those who could extract more revenue.

Without any question, the main burden of these new moral and economic pressures fell on the Company employees working in the Jagir. The image of the Jagir was also transformed to fill this important new role, not least because it constituted one of the first sizable pieces of territory that had come into the hands of the Company. Charles White, a member of the Madras Board of Revenue in 1793, wrote that the Jagir before the war of 1780 contained more than two thousand villages. Some of these he considered to have been substantial and populous towns. Moreover, the Jagir possessed the "finest soil and climate and contains between three and four thousand tanks [artificial reservoirs] with many means of fertilization."[37] In this view, then, the Jagir represented a fertile paradise. Because it was near Madras and its population could also supply the needs of the city, it had a ready market for its produce. At the same time, he showed that up to 1793 no Company employee had produced any useful information on the population or productivity of the Jagir. White noted that recent reports from the collectors of the northern and southern divisions of the Jagir were the "first documents of the kind." However, he felt that these reports were almost useless, not least because they had not utilized the material in Thomas Barnard's survey of harvest share distribution throughout the Jagir.[38] Indeed, he believed that "the necessity for this determination [of harvest-share distribution] is obvious as great irregularities have subsisted by reducing the circar [government] portion of the crop in some villages below the proper standard, where the renters [tax farmers] or revenue servants wished to favor particular inhabitants and by increasing it in other instances from motives of gain." He called for creation of a register indicating the shares due to the state and the cultivator respectively. With this record, he wanted the Company to reduce the number of tax-free concessions awarded to village officers and other important villagers. Without these measures, tax revenues produced by the Jagir since 1786 had therefore naturally been disappointing. He showed that the average tax income during that period amounted to pagodas 136,332 a year, far below what it had produced in taxes in 1763, a generation earlier. White concluded that the Jagir's "progressive improvement since the close of the second war with Hyder Ally [the war of 1780] from when a new era in the Jaghire may be said to have commenced, has not kept pace with what might have been expected."[39]

Yet recent reports from the collectors of the Jagir did not contain information regarding what land was occupied by cultivation, tanks, waterways, village sites, wasteland, and the like. The collectors had accepted figures taken uncritically from the reports of subordinates. White demonstrated, however, that these figures had been largely concocted. To remedy these mistakes, White called for much higher requirements to be imposed on Company employees to gather far more specific cultural and economic information. In particular, the Company needed information relating to control of the land; Darvall, one of the collectors of the Jagir (which had divided jurisdictions then), had called attention to the interminable quarrels regarding division of the shares of the crop at harvest. Company employees had to adjudicate these quarrels as well as to increase the revenue collection, and information was deemed essential for both functions.

The British made consistent efforts to understand the "taxable value" of the Jagir in the decade before 1793 but were totally unsuccessful in this endeavor. Part of the lack of success related to their methods and assumptions: they felt, both then and later, that they could discover the crucial information by means of precise economic methods. From this perspective, the lack of success could be attributed to the resistance by cultivators and other such persons as the Pāḷayakkārs (poligars) or "watchers" with whom the tax farmers dealt, who all prevented the Company from knowing the "true" taxable capacity of the Jagir. The "true" taxable capacity was, of course, a fictional amount in any case, with the amount collected representing ongoing (and always changing) negotiations between the state, its intermediaries, and local individuals. In the face of their inability to derive reliable figures, then, employees of the Company constructed the "taxable value" out of the Mughal normative tax accounts of the area as well as their own need for more money when the Company was in desperate financial difficulties. Both of these figures were totally fictional. Nevertheless, during the time of Collector Place between 1794 and 1798, the Company government became convinced for the first time that the Jagir could yield substantial taxes.

Collaborative Activities to Produce a Past for the Subcontinent

During the 1780s and the early 1790s, British employees of the Company had made no attempt to understand village culture in the Madras region. However, with the cession of the Baramahal, Malabar, and Dindigul in 1792, everything altered. For the first time on the subcontinent, the Company expected British officers to go personally to the villages of each area over which they had tax responsibility to assume direct charge of this activity. In this process, they also had to seek to control an agrarian population in a more direct political way than through the medium of an indigenous tax farmer. Often, in the process, these officers began to look on the local population as subjects of an increasingly unified government. They also had to form some kind of evaluative understanding of local agrarian culture. British officers who approached the society of the subcontinent with some vigor and who sought to "understand" brought to Madras certain assumptions about society and economy that were percolating through educated society in Britain at that time. This perspective constituted the basis of colonial domination.

One of the most important individuals who helped shape an understanding of the Jagir in the 1790s was Lionel Place. Central to the ideas that he brought to India were free trade notions derived from Adam Smith and attitudes toward religion based, it appears, on the assumptions of David Hume. When Place assessed Tamil society, many of these ideas came into play. However, in the productive process then ensuing no direct relationship existed between ideas brought from England and those articulated by Place. Instead, Place and others like him immediately framed their concepts in ways that built on ideas already presumed or contested in the local environment. It is important that the ideas of Place and his colleagues not be characterized as "western" nor the ideas available locally "indigenous." Both sets of assumptions were bound up so intimately with each other as to make it impossible to locate authorship. British officers and local individuals operated as part of one epistemic field.

Not least of the implications behind this caution is the fact that we must not essentialize the intellectual positions occupied by a myriad of British and local actors. Beyond individual differences of temperament, outlook, and function, we discover differences in the institutional viewpoints of the Board of Revenue, the governor in council, and others. Similarly, we do not want to essentialize the contributions made to this project even by the group of Mirasidars (who differed in their relationships to British officers), let alone by other local actors such as the Dubashes or the paraiyārs. Authorship is so diffused as to be unlocatable. What we can uncover, however, is that each of the participants involved occupied a different subject position in different contexts. Moreover, whatever the intention of specific contributions made to the dialogue, the result was used, changed, and manipulated by the person or group to whom it had been directed. This chapter tries to examine various events to show how this process worked.

One mental orientation that Place and other British actors brought with them rested in messianic and millennial ideas. As Place and his fellows appraised society, they perceived that society was in decay and assumed that a purer, more admirable society had existed in the distant past. More precisely, they envisioned their work as contributing to a cleansed society, one that bore many similarities with the society they perceived to have existed in the English past. Indeed, the only way they could relate to Tamil society was to deal with a constructed past Tamil society. This essentialized, unchanging Tamil past took on a meaning that was more important than all the "previous pasts" of Tamil society. Similarly, the only way by which the Tamils—and an increasing number of local individuals perceived things in this way—could relate to the British colonial state was by a consideration of their own constructed past in the heteroglot and interactive terms that were being generated by this cultural negotiation. This obtained not only for the millennial vision of Place but also for a wide variety of cultural definitions and institutions explored during the late eighteenth and early nineteenth centuries in South India. The work of Colonel Colin Mackenzie, for instance, depended on both the field work and the assumptions of his local non-European assistants, who collected thousands of oral histories and "wrote" or "translated" them into a form that was understandable, attractive, or acceptable both to the local individuals who provided these materials and to Mackenzie or other British officers of the Company. The interactive process differed only as to time and place and not as to goal. Therefore, the Tamil past and the past constructed for all of the southern part of the subcontinent assumed a political, psychic, and economic importance for members of the society that it previously had not had. This deforming and naturalizing process went on in an unseen way. Crucial definitions of the society and changes it had undergone, like those created for Tamil society, resulted from collaborative projects that involved both local actors from the area and British officials.

Let us now consider a particular set of interactions between the British, local land controllers, tenants, and the paraiyar (a caste name) or palli (a caste name) Paṇṇaiyāḷs, bonded laborers known in British historiography as "agrestic slaves." These interactions may help to suggest some of the larger dialogic processes we have identified, and will convey the complex nature of this multiauthored construction of the past.

The Nature of the "Mirasidar Insurrection" of 1795–96

The "site" of these activities was what the local records referred to as an "insurrection." This protest on the part of the land controllers of the Jagir was both a ritual and a political attempt by the land controllers and their Pannaiyals to resist British intervention in order to remain undisturbed in their activities. The "insurrection" began in October and November 1795 as an unwillingness by the land controllers located to the west of Fort St. George to accept Place's new tax assessments. In November of that year, some of these land controllers, accompanied by their bonded and daily laborers from this Poonamallee area, began to desert the Jagir for the territory of the Nawab of Arcot further to the west. In the same month, a destructive cyclonic storm dumped large amounts of rain on the area and broke many tanks and artificial reservoirs. In April and May 1796 the desertion intensified, spreading to other areas, particularly to the Karanguli area southwest of Madras. During this time, Collector Place made desperate attempts to get the Mirasidars and their bonded and daily laborers to return, first by distraining their movable property (cattle, grain, and the like) and then by banishing those Mirasidars who would not come back. In an effort to dominate and control the process of interaction, Place chose as his principle mechanism of coercion the threat of taking away the hereditary right of these "insurrectionary" Mirasidars to a share of the village product and granting it to more "loyal" occupancy tenants. A critical element was the action taken by the debt-bonded and daily laborers (mostly paraiyar or untouchable) whose flight and demands for more rice from the harvest grain-heap drew the intense scrutiny of the government.

Place's attention was caught partly because the paraiyar were, and could be, used to employ violence against Company employees and other Europeans by their mirasidar masters. Indeed, some of these paraiyar Pannaiyals and Paḍiyāḷs—laborers who worked for paḍis ("measures" of about 100 cubic inches each) of rice or payment in kind—were imprisoned by the Company because they were considered to have been ringleaders in fomenting the flight of the paraiyars from the Jagir. Between September and November, in the growing season of 1796, the Mirasidars of the Poonamallee area had surreptitiously let water out of the irrigation tanks and intentionally did not use the water so that there would be no crops to tax. Even beyond the explicit resistance of flight and noncultivation, part of the action of this "insurrection" involved the ways in which the Mirasidars and their agents helped to set Place and his superiors at odds. This strategy began when they induced Place's own tax-gathering staff not to inform him of their manipulation of irrigation practices to ensure that crops would not be grown.

Amorality as Strategy, Amorality as Decay

As noted in the Introduction, a critical element in the cultural definition of moral decay among the villages around Madras was that deception and immorality permeated local society. Both British Company employees, particularly Place, and local individuals pointed to this behavior as a product of cultural decline. Though these perceptions suggested also that "corruption" permeated not only "low" village society but "high" politics as well, and that the one side helped perpetuate the other, they still appeared to be in desperate need of reformation. The model provided to guide this reformation was the "golden age" past.

A modern social science rendition of this problem has been formulated by F. G. Bailey in *Stratagems and Spoils* and other writings. Rather than seeing amoral behavior as either part of a decadent culture or reprehensible, Bailey characterizes these "deceptive" activities as ways to ideologically order the life of politics and hence to survive. He looks on these rules as pragmatic dictates that govern political activity, pointing out that though politics is serious (in that it involves people's lives and valuable resources) it can most productively be seen as a game. Any game, he suggests, is ordered by a commonly accepted set of rules. Among these presumptions is the fact that competitors should be evenly matched so that the weaker player will have some chance of winning.

Moreover, any kind of behavior that would totally eliminate the opponent—so that the game would never be played again—is forbidden.[40] Unlike normative rules, the rules Bailey suggests operate in political contests that present prizes to win. Therefore, he argues, participants in these contests follow a strategy that allows moral rules to apply only to the contestant's family relations or his core following. Outside that core and set of family relations, it is quite acceptable to use amoral tactics and deception to win.[41]

As we will see in the account that follows, the "amoral tactics and deception"—that is, the game Bailey ascribes to a legitimate, productive, and pragmatic peasant strategy—was looked on by Place as simply a sign of moral decline. It seems likely that for Place social and political relations did not constitute a game. Thus, while Bailey's general social science characterization can explain an outsider's view of village relations both in the present and the past, it is less useful in understanding the meanings that were attributed to it in this specific historical situation by all the participants. We must see the processes by which society came to be analyzed and described as resulting from a profound change of ideas based on new historical requirements. In the interactive construction of knowledge that developed, these contemporary "amoral and corrupt" behaviors were regarded as not part of the ancient past and, therefore, as not legitimate; they could not serve as a useful model for shaping future society. We will see in this chapter and in Chapter 2 that these and other gestures were used as part of a general project to construct knowledge not only about the past of the cultural area around Madras and, in a way, for the subcontinent generally but also to some extent to construct knowledge about Britain as well. Therefore, Bailey's ideas, though useful as a modern social scientific explanation, do not take into account this dynamic kind of dialogic activity whose main goal was to construct the past as a way to prefigure the future.

Dominant agrarian groups in late eighteenth-century South India thus were perceived by Company employees as observing these "deceptive" and "amoral" rules. When the Company took over the Jagir, the employees of the Company were confronted for many years by a sustained and effective opposition to their attempt to control the activities and gather the taxes of the 2,241 villages in the area. This behavior not only thwarted the straightforward project undertaken by Place and others but also insisted on an active role in the process being assigned to local actors.

Land and Society; Mirasidars and Dubashes

Then, as now, the area of the Jagir was dotted by more than three thousand artificial reservoirs called tanks—some quite large—built to catch rainwater. Rain in this part of the subcontinent fell mostly between September and December, and the main rice crop was harvested between January and March. In 1796, the total arable land of the Jagir was divided between that considered to be irrigable (nañcai) or wet (212,155 kanis or about 636,465 acres) and that which was considered to be unirrigable (puñcai) or dry (129,631 kanis or about 388,893 acres); only 70,718 kanis (about 212,154 acres) or 37.1 percent of the nañcai or wet paddy land was actually being cultivated at the time. Likewise, at that time only 28,806 kanis (about 89,418 acres), or 22.22 percent of the dry, unirrigable dry or puñcai land was being cultivated.[42]

Rice cultivation demanded irrigation and intensive labor. In this area, dominant groups—those who belonged to the higher status groups in the caste system—would not touch the plough and did not do the actual cultivation themselves. Evidence from the late eighteenth century as well as more recent information gathered by anthropologists and others suggests that two of the most important groups of dominant subcastes, or jātis, in this area were brahmans—some of whom had been given grants by kings around the sacred center of Kanchipuram forty-five miles west of Madras town—and Koṇḍaikaṭṭi vēḷḷāḷas. Called the kāṇiyāṭci system in Tamil documents and parlance, in the 1790s the system of dividing the crop into shares was known as the mirāsi system. Though the mirāsi system differed from area to area in the coastal Tamil region, the basic premise was that the harvest of the fields in the village was divided into a series of shares. Persons who possessed one or a part of a share were called Mirāsidars because they had what was termed a mirās. In the Jagir, assessments of the land tax by the state were made with the Mirasidars of each village collectively (in a village settlement) for what was called the mēlvāram (the state share) of the village agrarian product. In the pre-British system, mirasi land in the Tondai country (a sociocultural region in the north of the Tamil-speaking area) seems to have largely circulated among members of the coparcenary group in each village. "Circulated" means that there was no particular piece of land associated with any particular individual or family; instead, land was redistributed either every year or every few years. A later commentator, F. W. Ellis, tried to show in 1814 that it was possible to alienate the rights to mirasi land; he succeeded in calling the mirasi system a form of real property.

This seemed more convincing by the last decade of the eighteenth century, because the custom of redistributing the land operated with less force by that time.

Both brahman and Kondaikatti vellala Mirasidars enjoyed the hereditary right to a share of the produce of the land and the work of their bonded laborers or Pannaiyals. The dominant groups in this relationship were called Kāṇiyāṭcikkārars or Mirasidars (a later Arabic and Urdu term taken into Tamil). According to this evidence, Kondaikatti vellala Mirasidars usually had Pannaiyals from the paraiyar caste while brahman Mirasidars had Pannaiyals who were pallis. Pallis as a caste group were located above the untouchability line in status and were later self-ascribed as vanikula kshatriyas. In fact some pallis had managed to become Mirasidars themselves.[43] The term "Pannaiyal" applied to laborers who, as individuals, were permanently tied to the land or to specific Mirasidars by debt bondage. Mirasidars could and did use violence to force Pannaiyals to do what they wanted them to do: evidence from the earlier period makes it clear that violence was used both in agrarian and domestic slavery.[44] As we will see, though debt bondage and the Pannaiyal system ended in the 1940s, even as late as the 1970s paraiyar laborers in Chingleput district were quite conscious of the landlords to whom they were connected. At the same time, because the labor of the Pannaiyals had become valuable, they could no longer be abused.

In this mix there was also a group of individuals called Padiyals from both the paraiyar and palli castes who were hired agricultural laborers. Padiyals were an important part of the intensive cultivation system and received wages in kind.[45] Padiyals usually made an agreement for their labor with Mirasidars annually at the start of the cultivation and tax year, in the middle of July. Though Padiyals did not occupy a position of debt bondage much, evidence suggests that relations between Mirasidars and Padiyals were not good. Generally speaking, Pannaiyals and Padiyals were referred to by eighteenth-century Company documents as "farm laborers" or "farm servants." By the beginning of the nineteenth century, however, Pannaiyals particularly came to be referred to as "slaves."[46] As we will see in Chapter 4, British and Indian reformers became concerned with the condition of these Pannaiyals, whom they too called slaves. If we anticipate these discussions a bit, we may say that the "emancipation" of these Pannaiyals simply took the right to use violence against these debt-bonded laborers away from the Mirasidars and gave it to the state.

Relations between the Mirasidar patrons and the Padiyals and Pannaiyals thus constituted one of the most important vertical relationships
in the Jagir; these relationships were based in the village. However, Mirasidars also had social and marriage networks that stretched to many
parts of the Jagir and to Madras town. For instance, some of the Kondaikatti vellalas had been employed as government servants under the
Nawab of Arcot.[47] During the time when the Nawab leased the Jagir
from the Company (1763–82) and during the early years after the Company took it over, many Kondaikatti vellalas gained privileges to cultivate land at a reduced land tax or at no tax at all.[48] These rights were
called māniyams and surottiriyams (Tamil "curōttiriyam"), ināms, and
the like. One of the main conflicts between the Company and these
Mirasidars concerned the resumption by the Company of these privileges, many of which the Company officials believed had been usurped
illegally. Even when legally held, these tax privileges were viewed by the
Company as part of a general process by which Mirasidars and Palayakkars, who had been employed to "police" or "watch" villages under
the pre-British system, defrauded the Company of substantial amounts
of money. Indeed, Poonamallee, one of the areas under Company control from 1749 onward, formed a base for the growth of power of many
Kondaikatti vellala families. Poonamallee had been granted to the Company by the Nawab in 1749; named for a village called Pūntamalli,
located about fourteen miles from St. George in Madras, the Poonamallee territory was characterized by the presence of many Kondaikattis
who had established themselves through these "usurped" privileges.

As important as the village-based vertical ties of the Mirasidars were
the horizontal relationships developed between the Mirasidars and their
literate kin, called Dubashes, who lived in Madras. A Dubash was a
person who knew two languages; generally, the term was employed by
the British in Madras to refer to a group of individuals who knew English and Tamil or Telugu.[49] Usually Dubashes acted as agents or bro-
kers either for individuals or as employees of the British and other European Companies. Even today, modern companies in Madras that have
origins in the eighteenth century have a senior official called a Dubash,
a vestige of this practice. Most of the Dubashes in late eighteenth-century
Madras were Telugu brahmans or Telugu perikavārs, Tamil kanna-
kappillais, Tamil yādhavas, or Tamil Kondaikatti vellalas.[50] Many of
these Kondaikatti vellala Dubashes were connected by kinship to Kondaikatti vellala Mirasidars in the Poonamallee and other rural areas of
the Jagir. In contemporary documents, these Kondaikattis were known

as Mudalis—later lengthened to "Mudaliyār"—a term that literally meant a person of first rank. However, in the view of many of the Company officers, the term "Mudali" carried a pejorative meaning. Mudalis were despised by the British because they were considered both essential actors and great threats to individual British and Company operations. Place said that almost every domestic servant down to the lowest menial employed by a European gentleman could be included in the network of connections deployed by these Dubashes. According to him, the Mudalis were able to use their contacts and knowledge of Europeans to retain "every inhabitant [in their own villages] in complete subjection."[51]

Thus, it is in regard to this nexus of relationships previously established by Mirasidars that a new, interactive process of reconstituting the past was brought to bear. The dialogic process that emerged at this crucial point in time had no single prize to be won at the end of the negotiations. Indeed, the process itself was the game, and the result of the negotiations at any point shaped the next phase of interaction. As noted, it was not only the nature of local players and the past that was altered by the dialogue; the conceptualization of British society at home as well as in a colonial context was also subject to naturalization and reconstruction.

Mirasidar and Pannaiyal Survival Strategies

To understand the nature of the contest between the Company and, respectively, the rural Mirasidars and their urban Dubash connections, we must look at the way in which these relations developed in the 1780s. When the British first took over the Jagir directly in January 1782, all but a few villages were uninhabited and their fields largely uncultivated because of the invasion of Hyder Ali and his horsemen. Without cultivation, it was impossible to collect land taxes. During 1782, villagers gradually returned to their homes in the Jagir. Because the confusion and aftermath of the war allowed families to establish themselves in new, dominant positions, disputes often arose. In the village of Viravorum near Manimangalam (sixteen miles southwest of Madras town), for instance, a dispute arose between two peasant communities, the agamudaiyars and the reddis. According to the agamudaiyars, the Mirasidar rights of the reddis had been sold during the war against Hyder Ali. After the war, the agamudaiyars were unwilling to allow the reddis to rebuild their houses in the village. Richard Dighton investigated the matter, believing that the reddis should be allowed to rebuild their houses as before and to cultivate their fields. Dighton sent a Company servant to enforce the Company's order, but this inferior servant was beaten almost to death by the agamudaiyars, who were joined by their fellows from a village twenty-five miles to the northwest. Indeed, in this period agents of the Company often had great difficulty in imposing control over the Jagir. Dighton concluded that in the future it would be necessary for a band of armed sepoys to execute the Company's orders.[52]

Besides the confusion brought on by the war with Hyder Ali and the opportunity seized by some peasants to improve their status, postwar circumstances benefited other villagers, such as artisans who found employment in the Company military establishments. This seems to represent a newfound freedom; before the chaos brought on by the war, artisans, it was said, had not been allowed to leave their villages. Even in the middle of the 1790s, Place found that artisans who had mirasis or hereditary rights to the product of land in villages were unwilling to return to their villages to perform needed services.[53] This confusion contributed to the new rules for the interaction forged in this period.

For the British employees of the Company, as for both the Mirasidars and their Pannaiyals and Padiyals, the land revenue or state share of the grain was one of several valuable resources located in the rural environment. When the land tax was collected between February and June of every year (in several installments called "kists"), and after several deductions had been made for the Padiyals and Pannaiyals and other sums had been subtracted for the upkeep of the village, the grain pile was divided into the cultivator's share (kuṭivāram) and the state share (melvaram). We can discern how Bailey's "game" came to be played by the Mirasidars and the government if we look first at an account of the way the Nawab of Arcot collected the land taxes before the British took over the Jagir.

Under the Nawab of Arcot, according to Lionel Place, the cultivator was given an agreement ("cowle," or Tamil "kavul" from the Arabic) at the beginning of the agricultural year in August or September to assure him of getting a share of the crops. When the harvest was underway, an estimate ("dowle," or Tamil "tavul") was made of the state share of the grain on the ground. Prices for this grain were also fixed by the head inhabitants of a village and the revenue officer of the state called the Amildar. According to Place's account, the head villagers received a favorable tax assessment and the cultivators, who had less land, paid proportionately more. At this point, the amildar was given a gratuity by the head villagers.

Then, both the amildar and the head villagers waited at the revenue office (Tamil "kacceri") of the Nawab, where the estimate was examined by the Nawab's manager and other revenue servants. The manager and the head revenue servants of the Nawab would then be influenced in their decision by promise of a present (called a darbār karccu). On the recommendation of the manager, "since the Nabob [Nawab] could not investigate it himself," the Nawab confirmed it. The Nawab suspected collusion between the head villagers, the amildar, and his own revenue staff to depress the amount agreed on. As a result, to get closer to the "actual" revenue capacity, the Nawab would then tell his manager that in return for agreeing to the assessment he expected a handsome gift (or nazzar) in return. The Nawab's sons also added their own demands.

Cultivators were cajoled and coerced into accepting the estimate. Otherwise, the grain stayed on the ground and losses were incurred by everybody. Because of all these demands from officials and from the Nawab, a heavy balance usually lay against the cultivator's (i.e., the Mirasidar's) name; this demand "absorbs what he set aside for subsistence." The cultivator was therefore confronted by two options—either to be satisfied with the small amount he got out of his land or to desert it altogether. From this point of view, the cultivator or the Mirasidar (called a cultivator even though he did not touch the plough) was someone to exploit. This description by Place seems fairly straightforward and reliable, insofar as it describes actions taken by the players. But what did Place make of these actions, and what motivations did he attribute to the actors?

As Bailey would say, in all peasant environments only close relatives of a peasant are within a moral core. All outsiders must be manipulated to enable one to survive, and Amildars and other officers of the state fell in the "outsider" category.[54] According to this model of behavior, Mirasidars felt no compunction about deceiving outsiders to protect themselves. From Place's perspective, however, the cultivator may be seen as one who "devises as many deceptions on the Circar [the state] as are put in practice against himself." A Mirasidar would combine with the village recordkeeper (Tamil "kanakappillai") to alter the accounts. He would also hide part of the crops he had cultivated. He combined with the other agents of the state—the tarafdars and the peons—to plunder the heaps of grain on the ground.[55] "Throughout," said Place, "is collusion." Here we can see that though the process seemed rational and pragmatic to the Mirasidars and other local individuals holding both high and low positions, Place looked on it as a form of moral decay because it did not conform to his idea of civil society. From Place's interpretation, therefore, though it appeared that the entire surplus of a village had been taken up to pay the state share or melvaram, the state assumed that the cultivator had managed to set aside enough for himself and his family to live on.

According to Place, in a system such as this a cultivator or Mirasidar was forced to set up pretensions that would provide enough protection to offset the purposely exorbitant demands made by the state. A Mirasidar and his local Padiyals and Pannaiyals were also forced to conceal their wealth in a limited good environment; otherwise, this wealth would draw too much attention. "Theft and fraud therefore he was driven to resort to as his only means of existence."[56] It was natural, as Bailey would say, that when the Company took over the Jagir the villagers would seek to employ many of the same tactics, continuing the game simply to survive. In the face of these strategies, the effort to characterize society as "morally decayed" was important as a way by which the newly "honest" British bureaucratic moral ideas of the public sphere could be openly delineated and the future of the local society formulated.

In the 1780s, then, British employees of the Company were certainly not in any stronger position to collect the taxes from the Jagir than they had been before. This resulted from both the economic condition of the area and the ability of cultivators to resist Company pressures. In 1775, one report of the area spoke of the great vulnerability under which villagers operated. Poor people "have [so] long been used to the hand of oppression that few have an idea of such a mode of redress [to any higher court or authority]." These people were always afraid that the person called the "renter [a tax farmer] or some principal Nautwars [Nattars or heads of right subcastes, such as the Kondaikatti vellalas, controllers of nāḍus] . . . may not with impunity deprive them of their property."[57] When a local Tamil employee of the Company abused and maltreated villagers near Chingleput, about thirty miles southeast of Madras town, the Company was quite willing to dismiss him.[58] However, when the Company itself started to demand services in a way that was increasingly unacceptable to local Tamil moral ideas, villagers had few alternatives but to employ what many British perceived as "disloyal" and "dishonest" stratagems simply to exist. In 1791, John Clerk, collector of what then constituted the northern division of the Jagir, had been asked by the military department to provide horsekeepers and grasscutters for the Company's cavalry. Clerk dutifully "impressed several men [paraiyar

Pannaiyals and Padiyals] for this service." He found that they were unwilling to serve in the cavalry camp:

> Such is their aversion to go to camp that a general insurrection among
> the ryots [cultivators, but Clerk here means paraiyar Pannaiyals and Padi-
> yals] has taken place who declare they will immediately abandon cultivation
> if any one of them are [sic] taken from their villages. Having experienced the
> consequence of a revolt among the lower class of inhabitants on a former
> occasion, I have every reason to believe, if coercive measures are continued
> the ryots [Pannaiyals and Padiyals] will totally desert the cultivation whereby
> the Revenue will be entirely lost.[59]

Clerk noted that these men he had impressed for work as horsekeepers
and grasscutters were confined "in their own areas" since his own armed
peons were unable to oppose the "mob of parriars [paraiyar Pannaiyals
and Padiyals] assembled to prevent them from being taken away."[60]
Thus, Pannaiyals and Padiyals, acting on the orders of their Mirasidar
master (who would lose the labor of the men), sought to impose their
will on the Company's directive by hitting them where it hurt the most—
by threatening to desert the land so that there would be neither crops
nor taxes to collect.

Rural Relations: Mirasidars, Pannaiyals, Padiyals, Renters, and Courts

Company attempts to get at the land taxes of the Jagir could only be
successful if its own lower-paid revenue employees were pulled into its
project along with others possessing the influence and land power bases
in the villages. The roster of these local authors of the project is large,
including such figures as Nattars (caste headmen), tax farmers, and their
renters. Perhaps the most important lower tax employee used by the
Company was the Amildar. In addition, among the villagers themselves
was a village resident whom the Company officials sought to make an
employee of the state—the Nattar, head of a righthand subcaste group
such as the Kondaikatti vellalas. In 1796, the Company hoped that Nattars would be useful "to assist Government in the settlement [tax as-
sessment] and realization of the Revenue from the villages"—a feeling
that continued for the next half century. At the same time, however, it
noted that "this Class of people [has] . . . assumed so pernicious and
corrupt an influence over the ryots [Mirasidars]."[61] In the early 1780s,
therefore, Nattars were considered a "necessary evil" by Company of-

ficers. They seemed indispensable because they assisted in collecting the land revenue from rural areas; before the British arrival, they were paid for their services by grants of land that carried little or no tax liability. Company officers repeatedly found that Nattars used this land—and particularly the people who worked on it—as a political base to blunt the force of the Company's initiatives in local areas. Nattars in the Jagir were important Mirasidars who naturally sought to enhance their own local position any way they could.

Like all Mirasidars, Nattars also had Padiyals and Pannaiyals, important in this context because of the claim they exercised over a portion of the harvest. If the Nattar or Mirasidar was a Kondaikatti vellala, his Pannaiyals and Padiyals would be paraiyars. Pannaiyals and Padiyals were rewarded in two ways for their agricultural work. Even before the grain on the threshing floor was divided between the state share (melvaram) and the cultivator's share (kutivaram), several deductions were made, including one for these paraiyar Padiyals and Pannaiyals. Known variously as tuntu (remnant) or kalavāsam (Tamil "kalavācam"), the contribution for Pannaiyals and Padiyals was claimed as customary ("māmūl," an Arabic term taken over into Tamil through Persian and later Urdu). Between two and three marakkāls (depending on the village) of grain for every ten kalams of grain beaten out on the threshing floor were taken; this amounted to between 1.6 and 2.6 percent of the threshed crop.[62] In fact, the Mirasidar usually gave extra amounts to his Padiyals and Pannaiyals during the year because the amounts given on the threshing floor as kalavasam or tuntu were insufficient.[63]

However, anything that was "customary" could be manipulated according to need. In the mid-1790s, it was noted that the word "mamul" meant "custom" unbroken by any kind of innovation but could also mean "law" or "rule." Ultimately, it was believed that it could be looked on as "mere usage" or "prevailing habit," and that was conceived by the British to mean "generally but not universally adopted and which gains assent only if convenient."[64] In other words, they realized that "past usage" or mamul (and the past in general) was a malleable commodity that could be changed to serve contemporary, historically contingent requirements. In many confrontations between Company servants and local villagers, the villagers invoked what was mamul as a way to legitimate their claims, although some Company officers discounted the validity of the term. Company land tax and other policy came to be based on what was "past usage." This standard in the eyes of Company officials was more "likely to produce an equitable division [into state and the cultivator's share] than any general regulation formed without a possibility of embracing so many local considerations," which in turn would greatly simplify the way in which fees were deducted.[65] Locally powerful Mirasidars and their Pannaiyals and Padiyals recognized the susceptibility of Company officers to the claim of customary usage and manipulated the concept for their own purposes. The same goal operated in relations between the Pannaiyals and Padiyals on the one hand and the Mirasidars themselves on the other.

Other groups with local interests were those involved in tax revenue relationships. From early in the 1780s, the Company gave the Jagir out in segments to individuals called renters who contracted to farm the land tax of the area. Renters were expected to deposit a certain amount of money as security against future payments for the tax they collected. These men also were expected to provide money for short-term taccavi (Tamil "takāvi") loans (money advances) to villagers and to spend a certain amount of money every year in repairing the tanks, reservoirs, and waterways in their area. However, renters never repaired the tanks or waterways and gave only minimal short-term loans to the cultivators. Though many of the renters in the early years appear to have been former dependents of the Company, many more had formed close connections with the Mirasidars, from whom the Company officers had much difficulty extracting the land tax. Relative to our concerns, these renters nevertheless were important to the British because they also attracted cultivators to the land—tenants or Payirkkaris—who functioned as additional authors of the land revenue-based social and political values being created. One of the Company's goals in the 1780s was to extend the cultivation in the Jagir because of the dislocation caused by war between 1780 and 1784. Renters were therefore used to invite tenants to take over plots of land. In local terminology, these occupancy tenants were called Payirkkaris. However, Mirasidars looked on these men and their families as strangers and newcomers whose claims to a hereditary portion of the product of the soil were stoutly rebuffed because of their attempts to claim status as Mirasidars. Indeed, the antagonism between the Mirasidars and the Payirkkaris became a central aspect of rural relations in the Jagir area for the next century and a half.

Whatever the origin of Payirkkaris, Mirasidars believed that all such outsiders, and particularly agents of the state, were to be manipulated in whatever way possible. Mirasidars first wanted to protect any privileges they had acquired as a result of the confusion that occurred in many areas between 1763 and 1782. Such privileges included the grants of land to them as Nattars on a reduced-tax basis. Not only did Nattar status thus liberate them from paying the state's portion of what was produced but it also gave them power over those who worked the lands. At the same time, Mirasidars sought to shift to Company officers the task of repairing tanks and waterways so that the land tax would not be increased by the tax farmers. In 1784, Company officials had already recommended that the tanks in the Jagir be repaired.[66] Two important villagers in the Poonamallee area—Mangadu Oppa Mudali and Eva-lappa Mudali, both Kondaikatti vellala Mirasidars—used that knowledge to manipulate the Company into assuming responsibility for tank repair. They argued that they were unable to do anything themselves but also asked the Company not to demand too high a land revenue on this account.[67] Thus, Mirasidars understood and used the vulnerabilities of the Company in negotiations regarding a task that should have been undertaken by the Mirasidars themselves (because a specific sum that was part of the village product, the ēri mērai, or tank fee, already went to them earmarked for the repair of the tank).

Mirasidars also manipulated the coercive mechanism of the state to harass their opponents, particularly in the Poonamallee area. Perhaps the most outstanding example of this was by the local Mirasidars of the Mayor's Court in Madras town, who beat down unsuspecting victims.[68] Because the area over which the court's jurisdiction held sway was poorly defined, Mirasidars and their urban connections used this ambivalence to harass opponents in the Poonamallee area and to increase their hold on that area.[69] Indeed, many individuals were able to manipulate agents of the state because they could anticipate their movements by information received through confidential contacts with the Company's servants in the Madras bureaucracy. On one occasion, Richard Dighton, who was in charge of the Jagir in January 1786, had been told to take over the revenue collection of several areas. Collection had been previously contracted by tax farmers, who were now unable to make their payments to the Company. However, though Dighton instructed Company Tahsildars (tax collectors) to take tax authority over the areas as soon as they received his instructions from Madras, the renters had knowledge of the takeover even before Dighton himself had received word. He reported that the renter of Manimangalam, south of Poonamallee, had by some means come to know about the appointment of the Company Tahsildars. As a result, even before the Company Tahsildar arrived to take charge from the renter, the renter had already sent away a sum of pagodas 60 that he had collected just the previous day so that the Company could not repossess it.[70]

Still another device used to undercut the authority of the Company government in a village was to submit a petition to superior authorities in Madras about a Company official or his representatives in the Jagir. For instance, on one occasion in December 1785, a senior official in Madras received a petition from the "Inhabitants of Poonamallee." The petition, composed by Evalappa Mudali, attempted to reduce the credibility of De Souza, a wealthy man and former employee of the Company who served as renter or tax farmer of Poonamallee. Evalappa Mudali had the surottiriyam (called "shotrum" in the records) or the right to rent the pēṭṭai (market area) of Poonamallee at a reduced tax and submitted the petition specifically to prevent De Souza from introducing new Payirkkaris into the area. Charles Oakley, who received the petition for the board of revenue in Madras, concluded that it contained no legitimate grievance. However, he decided to give the right to rent the pettai of Poonamallee on amāni to De Souza, who could then collect the taxes directly from the shopkeepers and other taxpayers, deduct the surottiriyam rent, and pay the surplus to Evalappa Mudali.[71] In this way, Evalappa Mudali would "receive the produce of the privilege he has usually enjoyed, without that influence or authority [over laborers and village officials] by which he has occasioned so much mischief."[72] All the local residents and cultivators in Poonamallee were instructed as well to deal directly with the Company's representative in the Jagir instead of sending petitions over his head to Fort St. George in Madras. In a similar move, Evalappa Mudali had disarmed Dighton by blaming the paraiyar Pannaiyals and Padiyals for defrauding the state, claiming that they were "taking away without measuring that part of the paddy [unhusked rice] that remains under the heap on the spot where it is beat out, a practice very prejudicial to Government since it allows fraud that is very difficult to prevent and which fraud Eevalappah Moodelly was active in pointing out."[73] Here, as in many other situations in this period, the Mirasidars tried to convince Company officers that the paraiyar Pannaiyals and Padiyals had independent responsibility for activities that would undercut the power of state agents. It is clear from the evidence, however, that the paraiyars followed the orders of their Mirasidar masters in these actions.

Whatever the case, Mirasidars used the sensibilities, structures, and vulnerabilities of the Company to mislead officials and to feed its fears about its vulnerability in being deceived and defrauded by those at the bottom of the social hierarchy. Though the British occupied the dominant role and sought to exploit the environment, they were subject to survival strategies that cut away at the power of the state. Moreover, in the aggregate, these activities, whether undertaken by local individuals or by British employees of the Company, helped to construct a knowledge of the Jagir that characterized local society as being in a state of great moral decay and in need of regeneration. As we will see, these mechanisms proved particularly valuable in inducing Company employees to believe that the paraiyars could engage in violence or other activities without reference to their masters. Here again, the use of violence (and therefore control) moved out of the hands of the state, as illustrated by a major disturbance that occurred in late 1785. It incorporated all these techniques that well illustrate the goals of local land-controlling interests as well as their use of Pannaiyals and Padiyals to further their aims.

The 1785 "Paraiyar Insurrection"

Richard Dighton in late 1785 had sought to do two things. First, he tried to impose the will of the Company government on the Poonamallee area by taking over the privileges of some of the Nattars, arguing that these had been "unjustly usurped from Government." He also confirmed some existing Nattars as instruments of the Company in the area. It was customary when implementing policy for an administrator to send a crier and a drummer whose purpose it was to publicize government orders to important villages; Dighton employed criers and drummers after he had confirmed the Nattars of Poonamallee to tell all those concerned that they were to come to him with any grievance and not to the Nattars. Shortly afterward, the Nattar Mudali and other head villagers in Poonamallee, some of whose privileges Dighton had taken away, "fabricated" a grievance petition and turned to other aggressive measures to undercut Dighton.[74]

Called an "insurrection" in the records, this agrarian disturbance consisted in leaders such as Evalappa Mudali withdrawing Pannaiyals and Padiyals from cultivation in November 1785 (the middle of the growing season) and gathering those Pannaiyals and Padiyals together. Once collected, these laborers threatened violence against Company officers. Mirasidar Evalappa Mudali had up to that time been able to control the lower Company employees (who were local individuals) in the area. Indeed, in his efforts to monopolize the vegetable oil trade, on one occasion Evalappa Mudali's own employees had beaten some Company sepoys sent from the nearby cantonment to buy cooking oil. Another locally important Kondaikatti vellala Mirasidar, Mangadu Oppa Mudali (as his name suggests, originally from the nearby village of Mangadu), had written letters to several villagers about the proposed disturbance.[75] These men chose the middle of the growing season to withdraw their Pannaiyals and Padiyals from cultivation, "when their whole attention is so immediately necessary," to create the maximum effect on Company officers who feared the losses to state tax revenues.[76] As soon as Dighton discovered these activities, he went to Poonamallee to imprison the leaders. In this he was backed by the authority of Charles Oakley, a senior official in the Company who told Dighton that "every attempt to compel Government into a compliance with just or unjust desires at the expense of the Revenue must be positively forbid and discouraged."[77]

When Dighton got to Poonamallee, he found the paraiyar Pannaiyals and Padiyals gathered in one place, intent on a grievance of their own that did not appear to relate to that directly mounted by the Mirasidars. None of them, they said, would "work unless they are allowed the Parrah Callus [paraiyar kalavasam] as usual." As suggested earlier, however, their masters had told these Pannaiyals and Padiyals to collect together as a way to demand that they be allowed a portion of the grain heap without any kind of measurement.[78] The result was not so much a challenge by agricultural laborers as an attempt to establish local dominance over the Company by the Mirasidars through the threat of violence and the loss of control that the Pannaiyals and Padiyals represented. Dighton was deeply concerned. The leaders of this disturbance (including also Muttu Kumarappa Mudali and Ambattur Vira Perumal from nearby villages) had all left town. Dighton even feared for his life and the safety of his office at Chetput outside Madras. Oakley the next day requested from the governor a company of sepoys under a "prudent" officer for protection against possible attack by the paraiyar Pannaiyals and Padiyals.[79] Both at this time and later, then, British officers were greatly intimidated by the Mirasidar control of Pannaiyals and Padiyals. Nevertheless, the separate interests of these laborers had also played a part in the confrontation in such a way that we may recognize the latter as authors of the resulting meaning constructed about the function of the event.

By the end of this episode, the essential grounds of dispute had been clearly drawn and the respective roles to be played by the antagonists clearly laid out. Company officials sought to cut away at Mirasidar juridical power. Mirasidars sought to establish themselves as the rightful local leaders by demonstrating their juridical power through their control of their Pannaiyals and Padiyals. For their part, Payirkkaris looked on these struggles and interactions as opportunities to strengthen their own position, though the paraiyar and palli Pannaiyals and Padiyals were tied to or had agreements with given Mirasidars. These important local leaders could get the same Pannaiyals and Padiyals to also threaten the use of violence even against Company officers unless "customary" practices were followed.

It is apparent that the "rules of the game" were largely known by both the British and the local population. Still, the "game" remained intimidating to the British, even though they dominated the area politically. This resulted from the fact that in this "game" the state often exercised less control than the British would have liked. Company officers realized that they were more dependent on the Mirasidars, Padiyals, and Pannaiyals than they wanted to be. This tension formed the basis of much production of meaning in this area. All the rules, of course, resulted from interaction between previous rulers and both Mirasidars and the laborers; these rules changed almost daily because of new requirements. If we accept Bailey's perspective, Place's account of the techniques employed by Mirasidars and others under the Nawab of Arcot indicates that a moral complementarity existed between all the parties to the tax gathering process, whether this was "amoral" or not.

Naturally, therefore, most of the actions of the players in the "game" were largely predictable since the players had trained each other over a long period of time. Not only were the actions of the players anticipated, but each contestant had prepared himself (most of these players were men) psychically for the outcome as well. This mental preparation, however, continued to be subject to new ambivalences. For the Company, the land tax was essential for its operation, burdened as it was by the debts of war in 1780 and the diminution in income from trade. In this context, it was essential for the Mirasidars to collude to maintain the game. From their perspective, Company resources were essential to the Mirasidars to repair tanks and the channels leading to them so long as the tax demand was not increased. Finally, as in any environment in which wet irrigation is dominant, local Pannaiyals and Padiyals were essential as the source of the intensive labor associated with rice cultivation.

Company Frustrations and Resulting New Tax Schemes

The main point of contention between the Company and the Mirasidars, however, was over the division of the respective shares of the harvest for the cultivator and the state. As we have seen, Richard Dighton had great difficulty trying to collect the state share in 1785. Although he had promulgated an order that each village in the Jagir should have an account of the distribution between the state and the cultivator's shares, it was never put into effect. The following year, Dighton sought to establish a new division of shares, but this again prompted many complaints. Besides the fact that the order did not take into account local usage, it also imposed too heavy a burden on the paraiyar Talaiyāris or village watchmen. Nor did it extend any incentive to return to artisans who had left their villages for employment both in Madras town and the military cantonments where their skills yielded good income. Though attempts were made to rectify these alleged shortcomings, ultimately the only places where the new government standard for the division of shares was accepted were villages where it was more favorable to the Mirasidar than the local mamul or "customary" shares had been. Renters found it more advantageous to stick to the old system because doing so avoided disputes with villagers and the necessity to use coercion to enforce this new distribution scheme. Finally, in 1790 the new allocation of shares, or vāram scheme, was annulled and the previous mamul system officially reimposed.

Some Board of Revenue members protested this strongly, feeling that the complaints represented purely the arguments of "the richer inhabitants to the great detriment of the Company's tax revenue." Roger Darvall, collector of what was then the southern division of the Jagir, reported that the mamul system, now reimposed for share division, was deleterious both to the Company's tax income and to the peace of the area. In 1792, a decision was made to fall back on the division of shares reported in the earliest survey of the Jagir conducted by Company officer Colonel Thomas Barnard in the 1770s (described above). With this adoption of Barnard's survey in 1792, the Company collectors in the Jagir were told to gather information to establish a "permanent equitable standard of division."[80] Then, once again, this abortive effort to expand the revenue base foundered on three interrelated aspects of the changing conditions. First, even the construction of new knowledge about the Jagir came up for grabs; no consensus emerged among the

British officers about the extent of benefits likely to accrue to the Company under the various share schemes. Second, the physical force and other coercive measures necessary to impose the state's revenue demands on the area far exceeded the Company's capacity. And third, the contestatory nature of the negotiations did not create a real winner among the British, Mirasidars, and other local interests. The no-win game continued, and the dialogue shifted to other issues and grounds.

Seeking to Reduce Dubash Power: The Appointment of Place

In late 1794, the Board of Revenue decided to make an all-out attempt to reduce the power of the Jagir Mirasidars and their Madras Dubash connections. They appointed a person of exceptional vigor and knowledge to undertake this job: Lionel Place had been what was called a "writer" in the Company's service in 1783 but rose rapidly to a position of importance within the Company's bureaucracy in Madras. Before his appointment as collector of the Jagir in November 1794, he made a name for himself as accountant to the Board of Revenue.[81] It was assumed at the time of his appointment as collector that he would encounter some difficulty in the course of his attempts to impose a new tax system on the Mirasidars of the Jagir.

In October 1795, Place submitted his first report on his activities. Concerned with three areas of the Jagir—Karanguli to the south, Kanchipuram to the west, and Tirupaccur to the northeast—the report covered some 898 out of a total of 2,241 villages in the Jagir. Place found that in each of the three areas Mirasidars and their urban connections had been able to retain what he considered to be a disproportionate share of the product of their villages, well beyond the amount allotted to them by share division considered locally appropriate. Place said that the process of keeping this surplus out of the hands of the Company was done by either concealing the sale price of the grain payment (selling the grain for a higher price than that reported) or by "defalcation" (using various devices such as false accounts to prevent the Company government or circar from getting its full share). In Tirupaccur, Mirasidars had kept back 24 percent more than was "their share," in Karanguli it was almost 60 percent, and in Kanchipuram it was almost 49 percent.[82]

In submitting his report, Place also sought support from the Board of Revenue for his work. Though the Board was impressed with the tremendous scope of the reform and the fact that the taxes from the

Jagir for the previous year exceeded the levels reached in 1772–77, "when the country was in its most flourishing state," it urged him to proceed with caution. This was to "prevent the measures adopted from being stamped with further apparent instability." Much of the Board's reaction probably resulted from the fact that though it sought a higher tax revenue from the Jagir, its primary goal was political stability. For instance, Place had indicated the necessity to regulate and tax the pilgrim traffic to the temples at Tiruvallur and what was then called Peddapalayam in order to acquire the funds needed to repair the temples. The Board concluded that "an adherence to those rules and maxims that prevailed in the well-regulated periods of the Hindu government cannot but be . . . satisfactory to the native and most conducive to the British dominion in India."[83] If there was one goal that could unify the Board, the Company, and many local individuals at this time it was the effort to construct a "well-regulated Hindu past" to solve contemporary problems. To continue their presence, however, the British depended on a large number of local inhabitants, a fact conclusively demonstrated by Place's later experience in the Jagir. This interdependence grew considerably over the next century and helped to restrain the behavior of everyone involved.

On the basis of his report, Place was permitted to conclude agreements with Mirasidars in the Jagir over proposed land taxes. However, on 26 November 1795, Place wrote to the Board of Revenue that, though he appeared to have made progress in making assessments with villages in Tirupaccur and Poonamallee parganas or subdivisions, he found a sudden unwillingness among the Mirasidars to agree to the proposed tax. In several villages Place cited as examples, he had taken care to offer tax agreements that were either the same as the previous year's or even below them. In his investigations, however, Place found that in each of these villages, where lands were largely in the hands of several Mirasidars who had connections with Dubashes in Madras town, the Mirasidars would not agree to Place's new tax rates; these Mirasidars opposing his attempts included Mangadu Oppa Mudali and several others who had also opposed Richard Dighton in 1785.

Confronted by this opposition to his plans, Place informed the Mirasidars that if they continued their unwillingness to agree to the tax assessments on their villages, they would have to relinquish their mirāsi (the hereditary right of the product of the village) in favor of somebody who would. Place had concluded that when he "found such opposition and intrigue thrown in . . . [his] way," he had little alternative but to abandon further attempts to make tax agreements with the villages in the Poonamallee area.[84] Indeed, although he had sought in some desperation assistance from the Nattars of the area in making tax agreements with the villages, he found "so manifest and determined a particularity to their own villages" that he decided to take over even their privileges on granted lands that had lower taxes.

Once again, the Mirasidars and other land controllers sought to reduce the authority of a Company official by submitting a petition over his head to the Board of Revenue. On 25 November 1795, one of Place's informants told him that such a petition had been submitted to the Board criticizing his policies. On the following day, Place decided to write to the Board about his own discoveries regarding the obstructions to his work.

Perhaps Place's major complaint against the leading Mirasidars and their Madras connections was that they effectively supplanted any outside authority. They achieved this, he wrote, through their connections with Dubashes in Madras. A Dubash, said Place, made dependents

> consider him their sanctuary in all difficulties, makes them his instruments in all dark plots and intrigues and as they acquire the habit of flying to his protection or for his advice, whenever a superior authority threatens to affect their mutual interest. [These interests form] an invariable opposition to every measure that has at any time been proposed by Government.[85]

He found Mirasidars willing to have false accounts prepared with fictitious entries for cultivators, "not merely in the names of persons residing in other parts of the Carnatic, but [even] of a man who has been dead these twenty years." Moreover, many of the leading Mirasidars whom Place encountered in the Poonamallee area in late 1795 were convinced that his superiors would never agree to Place's use of the forfeiture of mirasi rights as a penalty for not agreeing to his tax proposals. These Mirasidars told him that if the Board of Revenue were to agree to it, "the sacrifice would be but temporary since they [the Mirasidars] have on former occasions found a day of retribution will come and therefore that present resistance with whatever consequences they may be threatened will in the end not only recover their meerassee but everlastingly ensure by the precedent it will afford, their own villages."[86] Mirasidars also realized that if everything else failed they could simply desert their villages with their Pannaiyals and Padiyals. What is important is that they were aware of the Company's tremendous susceptibility to threats of political disruption and the withholding of taxes by flight.

Manipulating Company Values and Institutions

Perhaps, then, the most unusual characteristic of the Mirasidars and their agents who were Company employees was that they understood and used both the structure and goals of the Company to their own advantage. They manipulated the very values of the Company to foil any attempt to impose a stiffer tax settlement on them, realizing that any person against whom a petition was written would have to deal with the charges in it. This understanding made it essential for the Mirasidars to go to Place's superiors, the Board of Revenue. Moreover, when they looked for grievances to put forward, they couched these in terms and values articulated by the Company itself. For instance, collectors and other Company officers were expected to pay for all supplies requested in their tours through the district. Collectors were also subjected to many other informal moral constraints by the Board. A petition, if it was going to be effective against a Company officer, thus had to invoke the apparent values that the British themselves honored and contain charges that would be almost impossible to deal with. In this interaction, the Mirasidars not only helped to change what the British seemed to have meant by anticipating their response but also shaped the outcome so that those values were neither European nor local and "indigenous."

If what came to be called the Poonamallee Petition had these things as goals, it succeeded beyond possibly even the expectations of its formulators. In it Place was criticized not only for violating many customary arrangements but for having flogged villagers to get his way. In the famous sacred Vaishnava center of Tirumalisai, the petition claimed, Place had demanded that the inhabitants provide him with food, firewood, and fodder free of charge. The petitioners also claimed that Place had forced villagers in the settlements around the large Chembrambakkam irrigation tank to use bricks and stones taken from temples to repair the embankments of the tank. He then divided the cost of repairing these embankments (rupees 4,000) among the villages who benefited from the repair. As a result, the tax on these villages was necessarily doubled to recoup the costs of repairing the tank. When villagers refused to agree to the tax rates proposed, Place (said the petitioners) told the Mirasidars to sign a document indicating the forfeiture of their mirasi rights. Perhaps the greatest grievance cited against Place was that he decided to eliminate one category of deduction that favored the Mirasidars called badarnavīsi, particularly in Tirumalisai village. He himself described these deductions as "suppressions of the produce of lands, defalcations, and excisions from the Government dues, traced by examination into the state of cultivation, and by a wanton coincidence in the several circumstances connected with it, termed . . . Budernavees, a compound Persian word conveying precisely the above signification."[87] Place included in these miscellaneous deductions what the petitioners characterized as backyards or pulakkadais, where they grew their chilies, other spices, and fruit trees. Finally, the petitioners argued that tank fees (eri merais), which were usually collected as part of the taxation system, should be augmented to pay for the repair of the tanks instead of Place's practice of repairing the tanks and then foisting a higher assessment on the village benefiting from the repair. Mirasidars should also not be forced to allow Payirkkaris to begin cultivation in a village and claim a share of the produce. Rather, the Mirasidars should be allowed to accept these Payirkkaris or tenants only if they wished to.[88]

How problematic were these attacks on Place's behavior? It is quite true that Place used corporal punishment such as flogging on many occasions.[89] Place also used everything he could lay his hands on to repair the Chembrambakkam tank or reservoir.[90] He certainly sought to intimidate Mirasidars by trying to force them to sign a document forfeiting the mirasi rights if they would not agree to his demands. More important than these specifics, however, was the fact that Place appears to have sought to impose his will in a style that was far more vigorous than any of his predecessors.[91] This was the main reason why the petition was submitted.

And how successful was the petitioner's strategy? When Place was confronted with the grievances, he said that he had "anticipated in great part the information thereby required" in the letter that he had already written to the Board. He accordingly requested a personal interview with the Board to clear up the grievances detailed in the petition, but this was denied.[92] One of the reasons why the Board treated Place's request for an interview so coolly was because Place had noted that he was forcing Mirasidars to forfeit their mirasi rights (conceived of by the Board as private property) if they did not accept his tax assessment of the village.[93] In this instance, the Board of Revenue shared the horror felt by the Mirasidars. Consequently, Place was told that "in the present constitution of the [Company's] service the Inhabitants can have no security unless the Collector afford an early answer when called upon for explanations to complaints of grievance appealed to the Board of Revenue."[94] Place, obviously irritated with the Board's decision, wondered whether it was possible for a Collector to "stem the torrent of Interest, intrigue and opposition that they [the Dubashes and Mirasidars] are capable of letting loose unless he is upheld by the strenuous and uniform support of superior authority." He felt that in demanding a great variety of specific information in answer to the Poonamallee Petition, "the combination of Dubashes . . . will have gained their principal object. They will not only have prolonged the settlement [tax assessment] but will have successfully resisted the authority of your Collector."[95]

Describing the "Amoral" Dubash and the "Wise" British Government to Create a New Civil Society

If the Poonamallee Petition had set the collector against the Mirasidar petitioners, it had also set the Board of Revenue against Place. Moreover, when the Board denied an interview to Place, it became pitted against its own superiors, the Governor in Council. In the view of the Governor in Council, if the Company did not have at its disposal rewards and punishments, it would not have any revenue and would therefore not survive. If Place were to effect any new reform, he had to have the juridical power to grant the mirasi right to whoever would accept his tax assessment. It was, in their view, essential that Place be able to dominate those Mirasidars who were seeking to subvert the state's new tax system.

We may see, therefore, the way in which Place characterized the "artifice and cunning of the Dubashes of Madras" as "restless and insatiable," as just another attempt to create a series of absolute, monologic, normative, and utopian values.[96] Dubashes had "been in the constant habit of perverting the wise and human principles of the British Government to answer their own insidious ends." In a letter of March 1796, Place said that he felt that the Palayakkars of Ponneri should be punished for the humiliations that they had imposed on him. At the same time, he sought the assistance of the government in punishing certain individuals whom he called the "artful, designing, and culpable part of the inhabitants." He said, for instance, "To create an interest in the pretended hardships of the inhabitants of Poonamallee, they [the Dubashes] have represented them [the hardships] of that species the most abhorrent to the lenient and just character of the British Government."[97] On another occasion, Place argued that the Board of Revenue, "still and with superadded reason, strengthened with their voice of approbation" the "animosity which these successful endeavours [by Place had] occasioned." In this the Board was "aided by the insidious practices and circumventive arts of the whole Dubash Influence of Madras."[98]

Much of the social description that both Place and local individuals produced, therefore, was an attempt not necessarily to describe what they saw but rather to state what they wanted or needed to see in order to perform historical tasks. The "amorality" of village society, like that of the "insidious Dubashi culture," was another social space, an intellectual niche in which both British and local commentators were able to find what they hoped to find: a decayed society without morals. In all these cases, the primary goal was not only to carry out a tax assessment of the Jagir but also to monologically essentialize utopian and normative "standards" and to typify what was chaotic and what needed transformation and renewal. Here, Place momentarily sought to impose his "standards," to speak authoritatively and monologically. The Jagir was merely an epistemological site, an intellectual laboratory at which to produce "truth" for a future civil society.

Pannaiyal and Padiyal Protest Strategies as a Way to Exploit British Fear of Paraiyar Violence

Not only did the Dubashes and their rural connections blunt the reforming and rationalizing edge of the Company, but they actively participated in the construction of knowledge about both the presumedly decayed present and the more pristine past of the Jagir. At the same time, they used the linguistic and cultural ignorance and confusion of British collectors to their own advantage, working with substantial amounts of confidential information available through their dependents. This access gave them a "complete knowledge" not only of the "practical part of the business of our Government, but of the principles from whence it flowed."[99] That is, day-to-day activities rested in the control of individuals who did not share the goals of the British; but these same individuals understood, and could manipulate, the presumptions informing these activities. It was therefore natural that if Place sought to reduce what he called the "evils" perpetrated by the Dubashes and Mirasidars, he would logically be opposed by a "combination" of these men. These "abuses" and the "real taxable nature" of the Jagir had been effectively concealed from the "knowledge of the Government." It was also not possible to prove Place's assertions of the "abuses" very easily. If they could be proved, they could be identified and eliminated. After all, if an individual was to investigate all the complaints raised by the Dubashes, "there is no constitution or body, nor steadiness of mind that will be equal to the task of making such a [tax] settlement as the Company under the information acquired by the indefatigable exertions of Mr. Place have a right to expect."[100]

Of great interest in this interchange is the illustration of the juridical weakness of colonial governments, whether in India or elsewhere. It suggests the inability of any colonial government, though politically dominant, to be in control of the areas over which it claims sovereignty. Place's attempt to impose a tax assessment on the Jagir represented the first major confrontation between a bureaucratizing Company and a patrimonial Mirasidar-Dubash connection. On the one hand, the Board of Revenue decided to invoke the normative rules and constructed knowledge associated with the newly emerging civil service. On the other hand, the Governor in Council believed that if the Company was to achieve its immediate goal of making a tax assessment of the Jagir, it would have to give Place the right to assume something that he could not prove. They had to believe that behind the disturbance in the Poonamallee pargana were individuals who could manipulate both the day-to-day functioning of the Company's government and its presumptions in order to consistently subvert the state.

In their Minute condemning the denial of an interview to Place, the Governor in Council in Madras said that "the ultimate resource against the oppression of a zamindar [superior land controller] is the depopulation of his estate." No government could engage in activities that would force cultivators to leave the land.[101] Within two months of the Governor in Council's deliberation, however, Place had to report that the Pannaiyals and Padiyals of several villages in the Poonamallee area were unwilling to harvest the crops. Once again, in 1796 as in 1785, they threatened to desert the villages altogether unless Place and the other subordinate tax officers of the state gave them a larger portion of the kalavasam (their portion of the grain heap at harvest time). Place was greatly concerned about the delay in harvesting the crop and sought to prevent their desertion by requesting authority to issue a proclamation penalizing those who deserted their villages.[102] Ultimately, he issued a proclamation that was not confirmed by his superiors that required the return of the Mirasidars "on pain of otherwise forfeiting their village right [mirasi] to others who may be willing to cultivate the ground."

Though he tried to forbid desertion through a proclamation using drummers and criers, paraiyar Pannaiyals and Padiyals nonetheless became very strident in their demands. They demanded more than the two

marakkals of unhusked rice or paddy for every ten kalams of rice, or
1.66 percent of the total, to which they had previously been entitled.
They attempted to expand their shares by various techniques; for example, Place noted:

> There are mamool [customary] places for beating out the grain in every
> village but owing to a general disregard of all the prescribed rules of Revenue
> management, the Pariars [paraiyars] either will not be confined to them or
> reject the regulation that these spots should be previously cleared of grass
> that is purposely allowed to grow in order that the greater quantity of grain
> may be concealed under it.[103]

Whenever they had done this in the past, the total deduction for kalavasam rose as high as 10 or 12 percent of the crop and caused a substantial reduction in the state's share.

Mirasidars and their Dubash connections clearly understood how
vulnerable was the Company in the Jagir. They also understood how to
use British understandings and perceptions of local society to their own
advantage. Among the most important aspects of this knowledge was
awareness by British administrators that local Tamil society was organized by vertical lines of patronage as well as by horizontal lines of
kinship. According to the Company view, local kin connections were
powerful. Company employees also believed that all subcaste kin connections, whether for the Kondaikatti vellalas, the paraiyars, the pallis,
or any other, were broad, extending across the entire Jagir and beyond.
This was not the case. The only thing that we can say is that, though
vellala spatial orientations were narrow, they appear to have been somewhat wider than those of the paraiyar, which were even more constrained.[104] However, the British were not aware of this and assumed,
for instance, that it was quite possible for a paraiyar subcaste head in
Madras to issue an order to paraiyar castemates in the Poonamallee area
or in Karanguli, about forty miles to the south, to gather the paraiyar
to the city. Thus, although these paraiyar subcaste heads had much shal-
lower bases of jurisdiction, communication, and power than the British
knew, Mirasidars and Dubashes played on the fears and presuppositions
of the British and deliberately employed techniques to intimidate
them.[105] These interactions and vulnerabilities all formed part of the
mechanism for constructing "truth."

Place quickly discovered that the paraiyar Pannaiyals and Padiyals
were being told by their Mirasidar masters to threaten desertion and
violence. Initially, Place's source was a group of paraiyars going to join
other Pannaiyals and Padiyals in the Poonamallee area; they said that

they had been told to "revolt by the principal paraiyas of the [Poona-mallee] district named Petiah Toty, Poonamallee Cooty, and Mangau-doo Combon, and Pummel Cunnyan."[106] These are recognizable par-aiyar names and Pammal and Mangadu are both villages in the immediate Poonamallee area. However, when Place and his assistants sought to locate these men by posting rewards for their capture, he said that he realized that they had left the area altogether. A Talaivar or head of a paraiyar subcaste group in the village of Sirukulattur, on the border of the Chembrambakkam tank in the Poonamallee area, said that "un-less persuaded and allowed by their master [a Kondaikatti vellala Mir-asidar] the Pariars would never have thought to assemble in the manner that they did."[107] There was no question but that economic and social relationships between Mirasidar and Pannaiyal and Padiyal provided the important ingredients in the "insurrection." This was not a paraiyar rebellion per se.

In support of his contention, Place submitted several documents to the Board of Revenue. One of these was a cadjan—a letter written, as was the custom in those days, on a palm leaf or ōlai inserted in a special case—from a Kondaikatti vellala temple official in the sacred center of Tiruvallur (located fifteen miles to the northwest of Poonamallee). The cadjan, addressed to his gomasta (Tamil "kumasta" or "agent") who managed a village for him in the Poonamallee area, said among other things:

> It has been beaten [by drummers] through the whole place [by the Com-pany] directing the inhabitants not to assist the Pariars and is meant only to prevent the Pariars from crowding together and [not] with any other view. Nevertheless the Pariars have assembled everywhere. I think in a few days his taudoo [Telugu "tāḍu"] will be entirely cut off. He will be displeased. Do not however publish this. The Company's peons have been placed over him to press for payment.

When asked what was the meaning of the reference to his tadu being cut off, the gomasta said that tadu was the Telugu word for that device tied to the neck of a bride by a bridegroom. When a woman lost her husband it was taken off. He also pointed out that "it was also used to signify the loss of employment and reputation." It was in this sense that Place construed the letter—that everyone expected Place to be dismissed from his position because of the paraiyar disturbance.

At almost the same time, his difficult position was reflected in his inability to get the Palayakkars or "watchers" even to come to an in-terview at his office. Place, in his attempts to deal with these men, had made trips to Madras with his own local informants. On one of these trips, Place saw a Palayakkar from the Ponneri pargana—a subdivision of the Jagir to the north of the city—whose fees for "watching" villages Place had already confiscated. When he saw this Palayakkar named Maddikayala Teppalraj with eleven kāvali villages "to watch or police" and other income of pagodas 2,029 a year, Place said that he "commanded him to attend at my cutcheree [office] on pain of forfeiting his office, but he paid no regard to me." Place also discovered the spot in Blacktown where a number of the Palayakkars gathered. There, again, he told these Palayakkars to come to his office, "but in the most aggravating manner they disregarded my authority and peremptorily said they would not attend." Place concluded his comment by saying:

> If an example were sought for the licentiousness and violation of order and regularity that so commonly break out among the subordinate gradation of natives of this country whenever that authority to which they owe obedience suffers any temporary diminution of power or whenever it may seem to be threatened with extinction, it is afforded in the conduct of these and other Poligars.[108]

We may see that the ambivalent position in which Place found himself on this and many other occasions provided another productive environment in which to construct ideas about authority, including that of an "Asiatic despot."

Of equal interest was another cadjan letter found later to have been forged. It was signed by several individuals called "Uttakartan Mastry, son of Kolukaren Mastry, Tondava Mastry, [and] Velliam Mastry to their relations or Caste people in the Carangooly [Karanguli] district." The message ran: "On receipt of this cadjan [letter] you must repair to Madras. If you neglect doing so your punishment will be the disgrace of having dung thrown upon your faces [i.e., to be made outcasts] and your cast dishonored. Come to Vundra Mangalam and send an answer to this letter [as to] how we are to act."

This letter was a purported call from individuals, two of whom were later identified as having been dead for at least a year, believed to be the Talaivars or paraiyar caste leaders in Madras town to their caste fellows in the Karanguli area, located forty miles southeast of Madras. As we will see later, a second letter was written not by a paraiyar but by someone connected to the upper-caste Mirasidars in the Poonamallee area. Its intention was also to frighten and intimidate the British by confronting them with a summons by supposed Talaivars of Madras town paraiyars to other paraiyars in Karanguli using the threat of outcasting and kin connections as their tools.

In this strategy, the instigators played on the reconstruction of the past in which Company officers utilized a few instances of small-scale physical attacks to demonstrate the violent nature of South Indian society, for British officers were terrified above all of the violence that they feared the paraiyars would employ to attain their ends. Only nine months before Place was appointed as collector of the Jagir, there had been a dispute over a piece of land in what is now Tondiarpet, north of the Fort St. George area of Madras town. Disputants to the land included some Kondaikatti vellala Mirasidars and some Gramani or Shanar tenants, whose traditional occupation involved collecting the sap of the toddy palm to be converted into an intoxicating drink called toddy (an occupation called "toddy tapping"). An Englishman named Moore had purchased a part of the land from these Gramani tenants. When he enclosed it, he said that three Kondaikatti vellalas "ordered the [paraiyar] rabble to pursue and beat me. . . . At last they surrounded and seized me behind my back. Then they cut me with Bamboos and bruised me unmercifully."[109] Similarly, in January 1795, three months after Place had been named collector of the Jagir, the same Kondaikatti vellala Mirasidars made their paraiyar Pannaiyals and Padiyals attack some Gramani tenants at the time of the Pongal festival.[110] This action emerged from a dispute between the Kondaikatti vellala Mirasidars and the Gramani uḷkuḍi Payirkkudis, tenants whose roots as occupants went back to the 1770s. The attack by the vellalas served to counteract the decision of Place to allow the Gramani tenants who had fixity of tenure to actually sell lands in Tondiarpet without the permission of the vellalas, who had originally leased the land to the gramanis.[111] These and other experiences were well known to Company officials. Kondaikatti vellala Mirasidars both then and more recently have confidently used their paraiyar Pannaiyals and Padiyals to exhibit violence in harassing other dominant castes and all outsiders.[112]

New Conceptions of Loyalty out of Dependence on the British

The description of the facility of certain Mirasidars to manipulate British preconceptions and fears should not be taken as an indication that the British were outmaneuvered in this contest. That they could uncover information about the Mirasidars with which to combat their machinations, however, suggests other important local actors who also contributed to the project shaped by this dialogic process. As in any political situation in which the state is dependent on locally important patrons, the Company's regime in the Jagir required allies. One such supporter, a Kondaikatti vellala Mirasidar named Varadappa Mudali from Sirukulattur on the Chembrambakkam tank near Poonamallee, wanted to cultivate Place. Varadappa Mudali wrote to Place, "We are very poor and rely on the Gentleman's favor and protection. Some Malabars [Tamils] for the sake of their own advantage have excited the ignorant Pariars to commit disturbances, thereby bringing the whole disgrace upon the [Kondaikatti vellala] cast in the eyes of the Gentleman." Besides providing a list of all the other Mirasidars who were behind the disturbance in the Poonamallee region, Varadappa Mudali's paraiyar Pannaiyal named Rajan said, "As I belonged to Varadappah Moodelly [the other Mirasidars] never informed me [what they were doing]. . . . My Mudaliar cautioned me that if I reposed confidence in the gentleman [Place] and obtained his favor we should live happily. . . . This is my declaration and I expect the gentleman's favor."[113]

When Company officers tried to ascertain if paraiyar Talaivars or leaders had issued a call to other paraiyar Pannaiyals and Padiyals in Karanguli, the structure of the "insurrection" became much clearer. First, some lower servants of the Company went to see a paraiyar Talaivar named Periya Tambi. He lived in the "great paraiyar cheri" at the northern end of Pedda Nayyakenpet at Madras.[114] Called the Tottakaran Mestri, Periya Tambi was shown the letter supposed to have been written by Uttakartan, Tandava Mestri, and Velliam Mestri. Place reported that Periya Tambi said that he "found it [the letter] so clogged with compliments I was disgusted. We who gain our livelihood by cleaning gentlemen's shoes, can we pen such a letter? No. If the Company saw it they would put fetters on our hands and feet and transport us to Bencoolen [a British "factory" or warehouse settlement on the western coast of Sumatra in Southeast Asia, known as a penal colony]."[115] Periya Tambi was furious that the paraiyar leaders in Madras were being held responsible for the "insurrection" by upper-caste leaders. It is also possible that Periya Tambi invoked the idea of the illiterate and lowly paraiyars to take the pressure off his immediate community.[116] He told one of the men who accompanied the subordinate Company employee who bore the letter that he should "admonish" the paraiyar of Karanguli "not to raise such disturbances in the district."[117] Uttakartan Mestri of Periyamedu, the third supposed author of the call to the Karanguli paraiyar, said that the letter was a complete forgery and used as proof of this the fact that two of the supposed authors (Tandava Mestri and Velliyam Mestri) had both been dead for more than a year.[118] Thus, in the investigative process, additional information and allies emerged. The production of meaning continued.

The "Insurrection" as a Utopian Arena

In March and April 1796, as the investigations concerning the authorship of the former "paraiyar letter" were being undertaken, another major shift occurred in the relationship between Place and the Poonamallee villagers. On or about 21 March 1796, Place decided that the desertion of the villages in the Poonamallee area forced him to resort to a more dramatic expedient. "This was," said Place in his 1799 report, "at any rate a crisis which a variety of circumstances concurred to establish, as that upon which the possibility of introducing a better system of management into the Jaghir was to depend."[119] Whenever he tried to impose his will on the land controllers in the local environment, the strategies of Mirasidars and their Pannaiyals and Padiyals stymied Place:

> The common practice with the inhabitants on these occasions was to resist both [the state and the collector] by collecting and using their servants [paraiyar Pannaiyals and Padiyals], traversing the country in large bodies, and putting an entire stop to the cultivation and the harvest, until such control was withdrawn, and their demands arising out of it, however unreasonable they might be, are satisfied.[120]

"If by one strenuous effort," he believed, "I could liberate the population of the Jaghire from the shackles of Dubash dominion, and restore it to something like its former happy state," he felt that his efforts would have been worthwhile.[121] Like the "amoral" villagers, these Dubashes were simply a representation of the fallen condition of contemporary local culture. At the same time, the contestation became an opportunity to recreate the society.

As a result, Place tried to use what little coercive power he had at his disposal to bring back the Mirasidars, Pannaiyals, and Padiyals of Poonamallee. Contrary to the instructions of the Board of Revenue—who had given him permission to issue a proclamation offering more generous terms to those who had deserted—Place issued one that warned them even more severely. Place's proclamation banished a group of eight "head people" from the district, threatening to take away their grain and other movable property as well as their mirasi rights if they did not return to their villages within five days.[122] Place contended that he had issued the proclamation because the desertion of the Mirasidars had happened so suddenly as to have precluded any "general intercourse, so as to have united them in the pursuit of an uniform object," or to have understood the effect of their "temerity." He felt therefore that he could coerce them by "at once exposing the utmost evil that would befall them, to awaken the minds of the inferior classes to a comparison between what they sought, and what they relinquished and thereby to detach them from the guidance of eight individuals, who had to my certain knowledge agitated and occasioned the desertion."[123] His main goal was to detach a segment of the local population, invoking loyalty to the Company government. He felt that his presuppositions had been correct, for the villagers immediately began to return. This enabled him to make tax settlements with more than 250 villages. These particular villages were among the poorest villages in the entire Jagir; they had suffered most from a cyclonic storm in November 1795 at almost the same time that the Poonamallee Petition was submitted. They therefore had the best reason to leave, he said, "yet they voluntarily came to my cutcheree [office], entered into engagements of rent without the smallest deviation from the principle with which I had set out, and have paid so much of their rent as to owe but an immaterial balance."[124] By contrast Place noted that the Mirasidars who remained away came from perhaps the most productive villages of the entire Jagir and had already benefited by "getting their tanks and watercourses put into the most compleat and substantial repair [by the Company]." He contended that "these villages are what the leading men in this desertion have marked out for themselves, and upon their own terms, into which they would compel Government by instigating the inferior ryots [paraiyar Pannaiyals and Padiyals] to withdraw, and by threatening desolation of the lands, [if] their purpose be not attained."[125] Place believed that one central way the Company could create loyalty was by appointing individuals to the position of Nattar. This enabled the Company to benefit from these individuals' ability to manipulate the village environment in favor of the Company's interest. However, he pointed to one Appa Mudali, an important Nattar of the Poonamallee area, whose "influence was successfully used beyond the reach of the Collector and it was therefore that I strenuously solicited his dismission from the office of Nauttawars [Nattars]."[126] In Poonamallee, of all places, where the control of the Nattars had been taken over by the Dubashes, Nattars loyal to the Company were essential.

Place believed that faithful Nattars were critically important to the operation of the Company's tax collecting mechanism in the Jagir. A Nattar could resolve disputes, provide relief to individuals in the village when the public taxes increased, and relieve the anxieties and fears of those around them about anything that was new or "intended as an improvement." But, he said,

> If this influence is not in the hands of the Nauttawars, it will always [lie in the hands] of the most artful and designing men of the Purgunnah [territorial subdivision] and I would ask if it is not better that it should be with those who are attached to the circar, than with those who have every motive to detach themselves from it; indeed whose only benefit is derived from superceding and counteracting it.[127]

Where Nattars did not exist, the population was under the control of individuals who had assumed "unlimited power over them in so much that without a reason being given, they received sudden instructions to fly from the authority of the Circar, till the object of their leaders whatever it may be is attained" and they "dared not disobey."[128]

Place cited most recent experience to show that it was quite possible to use those who were dependent on the Company as a way to maintain peace and conclude tax settlements. In Karanguli, south of Madras, for example, the headman was considered to be too attached to Place himself to be consulted when the plot to desert was put together. In the night, the headman's dependents came to the headman to say that the "inhabitants" of the various territorial subdivisions "had received orders instantly to desert from the Jaghire" and asked whether they should do so as well. Place said that to this the headman "replied in the negative; that they could have no reason for doing so, and must remain obedient to the circar's [i.e., Company's] orders. They did so; every village in that magan [parganah or territorial subdivision] was rented out the next morning without the least murmur and objection and all the rent has been since paid."[129] As a result, he proposed giving a parwana or order that required the Nattar always to be watchful and inform himself about everything that was going on in the area. A Nattar would also be told to "conciliate the minds of the inhabitants to the circar, prevent all improper combinations . . . and inculcate obedience and make them understand the happiness that they enjoy under the protection and justice of the Company's Government." Finally, the Nattars would be informed that they themselves should always be "obedient to the circar" and carry out all the requirements of the job.[130] The central problem with which

Place and the Company were concerned was how to keep those in the countryside loyal and collect taxes in the years ahead.

Not surprisingly, Place's position in the Company's structure was seriously weakened as a result of this episode. He felt that, since his suggestions for solving the problem had not been taken seriously by the Board in the past, he had few options but to pursue the matter in the way he did. As a result, he simply noted in his diary that he had issued the proclamation "for the information of the Board when they think proper to pursue it."[131] On this occasion, when the matter was brought to their attention, both the Board of Revenue and its superiors the Governor in Council felt "constrained to rescue the people from the apprehension of a power [of banishment and confiscation] which cannot be vested in any Collector." Place was warned that unless he reformed he would be liable to dismissal from the service.[132] Here, Place had again assumed for himself a constructed authoritarian role of "Asiatic despot" who could outlaw people by fiat. The "insurrection" offered an appropriate opportunity to do so.

Analyzing the "Insurrection"

In September, October, and November 1796, Place felt that his own tax employees had deceived him. They had, he said, prevented him from discovering the fact that some of the same Mirasidars, living in villages around the large Chembrambakkam tank that he had repaired, had purposely not taken advantage of the early rains that year. Many of these people had also deserted their villages. In the months that followed, Place concluded tax assessments with many villages. Nevertheless, in many large areas of the Jagir such as Karanguli to the south and in both Uttiramerur and Kanchipuram to the west, a number of cultivators left their villages.[133]

Because Place had the support of the governor of Madras, he was able by November 1796, with the consent of his superiors, the Governor in Council, to carry out his threat of taking away the mirasis of those individuals if they did not return to their villages. When he reported the results of his actions in November 1796, he said that of the ninety-six Mirasidars who had been originally deprived of their mirasi right twenty-three had been reinstated, and that a total of seventy-three Mirasidars who were unwilling to return were deprived of their hereditary mirasi rights and replaced by others who were amenable to Place's tax demands.

Place's account located the initial desertions in the Poonamallee area in November 1795, where twenty-four Mirasidars later lost their mirasi. Then in April and May 1796, after the growing season was over, Mirasidars and their servants left from the Salivakkam pargana, a subdivision south of Madras (where one Mirasidar lost his mirasi), Kanchi to the west of Madras (where four lost their mirasis), and Karanguli to the south of Madras (where twenty-six lost their mirasis).[134] Although some of the original protesters in the Poonamallee Petition came from Tirumalisai village, none of the Mirasidars of that particular village lost their mirasis.[135] Of the 122 Mirasidars who deserted, only twenty-four lost their mirasis in early November 1795, whereas ninety-eight left between 12 April and 30 May 1796 after the harvest had been taken. In addition, there was a group of individuals who abandoned their mirasi rights "voluntarily" when Place sought to make a tax assessment on the area, as well as two who gave up the mirasi a year and a half earlier.[136] Moreover, one Mirasidar could not be found and five were deprived of their mirasi rights because the mirasi was "not justly theirs."[137] Finally, one Mirasidar was removed simply because he "always resides in Madras, and declaring that he could not attend to the cultivation consented that the meerassee should be transferred to these people [indicated by Place in his letter]."[138]

It is hard to identify the subcastes to which the main body of Mirasidars who were deprived of their mirasis belonged, except that they were apparently not brahmans. Of the group of twenty-four who left the Poonamallee pargana in November 1796, only four had Tondaimandala or Kondaikatti vellala surnames, while eight of them had as a surname "Pillai," which could refer to members of the karnam subcaste or to yadavas or even to pallis, later to be called vanikula kshatriyas. The twelve remaining had names that were undistinguished except that they were not brahman.[139]

Finally, on the basis of the figures of Mirasidars who deserted the Jagir, the numbers seem relatively small. According to Place's count, only 293 Mirasidars left the Jagir before July 1796, ninety-four of whom came from eighty-three villages in the Karanguli subdivision south of Madras. Of these ninety-four individuals, thirty-four came from only five villages and an average of only one Mirasidar deserted from each of the remaining seventy-eight villages. In addition, a total of thirty-eight Mirasidars had deserted from fourteen villages in Kanchi pargana or subdivision, seventy-three from twenty-four villages in Uttiramerur subdivision, and eighty-eight Mirasidars from twenty-five villages in Kavantandalam subdivision. All of these Mirasidars were men. In addition, many of the Pannaiyals and Padiyals left as well; women were associated with this group. It is hard to estimate the numbers of Pannaiyals and Padiyals who left the Jagir in late 1795 and early 1796. However, it seems likely that about ten Pannaiyals and Padiyals and their wives deserted for every Mirasidar; this would put the total number of Pannaiyals and Padiyals who deserted at six thousand, for a total desertion from the Jagir of about sixty-two hundred people in 1795–96.

Although all the villages Place associated with the "ringleaders" of the "insurrection" cannot be identified, those that can be identified all lie in a circumscribed area five to ten miles south of the village (later a town) of Madurantakam south of Madras. Among those individuals whom Place chose to call "ringleaders" there seems to have been no "caste connection" except for three Tondaimandala vellalas, one Telugu reddi and another "Nāyak," who was probably a palli or a Telugu balija naiḍu.

However, though the total numbers of Mirasidars were relatively small, they constituted an intimidating group to the Company. In quite serious financial straits, the Company desperately needed people to cultivate the fields of the Jagir and the tax revenues such cultivation generated. The desertion also occurred at the very point when Place and the Company were straining every nerve to attract back the population that had left the Jagir at the time of the 1780 war—a fact of which the Mirasidars were well aware.[140]

This insurrection became part of the folklore of the Jagir (what later came to be called the Chingleput district). For many years, whether among British or local commentators, the problems and "truth" that the interaction had raised formed part of the discussions concerning the area. These ideas were inscribed in both the records and the behaviors of British officers and local Mirasidars, Payirkkaris, Padiyals, and Pannaiyals. As we will see in the chapter that follows, Place not only had ideas about local culture but also sought to offer a model of how a Tamil "king" should behave. His behavior was answered and complemented by much activity by other local individuals whose understandings of what they were doing was thereby altered. These "local" and "subaltern" voices were active in the reconstruction of the society. It is to a consideration of that dynamic that we now turn.

CHAPTER 2

Using the Past to
Create the Future

Cultural "restoration" became an important shared project both for local inhabitants and for British administrators at the turn of the eighteenth century. For instance, key actors included Tamils concerned with explicating cultural identity for the region called Tondaimandalam (one of the five such cultural regions in the Tamil language area). For these Tamils, contestation around the nature of the sedentary base that rooted Tamil culture involved local vellalas, paraiyars, pallis, and Telugu peasant castes. Each of these contenders claimed a special (often "original") site in the landscape and fashioned a cultural representation of the area that flowed from this construction. Each also sought ways to collaborate or interact with colonial representations to further these constructions. Similarly, in transforming itself from a trading company to a bureaucratic state, the English East India Company confronted several problems. One of these was the need to ensure a regular source of tax revenue; another was to create a local populace loyal to the Company's government. Together, these interactions form another key epistemological moment in which the relations between a local population and a colonizing agent were worked out in a dialogic process. In this operation, "colonizing mechanisms," whether formed as knowledge or as juridical institutions, were neither British nor local. Rather, these new formulations and the institutions that arose from them had no clear intellectual or cultural origin.

This chapter will examine a series of political, economic, and cultural interactions in the Jagir. Part of the interest inherent in these cultural negotiations is that they occurred at a point when both the state and the local population rapidly formulated views about each other. These interactions, many of which occurred between 1795 and 1820, were of great importance for the future of the area encompassed by the Jagir. But this knowledge also affected behavior and the creation of a series of negotiated institutions in what came to be called the Madras presidency, as well as in what came to be India generally. Ultimately, I will argue, it profoundly affected the regional cultural movement to define and identify Tamil Nadu, a movement linked not to the concerns and goals of the colonial state but to those right and left castes working to reshape Tamil cultural identity by sedentarizing and sacralizing it.

An assumption made by many scholars about the Indo-British administration on the subcontinent is that it had, almost from the beginning, the capacity to exploit the environment to its advantage through violence and cultural imposition. What is not stated in this formulation is that all of these elements—important in creating bureaucratic devices such as special educational and employment facilities—resulted from intense cultural negotiation that took place over a long period of time. Even devices such as the development of juridical mechanisms to coerce the population were heteroglot creations, not simple impositions by European conquerors. In the eighteenth century, the British were often not in a position of juridical strength but rather were forced continually to modify their expectations of local social and political structures in order to remain "in power" or "legitimate." Negotiations took place in this and later contexts.

In the eighteenth and nineteenth centuries, many attempts were made to identify the important aspects of the region's history and former proprietary relations as a way to create a unitary state. Though this was in a sense a gradual affair, it came to be the main priority in the last decade of the eighteenth century and became even more important during the first two decades of the nineteenth century. A constant, gradual alteration in British expectations of the local population lay at the very basis of the transition in Company governmental style and behavior between 1795 and 1820.

British discontinuance of what were considered to be local cultural style and its expression through ritual exchanges took many forms. Starting in the 1780s, British officers of the Company abandoned the use of those behaviors associated with local culture considered to be unsophisticated. This, too, was not a wholly consistent process, for important projects were undertaken by the newly juridically dominant

British that seemingly compelled them to adopt, at least momentarily, some local styles. (The way in which Lionel Place took on the attributes of an "Asiatic despot" in the 1790s provides one example of this.) However, throughout the archival record the predominant attitude that emerges underscores the need felt by administrators to be more financially accountable to developing institutions by discontinuing costly ritual relationships. One instance of this kind of change comes from the record of a successor of Place as collector named Greenway. In the discussions surrounding the reorganization of the policing strategies to be followed by the Company's government, Greenway recommended pensioning off the old Palayakkar "watchers" and introducing a new system in which the new policemen would be paid directly by the state, not by each village as had been previous practice. This, wrote Greenway, would be undertaken "so as to render it perfectly efficient—to use a phrase recently adopted in modern language, the Police must be re-organized and it is necessary to do away with the present system."[1] Old ritual and local activities thus became "inefficient" and not in tune with the new bureaucratic requirements of the state. A direct relation was ultimately drawn between efficiency, the abandonment of rituals, and centralization.

The new emphasis marked a dramatic shift in the negotiating processes and relationships that had prevailed. During the previous century and a half, political relations had been based on the continual possibility of inversion, that is, of ritually taking the role of the other in order to extract a concession. Ritual activity included desertion, hunger strikes, confining an individual until that person gave you what you demanded, or depriving someone of food and supplies until he gave in and paid a debt. These inversions, which occurred often in eighteenth-century South India, rendered the body of an individual subject to public violence, as in the case of the Kallars in the Tamil area and the Bhats in the Gujarat region.[2] After 1795, by contrast, the British increasingly tried to prevent those activities, no matter what the local individuals hoped or thought. Open violence by local populations and by the state was increasingly frowned on, while the voluntary use of violence on an individual's body to force another person to pay a debt later became illegal. After 1795, the government tried to introduce a bureaucratic society and institutions based on the idea of perceived order and social irreversibility in an embedded interdependent society. This was a society in which an increasing division of labor and interdependence meant that individuals could not easily exchange places. Consequently, both the

British rulers and the local individuals would remain in their hierarchical positions. The British rulers would not find themselves in a position of momentary weakness and the local subjects correspondingly would not occupy a position of temporary strength. Increasingly, it became important that the rulers should remain juridically strong and locals remain juridically weak. Therefore, as the state became more centralized, social relations gradually became less reversible and the body could be less openly violated. Individuals were increasingly imprisoned instead of being flogged and killed openly. This was an interdependent society in which inequalities certainly did not cease but in which interdependence restrained those who were juridically strong as well as those who were juridically weak.

A focus on this increasingly fixed relationship through the exercise of juridical processes has distracted scholars from other forms of negotiations that continued to enable local participants to play dominant roles. One of the important interactive strategies that evolved from these developments related less to the question of political irreversibility in the present than to ways to conceive both the past and the future. A utopian vision of the past and the future pursued by both the British and the local inhabitants became the basis for the interactive construction of a new political order. "Golden age" ideas from both Britain and the area around Madras helped to provide conceptions about the past in order to build the future.

The Construction of a Utopian Past and Future

It is true that the strategy of reversing places in a carnival, a desertion, or other temporary situation of status reversal—in which the agent of authority was momentarily in a juridically vulnerable position and the ordinarily helpless person or group was in a position of dominance—became unacceptable to the British after the 1790s. However, throughout this period, whether before the 1790s or later, a continued dialogic production of ideas and creation of knowledge characterized the cultural encounters among the British, the local population, and others. This became apparent at precisely the time when Place had to analyze the problems that he faced in the months after the "insurrection of the Mirasidars." During this period, he sought answers to his questions from his local informants. From them he learned local cosmological ideas. In particular, he learned that, at least according to Sanskritic notions, cosmology divided the history of the world into four yugas that involved the gradual escalation in impiety, discontent, and immorality until the coming of the Dark Age or kali yuga. His information also was undoubtedly affected by Tamil cosmological ideas that involved periods of pervasive destructive deluges called ūlis.[3] The Sanskrit kāli yuga and the Tamil ūḷi are a Dark Age in which the local informants to whom Place talked situated Jagir society of the 1790s. To these local ideas, he added his own cosmological and urgent millennial notions and the need to reform both a degenerate British and a decadent local society.

According to the vision of local society that Place heard and wanted to believe, he lived in a dark and dissolute age. Place considered that philosophy and science in the Tamil area "were once in as flourishing a state in this country as any part of the world."[4] As a result of Muslim invasions, however, the arts were destroyed and culture in India became derivative. According to Place's ideas, Muslim conquests in the fourteenth century extracted much wealth from the Tamil country. "Individual wealth," said Place, "must have exceeded all bounds of calculation. . . . What an admirable form of government and happy race of people must have existed in those days to admit of so incredible a freedom from intestine broils." In Place's view, all the evidence demonstrated that in the fourteenth century the government and society of the Tamils were superior to anything in England at the time.[5] The interactive aspect of these ideas is well exemplified by a text published officially in 1908 called *Memoir on the Internal Revenue System of the Madras Presidency,* written by Bundla Ramaswami Naidoo in 1820, shortly after Place's time. In that memoir Ramaswami Naidoo noted:

> It is true, as all Europeans imagine, that we Indians, do not possess any recorded histories of our ancient civil and political matters but all that we have, are religious traits [tracts], mixed with political institutions, it must indeed be a matter of curiosity to the European world, as our books treat upon facts that occurred many thousand years before the Christian system of Chronology, under which, they believe that the world is aged only above five thousand years.[6]

Though the author noted in the next paragraph that the beginning of the kali yuga or Dark Age was A.D. 1817, most of the sources used in his memoir were either British accounts of local society or British translations of Sanskrit texts or other texts from the subcontinent. He believed that in many ways the culture of the subcontinent was more ancient and superior to British culture. At the same time, he participated in a cultural negotiation about the definition of local religious ideas and culture. In this account, we notice the elements that framed local knowledge about the past of the area, but these views were used in ways that make the origins of these ideas impossible to determine. They are already surrounded by an obscuring mist.

Both Place and Bundla Ramaswami Naidoo sought to come to terms with the same problem: the perceived decayed position of the contemporary local society and polity of the Jagir. They both induced this idea as a way to activate a profound competition between centrifugal local voices and centripetal unitary discourse.

In the 1790s, British employees of the Company and many others were able to see decay in every human being. One commentator described the behavior of these "decadent" people in Madras in a florid style. He wrote:

> And it may well be supposed as I live in a *fashionable*, public part of the Black Town [in Madras] that I am seldom at a loss for objects of speculation. The abundant *fineries* in all their variegated *modes, forms, colours* displayed either by *European ingenuity* or *native adoption* demonstrate very plainly that the present is the age of improvement. Mercy! what a *revolution*. The Revolution in France is a *Bagatelle* compared to it. Ten years have not been elapsed, never to return, when scarce a *dimpled Dubash* of this proud Presidency permitted his *unhallowed* limbs the luxury of a *palankeen. Hackeries* were the sober conveyance of his sableness, with a pair of sow oxen, typical of the master's habits, and no bad emblem of his temper. Hackeries! constructed on ancient principles and made for purposes very different from those of ostentation. From the wealthy, long-eared *Armenian*, to the slim and sable spright, his scribbler—from the jovial Country Captain who wrapt up his amphibious importance, bids defiance to all terrestrial being, to the *humble* attendant who lights his *cheroots* and presents his *grog*—from the *Beetle-chewing Dubash* who *builds Choultries* and *endows Pagodas*, to the swarthy menial who follows him—all—all! *are altered* [emphasis in original].[7]

Like this illustration from an account in the *Madras Courier* of 1792, everywhere Place looked in the 1790s he believed himself confronted by the creations of the Muslim and European conquerors, who had, he felt, debased the moral character of the local people. Perhaps the most outstanding instance of such a debased creation, in Place's view, was the Madras Dubash: "I know of no character more mischievous than what is understood by the term 'Madras dubash.' . . . Ignorant to an extreme, even in their religious duties, they almost all keep, what they call a Shastry Bramin, to direct and keep them in remembrance of their daily exercises, these sorts of knowledge which should seem necessary to their vocation are supplied by cunning and the art of circumvention."[8] Place wanted to liberate the population of the Jagir from what he called "the shackles of Dubash Dominion, and restore it to something like its former happy state."[9]

More than even the Mirasidars, the Dubashi (the institution of the Dubashes) provided a site important in the production of knowledge. Dubashes "organized the commission from merchants when contracts were sealed [in the eighteenth century] for the supply of textiles and from tax farmers when offers for farms were accepted, organised presents from and to hinterland officials, disposed goods traded in by their employers and kept their private accounts."[10] This institution, therefore, necessarily emerged with an extensive network reaching the area outside Madras town and developed along with the trade generated by Company employees trading on their own accounts. The Dubashi engages our interest because it expressed the requirements of the new public and bureaucratic culture formed during the last quarter of the eighteenth century, a development illustrated by the famous "Hollond affair" in Madras. John Hollond and Edward J. Hollond were senior Company employees; John had been governor and Edward John had been acting president of the council for a brief period. Avatanam Papaiya, a tax and betel farmer, served as John Hollond's Dubash.[11] At one point, Company employee David Haliburton lodged a case against Avatanam Papaiya, and in 1790 the inquiry found that Papaiya had had an improper influence on both the Hollonds and the transactions of the Madras council.[12] As a result, the Hollonds were suspended and Avatanam Papaiya punished. In another case, during a 1781 investigation into the dealings of Dubashes in Madras, the Dubashes, unwilling to be examined, refused to take the oath. They resisted, they said, because "if they were guilty of breach of confidence to their former masters no other person will employ them hereafter."[13] Both of these episodes illustrate the growing tension prompted by the increasing need to separate private and public life in the creation of a new civil society. In many ways, the episode between Place and the Mirasidars simply provides another illustration of that tension.

Dubashes thus stood simply as a symbol of British bewilderment and powerlessness in the face of an apparently inscrutable local system. In 1793, a member of the Madras Board of Revenue, C. N. White, wrote that Dubashes "seldom fail to avail themselves of their situation, to serve themselves and their connections at the expense of the Inhabitants and even without the least regard to the character of those who employ them [i.e., the British who should have been in control]." He was amazed at how many Company servants in the Madras area working in revenue matters had totally neglected learning any Indian languages to "save themselves from the disgrace of being constantly made the dupes of intriguing servants." (This in contrast to Bengal, where they had made "considerable progress in languages.") White suggested that British administrators were quite defenseless in dealing with their own colonial products, who were seen as totally amoral. White went on to say that learning Indian languages "must lead to a knowledge of the History and ancient customs of the people, who from what may be observed of them were in a state of improved civilization at as early a period as the inhabitants of any part of the Deccan or Hindustan, and while a great part of Europe was involved in ignorance and barbarity."[14]

Often the land itself was characterized in terms that allowed access to cultural answers from other eras. In another context, White described the Jagir "which formerly was and is still capable from its soil and situation of being rendered one of the most fertile spots in India, has within the last 10 or 12 years been the prey either of needy and rapacious renters, or of dishonest Dubashes and native revenue officers."[15] White, along with many other persons besides Place, believed that before the war of 1780 and particularly during the period of the Nawab Sadat Ali (d. 1732), the Jagir was in a "high state of improvement." Before the 1780 war, said White in 1793, the Jagir contained "upwards of two thousand villages with rich and populous towns." It also had "the finest soil and climate and contains between three and four thousand tanks . . . with many means of fertilization."[16] (We will see that a century later the Jagir came to be regarded as unproductive precisely because it was considered to have poor soils.)

White and other Company servants also believed that the town of Madras stripped this agrarian area of its wealth primarily to meet European colonial needs. In Place's 1795 account of the Jagir, he complained bitterly that European requirements for mutton virtually drained the Jagir of its animal wealth as well as the manure produced by sheep and goats; many of the sheep required for the Madras markets were "table sheep," which were invariably ewes with lambs.[17] Lord Hobart, the governor of Madras, in 1797 also established a police committee in Madras to deal specifically with European needs. In this case, Hobart set up the committee to reduce the prices of "bread, fish, beef, veal, mutton, kid, pork, poultry, wild fowle, fruit, hire of palanqeen [a box-litter carried by men for travel] boys, coolies, carts, etc."[18] All these services and products constituted perceived necessities for the European residents of Madras. Europeans believed that the high prices that they paid resulted from "deliberate fraud and collusion" by artisans, "but-lers," and "compradores" who, according to Susan Neild-Basu, histo-rian of Madras, "took advantage of the Europeans' dependence upon their services." These butlers demanded twice what they had received in the early 1780s, whereas "the necessaries of life to the poor are full as cheap now as they have been for many years past."[19] At the same time, the residents of Vepery and St. Thome in the western and southern reaches of Madras town complained particularly about the amildars and other revenue employees of Collector Place of the adjoining Jagir, who had been unwilling to "direct the dealers to supply the public at the reduced rates." Place's own tax employees had detained sheep on the Jagir roads leading to these city markets.[20] This suggests that in this area as well, Place's ideas about the devitalization of the Jagir by Madras enabled him to act to prevent it. At bottom he and others like him did not want people to move from the Jagir to Madras town. This was also part of a sedentarizing tendency. For the next three-quarters of a cen-tury, the British and others continued to attribute the decay of the Chin-gleput district to its proximity to Madras.[21]

We cannot trace this appeal to former epochs to the thinking of Place alone. As we have seen, many other British administrators of the Com-pany also created heteroglot knowledge using local ideas and considered it their mandate to restore both the Jagir and the subcontinent to what they perceived to be its "original" condition. In Bengal, during the 1770s, Warren Hastings employed the same tactics to retain what he considered to be the "indigenous" judicial system there. He encouraged Nathanial Halhed to translate the *Mānava Dharmaśāstra* or what is commonly called the *Code of Manu*. As has been pointed out, when Hastings "interfered" to reorganize the entire judicial system, he argued that "no essential change was made in the ancient constitution of the province. It was only brought back to its original principles."[22] Others have shown how this orientation toward the culture of the subcontinent began to change in the mid-1780s as the evangelicals illustrated the ways in which people of the subcontinent were depraved.[23] Structurally, little difference existed between a utopianist position that appealed to the culture of former eras and the evangelical position, because both of them structured knowledge in order to look on contemporary society on the subcontinent as decayed. Both sought to formulate the future. More-over, those with the utopian view simply perceived ideal and essential-ized institutions on the subcontinent (which they also connected with British structures) and used them to change local society, while the evangelicals tried to create what they considered to be British cultural ideas against the background of what they said was a decayed subcontinent. Neither of these approaches, however, can be said to have been "British." Their involvement with the local environment immediately produced interactions that provided an active role to local and other people who sought to "understand" these expositions.

In another British colonial context with many structural similarities to those under discussion, African village leaders in 1962 Northern Rhodesia noted that British officers did "not effectively communicate with villagers, who tell them what they think they want to hear." Moreover, George Foster reported that one of the main preoccupations of the British officers was "standards." In that environment, they invoked "standards" as a strategy to help make an effective boundary between British officers and Africans and to perpetuate a utopian land from a former epoch. Foster noted that he *"never heard an African praised for work done.* The usual evaluation of a performance was to explain to the African how he might have done the job better, and to mutter an aside to the visitor about 'the difficulties in teaching these chaps standards' [emphasis in original]." In the same context, Foster writes about the symbolic meaning of unrealistically high electrical standards in that environment. "All lamps and other appliances are grounded by a third wire, every lamp plug has a fuse, the socket into which it goes has another fuse, and the attempt to draw several lines from a single outlet, by means of multiple sockets, produces an electronic device suggestive of a minor satellite."[24] What this implies is that in Africa as well as in India, officers in the British administration had sought to create knowledge to convince themselves of the decayed condition of "indigenous institutions" unable to meet British normative and utopian "standards," standards stated in a monologic and authoritative voice.

Even in 1816, Francis White Ellis, a British collector of Madras remarking on James Mill's well-known *History of India*, wrote:

> The abilities and the usefulness of this writer are neutralized by the supercilious contempt he invariably manifests towards everything for which he cannot find a criterion in his own mind, or which he cannot reconcile to some customary standard of thought. . . . He has subjected the Hindu system to a comparison with an abstract standard of his own erection, and as might have been expected, has condemned it as being found wanting.[25]

This excerpt suggests that in the cases of James Mill and the 1960s Northern Rhodesia described by Foster, the "standards" based on monologic and momentarily authoritative language were unstable. This resembles what Norbert Elias called "the civilizing process." Elias has argued that "the concept of civilisation indicates quite clearly in its nineteenth-century usage that the process of civilization—or, more strictly speaking, a phase of this process—has been completed and forgotten. . . . To the upper and middle classes of their own [European] society, civilization appears as a firm possession."[26] Structurally speaking, the use made of texts by a group of people known as Orientalists to essentialize society in order to remove the discussion from the present to the past followed a similar strategy of forgetting the civilizing process. It removed the discussion from the everyday to the utopia of another era and place and was equated with the normative. In many ways, what Richard Fox calls "pejorative" or "negative" Orientalism was a way to forget the civilizing process in order to make room for other normative values and "standards."[27]

One way to illustrate the creation of a utopian appeal to another time in South India is to look at interactive constructions of knowledge about Indian villages. Contrary to what both the British and local individuals claimed in their normative, utopian descriptions, other documentation of village society shows that local populations were mobile before the coming of the British, migrating in response to wars and epidemics as well as in searches for work, trade, and water. Some of the movement took place within highly spatially defined areas, as with the kaikolar or sengunthar weavers in Tamil society.[28] We can also discern more movement among those lower in the ritual and economic hierarchy than was the case with those who had more investment in the land. Evidence prior to the desertion of the Jagir Mirasidars with their paraiyar Pannaiyals and Padiyals in 1795–97 points to many disputes among land controllers over mirasi rights when they returned to the Jagir following the war of 1780.[29] This evidence suggests that every time land controllers had to leave the region due to war, famine, or the like great fights arose over mirasi and other rights following their return.

Thus, the constructions of the normative past denied both physical mobility and social contestation in an effort to illustrate a decayed present and to suggest the characteristics necessary for the future. Though it may have been true, for example, that land controllers and their Padiyals and Pannaiyals engaged in ritual activities on an annual basis to strengthen their bonds of commitment and dependence, there is much other data that shows tense agrarian relations between these agrarian paraiyar Padiyals and their vellala Mirasidars that were certainly not permanently fixed in a particular mode.[30] Place wrote that the Padiyals

of the Mirasidars at Uttiramerur, southwest of Madras, "had been defrauded by their masters of the hire which was due to them, while working on the tank; and from the injustice thus done to them many have
deserted and others could not be prevailed upon to engage with them,
on an adjustment of the previous year's produce, every species of peculation also appeared to have been committed."[31] In Karanguli, south
of Madras town, Place said that the "inhabitants [Mirasidars] had allowed their servants [Padiyals] to go away after the expiration of Fasli
1204 [tax year 1794–95] and neither entered into new engagements with
them, nor procured substitutes till after the tank had filled."[32] Attempts
to claim for the villages in the Jagir sedentary and benignant Mirasidar-
Pannaiyal relations therefore face much evidence to the contrary. We
may also look at the desertion and reoccupation of the Jagir villages as
a constant process where old claims to a share of the grain and the right
to build houses in the village site were continually fought over and negotiated.[33] During the eighteenth and early nineteenth centuries, Company officers such as Place and many local inhabitants sought to create
for this uncertain situation the idea of a village society that always re-
constituted itself into discrete villages without argument. It was essentially to fulfill this idea of an unchanging and peaceful village society
that they collectively developed these normative and utopian ideas about
rural communities on the subcontinent.

This construction of knowledge provided a way to create an embedded, organic solidarity for the future for which the society of the area
needed to be sedentarized. Nor can we say that the creation was a willed
activity. People at all levels of local society participated in creating an
embedded, interdependent, and sedentarized village society of the future. To do this, they used locally available appeals to former epochs
and places, ideas that were themselves altered by contact with similar
notions from other sources. For, as we have seen, local writers conceived
of amoral village behavior as a recent development. Place, in embracing
ideas about a sedentarized village society, came in 1799 to believe that,
though these Mirasidars were "absent for years from their lands, [they]
did not fail to assert their claim to them." When Place first took over
the collectorship of the Jagir, for example, he found many of the villages
lacking Mirasidars altogether, "the parents, children, and relations being extirpated. . . . The idea of permanent property [ownership] was
such in the minds of the natives," Place wrote, "that they declined cultivating any fields thus appropriated, unless under the meerassee tenure."[34]

Making Religion More Useful

One of the ways by which Place tried to reorder society in the Jagir was by revitalizing Hindu religious life there. This would, he felt, make the population happier and correspondingly more productive, useful, and cooperative with each other. He funded the ceremonies and festivals of Hindu temples in the Jagir to attract back the dispersed population.[35] During his collectorship (1794–98), Place made a concerted attempt to revive the temple festivals at Kanchipuram, Tiruvallur to the west of Madras, and Peddapalayam to the north (now known by the Tamil equivalent of Periyapalayam).[36] Initially, after reporting on the condition of the Jagir in October 1795, Place convinced the Board of Revenue to make an allotment of pagodas 15,000 for the repair of the temples there. In addition, a temple fund called the pagoda mērai was collected in small amounts from about fourteen hundred of the more than two thousand villages in the Jagir. During the revenue years July 1795 to July 1798, the average yearly income from that fund was pagodas 15,566, a sum that was supposed to be devoted to the religious festivals of both the great temples in such places as Kanchi and village temples.

Place spent most of his energies and much money on the Kanchi Vaishnava Varadaraja temple in the part of the town called Little Kanchi. He noted that it "had been robbed of its most ornamental Pillars and other sculptural work" by Muslims to build a mosque. If, he said, the mosque had not been in a state of ruin, "I should have thought it a commendable act of retributive justice to have restored them [the pillars] to their original place [by destroying the mosque]."[37] (However, Place saw nothing wrong with taking parts of certain Hindu buildings for the purposes of constructing the dams for the artificial tanks of the Jagir.[38]) Many of the associated buildings of the Varadaraja temple, he said, had also been pulled down when materials were used by Muslims to construct mosques in other parts of the town.

In many ways, the phrase "restored them to their original place" indicated Place's view of the way to establish social and civil harmony in the Jagir. As he understood it, his mandate was to recreate the area in utopian terms so that it would flourish as it had in the past. He employed this mechanism to take advantage of the ideas regarding the past he had brought from England and mixed with local ideas. To that end, he sought to rebuild the Varadaraja temple and to participate in its principal festival in the Tamil month of Vaikāsi (mid-May to mid-June). His restorative sense was, quite naturally, a selective one informed by the British effort to achieve dominance and to establish an authoritative monologic definition of harmonious South Indian society in the future. This effort had many implications. For instance, Place's notion of restoration did not include the restoration of the mosque in Kanchi but did involve the renovation of artificial reservoirs or tanks that would remind people of the British presence. Similarly, in this context, he condemned the brahmans for not being good agriculturalists because they would not touch the plough:

> Those villages the meerasdars whereof are Bramins, are generally speaking, in the worst state of cultivation. Moreover, the religion of a Bramin forbids his tilling the ground. But he must do so by employing servants, his vocation is prayer and his subsistence otherwise so easily obtained . . . to make him indifferent about the cultivation of his lands. He is held in sacred reverence. . . . Multitudes are thus supported, and irretrievably consigned to idleness.[39]

For Place, at any rate, the relationship between idleness and religion was part of contemporary societal decay. He appears to have wanted to revive temple-centered Hinduism in which brahmans would mainly function more as temple priests than as Mirasidars.

One of his main approaches to this goal was to physically reconstruct what he felt the Muslim invaders had demolished. Place noted that the Varadaraja temple in Kanchi had been used on many occasions by Hyder Ali and Tipu Sultan during the war of 1780. For instance, he wrote, the "central dome under which the sacred idol was deposited had almost to be rebuilt." In addition, the fires that had been kindled in the interior had damaged many of the sections made out of granite and the floors had been torn up by Hyder's armies when they were looking for the treasure they believed was hidden there. "In short the whole interior was nothing more than what had escaped the dilapidations of time and neglect or the ravages of a devastating Enemy."

Place used these partially destroyed buildings to conjure up what he conceived to be the values of another time. The vestiges enabled Place to see local culture in clear and precise terms, to understand what were the "true standards of the past." These ruins, therefore, still functioned as a "stupendous" monument to the "munificence and benevolent care of the antient Hindoo Governments of the favorite object upon which the Industry and wealth of the People had been bestowed and in which their happiness was materially interested." We see, then, that both the existence and the psychic use of ruins—products of war, "disorder," and "despotism"—were critical to the development of constructed knowledge and institutions about local rural society in the Jagir and elsewhere. The old ruins of the temples, waterways, artificial tanks, towns, and cities of the Jagir pointed to a future society viewed in a new and more socially interdependent light. To Place, the attention that he personally paid to the annual festival of the Varadaraja temple in the part of town called Little Kanchi was rewarded by the great crowds that visited it. He noted especially "the harmony that prevailed among a concourse of people incredible to those who have never seen it, I do not think less than 300,000." The apparent "harmony" and sheer size of the temple crowds helped Place formulate his view of both the past and the more cooperative and interdependent future of Jagir society.[40] This order he saw as a kind of restored vestige of a previously happy and untroubled political and social system. On the occasions when he participated in these temple festivals, he said that he did not withhold his support or practice any kind of economy "but made it a practice to go almost to the utmost length of profusion." As a result, Place noted, he bestowed on the temples "jewels and plate" valued at pagodas 2,161 paid out of money from the temple fund.

Place looked on his role as collector as a mandate to serve as an example to the local society of the Jagir, illustrating how to behave cooperatively and harmoniously with each other. He aimed to create a new civil religion. He also appears to have looked on the revival of the temples as simply another way by which he could get the local population to be more productive. Thus, Place, with his new set of requirements, used heteroglot ideas about the Tamil past and local culture to demonstrate values from other times and other places to the local population. These values were neither European nor local, neither Western nor indigenous. Many of his ideas about how the local population had acted religiously emerged from what he chose to see and from ideas he derived from local informants. Nevertheless, his purpose in this construction was to see religion in a new way. He was, in effect, participating in the production of a new kind of knowledge about this religion that was later referred to as "Hinduism;" his formulation used religion to make people happy and effective persons.[41] In this sense, Place played a part in a general social process carrying out an important historical function to express epistemically what was happening in a society.

In many ways, Place appears to have operated as he felt a Tamil king would act in regard to temples. He saw flourishing religious centers as critical for creating a compatible and productive population and did everything at his disposal to regenerate what he presumed to be the original condition of these temples, in order to physically and morally recreate a well-regulated kingdom where subjects would be more inter-dependent. Specifically, he believed that the conditions of these temples would be greatly enhanced if he put the finances, and with them the ceremonies, into some kind of order. In 1799, he wrote:

> I considered the religious ceremonies of the Jaghire throughout a matter so intrinsically connected with the happiness of the people and the abuse of the funds appropriated for the support of Pagodas [temples] so much in need of reform that I gave general orders upon the subject to remedy the evils and neglect of which the Inhabitants almost universally complained. . . . I had frequent occasion to see that those who had the conduct of them [the religious ceremonies] required to be controuled in the expenditure of the funds with which they were also entrusted and although I cannot say that my orders produced all the effect intended I know that benefit so far resulted from them that the inhabitants took a more active part in those affairs.[42]

As we saw earlier, although he was able to have the Dharmakarta (or, as Place called him, the church warden) replaced, he was unable to resolve the disputes between the Vadakalai and the Tengalai Sri Vaish-nava brahmans over the use of the Varadarajaswami temple. This pre-sented a great problem, for Place felt that substantial religious dissention was one of the main obstacles to be overcome in the Jagir. Indeed, part of his perception of religion in this "decayed" cultural environment was that it created strife. Nevertheless, he concluded:

> Nothing is more difficult in any country than the adjustment of religious differences and nothing in this to which the best informed European can be more inadequate because they turn upon those intricacies in theological doc-trines and forms which he cannot enter into [.] Yet it is these which create the greatest animosities between parties. In adjusting the disputes between the two sects of Bramins belonging to little Conjeevaram Pagoda [the Little Kanchi Vaishnava Varadaraja temple], who, however, besides a variety of trifles are distinguished by the use of separate forms of prayer.[43]

Similarly, Place found that both the Varadaraja temple and the gar-den outside were in bad condition since, among other things, no gar-dener had been employed in many years. "But the one and the other [the temple and the gardens], however when I left the Jagheere, if they were the first were nevertheless magnificent monuments, worthy of the liberality of the Company's Government." All of this suggests that he believed that the money he spent (over pagodas 9,600), and particularly the money devoted to the eight gilt ornaments that stood five-and-a-half feet tall on the main dome of the Varadarajaswami temple, was wealth spent not only to establish the legitimacy of the Company but also to assure a sense of well-being among the people.

Place also repaired the temples at Karanguli, Peddapalayam, and Madurantakam because this would help bring back the dispersed population. Out of the total expense of repairing all of these temples (pagodas 12,366 from the pagoda merai or temple fund in addition to pagodas 15,000 authorized by the Company), more than pagodas 2,750 was spent on the Madurantakam temple itself. He also decided to set up rules for the "police for the correction of the various abuses that prevail in it [Kanchipuram] for the better preservation of property." At the same time, he wanted to establish both a prison and an office for the collector there to preserve records, since the office of the collector in Kanchipuram "consists of a few sticks and coconut leaves, neither proof against a shower of rain, nor capable of withstanding the gusts of wind usual at this season."[44]

Place had said that he helped to revive the temple ceremonies in Little Kanchi and elsewhere both to draw people there and to put at rest "the minds of the people."[45] But he wanted to do more than state these goals; he also sought to introduce these ideas into written agreements between taxpayers and the Company. One example of such an insertion can be seen in the agreement or muchalka signed by the Mirasidars in 1796. Inscribed there was the condition that the Mirasidars themselves would do "the utmost to restore such ceremonies [at the temples] as have been stopped, so that we may pray to God to make us happy and prosperous in our village."[46] Access to the sacred was equated with wealth and pleasure. Place sought to invoke a new interactively constructed knowledge about the true function of religion. Indeed, he apparently was the first person to request thirty Hindu sepoys commanded by a Hindu officer to serve as an honor guard for the procession of the Varadarajaswami temple.[47]

For Place's purposes, then, restored religion could be equated with orderly society. That this construction was not universally shared by Company officers may be easily documented. Though the Kanchi Varadarajaswami temple crowds seemed "orderly" and full of harmony, for instance, there were episodes in which these same groups appeared "disorderly"; these seemingly "unruly" episodes would not form part of a utopianist vision as exemplifying the values of the past. For instance, Greenway, one of Place's successors in the Jagir, reported in 1801 that as a result of a serious accident the costs of the "third day ceremony" at the Varadarajaswami temple in Little Kanchi had increased. He described the incident responsible for this increase:

> The gates of the Pagoda [temple] had as usual been open from early in the morning and free ingress and egress permitted when the idol was brought out of the Pagoda [temple] and carried to a Muntapum [stone portico] in the inside of the walls. At sunrise there was a general motion towards the gate [with] a large concourse happening unfortunately at this moment to press in from either side of the gateway in order to prostrate themselves. There the guard which was stationed at the entrance was overpowered, and the two crowds meeting, thirty-one men, women and children were trampled underfoot, three of whom only were recovered, the rest were all suffocated and it therefore became necessary to purify the place before the idol could be brought out.

As a result of the cost of the purification, which in this case came to pagodas 14, the Company had to pay a total of pagodas 313 for the third-day ceremonies, which included the cost of cleansing.[48] Temple crowds could therefore be seen either as a sign of order or a source of disharmony and expense, depending on the use to which this signification was put.

Expressions of the New Religion

The Company decided in February 1818 to discontinue the financial support of the festivals in Kanchipuram and elsewhere. Nonetheless, the involvement of the Company's government in the temples of the area continued for many years. Moreover, the effect of Place's early interest in the Varadaraja temple became reflected in local practice in a way that even he could not have imagined. This heteroglot result demonstrates clearly the tension within the British view of the project of religious restoration.

John Kaye's account of Christianity in India describes Place's activities with hostility. Writing his story of Place's behavior in the middle of the nineteenth century, Kaye sought specifically to demonstrate its effect on local practice in a period after which the Evangelicals had become an important force in state policy. In particular, Kaye's criticism focused on appropriate behavior for a government servant. Kaye quoted Place's argument from a report Place wrote about the need to support the temples in the Jagir:

> The management of the Church [Temple] Funds [Place had written] has heretofore been thought independent of the control of Government; for this

strange reason, that it receives no advantage from them; but inasmuch as it has an essential interest in promoting the happiness of its subjects and as the natives of this country know none superior to the good conduct and regularity of their religious ceremonies, which are liable to neglect without the interposition of an efficient authority, such control and interference becomes indispensable. In a moral and political sense, whether to dispose them to the practice of virtue, or to promote good order and subordination by conciliating their affections in regard to this matter is, I think, incumbent.[49]

Kaye said that Place proposed this policy "as tending to make better subjects, and more to conciliate the people. *What he recommended to Government he did himself,* as far as he could, by his own individual efforts [emphasis in original]."[50] Kaye then went on to report what Alexander Duff, the famous missionary, had found when he went to Kanchipuram in 1849. Duff had said:

> Probably no one bearing the honoured name of 'Christian,' has left behind him so distinguished a reputation for his services in the cause of idolatry as Mr. Place. When visiting Conjevaram last year (1849), I found his name still cherished with traditionary reverence by the votaries of Brahmanism. The nomenclature which he had introduced was still in vogue. The native officers spoke of the pagoda [temple] as the 'Established Church;' of the temple revenues as the 'church funds;' of the Brahman keepers of the idol shrines as the 'churchwardens.' In the neighborhood of one of the great temples a spacious garden was pointed out as the 'gift of Mr. Place to the god;' within was shown a gorgeous head ornament, begemmed with diamonds and other jewels, worth a thousand pounds, which Mr. Place had presented to the great idol. During his collectorate, he was wont to send for all the dancing girls, musicians, and instruments, elephants and horses attached to the different temples in the surrounding districts, in order to celebrate the Conjevaram festival with the greatest pomp. Attending in person, his habit was to distribute clothes to the dancing girls, suitable offerings to the officiating Brahmans, and a lace garment of considerable value to the god.[51]

"This," wrote Kaye, "is commonly cited as the first instance in which the British Government took upon itself the office of dry nurse to Vishnu." From his perspective, it was naturally inappropriate for the British administration to assist in these festivals.

This episode reveals perhaps more than any other the fact that almost every project undertaken by Place put certain behaviors and kinds of knowledge at risk while privileging others. Place found himself in the middle of a general process aimed at reformulating a variety of institutions and behaviors as part of the future by appealing to the values and behaviors for other social groups from other times and places. These behaviors and values were negotiated by "bazaar voices" whether local or other, thus demonstrating the effect of heteroglossia and Bakhtin's Rabelaisian laughter. The project involved the formulation of religion not as dissension but as a source of happiness and cooperation.

Let us now look at another area in which similar kinds of negotiation occurred: the way the state sought to remove the use of violence from lower-level authorities in order to control it from the center.

Uses of Violence and the Construction of the Asiatic Despot

One way to illustrate how juridical power operated in the pre-British context is to look at the Palayakkars in the Jagir. Palayakkars or what the British called poligars were individuals, mostly of Telugu warrior subcastes by origin, who had been given the "watching" or "police" jobs in South India before the European arrival. They formed vestiges of what can be called the nayak system, part of a larger segmentary structure called the Vijayanagar kingdom centered in the Kannada-speaking area west of Madras. In the late eighteenth century, the Pala-yakkars in the Jagir were concentrated in the northwestern and more physically elevated third of the area. This followed the pattern of settle-ment of Telugus in the Tamil country, well documented by the British in the 1931 *Census,* which showed that the largest concentrations of Telugus in the Tamil region were located in the upland regions, away from the coast. Both before and after the defeated Vijayanagar kings settled at Chandragiri as local kings or rajas of that place (about seventy-five miles north of what was to become Madras), various Telugu chief-tains established themselves in all parts of what was in the last decades of the eighteenth century called the Jagir. In 1672, Mughal forces under a general named Neknam Khan absorbed most of the Raja of Chandra-giri's territories but left him the town of Anagundi and a few villages.[52] Before Anagundi became the capital, the two centers of this polity were Chandragiri in the Telugu upland country just to the north and lowland Chingleput farther to the south, where a fort of substance was built.[53] In the middle of the seventeenth century, as opposed to the late eigh-teenth, Telugu-speaking Palayakkars resided in almost all parts of the Jagir, even the lowland areas.[54]

Many of these areas, Palayakkar centers in the seventeenth century, had disappeared by the late eighteenth century. According to Place, in some villages in the lowland regions of Kanchipuram, Karankuli, Uttir-amerur, and Poonamallee, the office of Palayakkar had been taken over by the more powerful village Tamil inhabitants who found ways to get the fees or privileges rightfully due to the Palayakkars.[55] In fact, under both the preceding Mughal government and the government set up by the Nawab of Arcot from the 1740s onward, the Palayakkars' villages were first taken over by the state and then a portion or all of them were regranted to them. During the Anglo-French wars, the Palayakkars operated in territories controlled by neither the French nor the British.

However, once the British took over the Jagir in 1783, each collector took the right of "watching" the villages away from the Palayakkars and then, as was the custom under previous polities, restored them. In 1794, when Lionel Place became collector, he decided to take over the grants to these Palayakkars and specifically not to restore some of them as had been customary. He did this, he said, because these Palayakkars had deserted the Jagir along with the Mirasidars to protest Place's new tax demands on the area.[56] However, Place took over the privileges or fees of the Palayakkars without authorization from the Board of Revenue, his superiors in Madras.

As we have seen, Place had two goals to be achieved by these actions. He wanted to increase the tax that went to the Company under his name. He also did not want any intervening political authority between himself and the villages. The Palayakkars immediately realized that these actions would alter the political arrangements dramatically regarding not only control over land but also control over the use of violence. That is, Place believed that the Palayakkars not only deprived the Company of a large amount of money but also were responsible for many disturbances and robberies. In April 1795, about six months after he was appointed, he wrote:

> A casual circumstance which came to my knowledge some time ago respecting a robbery committed at Madras afforded me some arrangements for the better security of property which has been so frequently exposed to open violence and concealed attacks. By having fortunately succeeded in securing the principal accomplices of the robbery in question I was progressively led to the apprehension of others who had been convicted on various similar occasions until I have now in confinement 35 persons who have been guilty of this crime.

He claimed to have traced a large network of persons whom he labeled as thieves and from whom he had recovered much stolen property. This, he said, had reduced the number of robberies both in the Jagir and elsewhere.[57]

Place's transactions with the Palayakkars related in part to the way in which public violence was used. As Thomas Munro wrote, "In cases of murder it was his [the Palayakkar's] duty to produce the murderer and in cases of theft to produce both the thief and the property stolen."[58] Even before Place became collector, another British official in the Jagir, Richard Dighton, had been uncomfortable with the way in which the Palayakkars used public violence and torture to find thieves and stolen objects. He felt, however, that there was no option but to leave the entire enquiry about thieves in the hands of the Palayakkars,

> in whose borders the robbery may have been committed and who are by the custom of the country bound to make good to the party the property stolen and in order to indemnify themselves to discover what is become of the stolen property. . . . [But, he said, to find out who had stolen the goods,] the Polygar often employs methods which according to our ideas of criminal justice appear very harsh and cruel. However I cannot help thinking that unless the Polygar had the liberty of exercising these punishments he would be very unwilling to make restitution for the loss sustained. I have hitherto avoided giving any authority to the practice of such methods, but left them unnoticed with a determination not to interfere, unless I should receive information of any excessive cruelties being used or any greater punishment being inflicted than the nature of the crime deserved and in doing this I am actuated by a conviction, that were no such punishment allowed, there would be no safety of property in these districts, as there are a certain tribe of people who make thievery a profession and who would not be induced to give up the stolen goods by a simple confinement of their persons.[59]

Dighton categorized certain "tribes" as criminals by birth as a way to rationalize the continued use of torture and violence by the Palayakkars.

Place's strategy regarding public violence moved beyond the construction of local knowledge to replication of local behavior. We have noted that, despite Place's efforts to project both the past and some aspects of present society of the local area as harmonious, he also proposed himself as a constructed version of an Asiatic despot. In that way, he often used flogging both to inflict pain and to humiliate. Place's conception of his authority emerged from the interaction of ideas he brought from England with Palayakkar behavior and other ideas of "Asiatic despotism" (themselves produced both on the subcontinent and elsewhere). In that persona or self-presentation, he felt that he should be able to punish and use violence against any villagers who sought to hide information about robberies or engaged in other activities that Place felt were "disorderly."

One incident illustrating this "despotic behavior" occurred at a village named Numbal in present-day Saidapettai taluk (of what later became the Chingleput district). Numbal was one of two villages granted by the Nawab of Arcot in 1763 to Shamier Sultan, an Armenian merchant located in Madras. Though located within the Jagir, which had been granted to the Company, Numbal was considered by Shamier Sultan to be outside the Company's authority. Therefore, when Place sought information about a group of thieves who had sheltered there, Shamier Sultan's local employees sent back "an impertinent message and got together some of the Nabob's Sepoys to set me at defiance."⁶⁰ Since it was possible that the Numbal villagers were connected with the robberies, it was, Place believed, quite appropriate for him to punish them for concealing the robbers. This incident is interesting, showing that Place felt that his own political function gave him the right to display the same license regarding public violence as did behavior of those very Palayakkars about whom Dighton had been so squeamish.

According to an account of the incident from the two sons of Shamier Sultan (named John and Nuzur Jacob Shamier), the difficulty started on 31 March 1798 when the Amil of Poonamallee (a Company tax-collecting employee and subordinate of Place) wrote a letter to the Amil of the "Shamiers of Numbel."⁶¹ The Amil wrote that the "Rajshree Thooryavarkal" (Place) wanted Venkatarayan, Shamier Sultan's Numbal amildar, and several others to go to Place's kacceri or office. On 4 April 1798, the Shamiers wrote, Venkatarayan was about to depart when a group of sepoys and Dalayats or armed messengers with Place's Amil from Poonamallee appeared "unexpectedly" at Numbal and asked Venkatarayan why he had not come to Place's office. Next, the sons of Shamier Sultan reported, the Poonamallee Amil asked the whereabouts of the other four people whom Place sought. They found one of them, a man named Aiyakutti, and took him and Venkatarayan to a spot about three hundred yards away where Place had arrived with his Dubash in a grove of trees. Later, they went to Place's office. When Venkatarayan and Aiyakutti were unwilling to provide information regarding the robbers who had been "plundering the district," Venkatarayan was flogged with forty stripes and Aiyakutti with thirty. (In fact, Venkatarayan was given a "sentence" of forty-eight minus eight stripes with a cane, and Ayakutti thirty-six minus six. Apparently, the deduction in the flogging was a way to indicate Place's "grace" or "mercy." This was similar to the function of the "mercy" of the English king in granting pardons to people condemned to death in eighteenth-century England.⁶²) The sons of Shamier reported that for security reasons some sepoys "belonging to his Highness the Nabob" customarily remained in the village, apparently because it was still considered to be a village in the gift of the Nawab, even though the Nawab had himself granted the entire Jagir to the British. When two of these sepoys appeared in the crowd, Place had both of them flogged with twelve stripes of a cane simply for being there. Moreover, Place is reported to have said that unless the sepoys left the village he would have them shot. In due course, Place also had a declaration taken from Venkatarayan, whom he suspected of participating in the marauding, and fined him and Aiyakutti rupees 25. Place then confined them both in Kunnattur, an important weaving village in the present-day Saidapettai taluk on the southern bank of the large Chembirambakkam artificial irrigation tank.

Place was specifically reprimanded by his superiors for being too severe in flogging Aiyakutti and Venkatarayan at Numbal.[63] Nevertheless, Place's purposes are clear. He intended to take the use of violence away from the Palayakkars by reserving it to himself in his role as an efficient, centralizing monarch. In another attempt to contain all juridical power within his person, he also tried, as we have seen, to induce all Palayakkars to come to his kacceri or office, where they were forced to demonstrate the validity of the privileges they claimed. In another connection, two British merchants, Henry Sewell and Richard Woolf, whose local position was threatened by Place's behavior in the 1790s, wrote that "we have no doubt that it has been and still is the desire of the Collector's servants to have all Europeans removed from any possessions in the country with a view by that means of exercising a more despotic sway over the natives, unrestrained by the presence of those who might report their conduct in its proper light."[64]

Place wanted his own authority to be visible and symbolic. For instance, he complained that the way in which the committee of police from Madras town operated in "his" Jagir reduced the prestige and legitimacy of the Jagir collector. He pointed to the fact that when the police committee made a proclamation about fixing the prices of articles for the Madras market, they did so by "beat of Tom [Tamil "tamukku"] in front of my Amildar's cutcherry [office] under the protection of a military force [and] to require the Buzar people to wait on them on the pain of a heavy fine. . . . The beating of a tom and levying of a fine . . . are privileges peculiarly belonging to a Collector in his own districts."[65] In the Jagir, particularly, Place felt that the collector's authority should be paramount over "every description of people." Place's idea was that a collector's authority should be more or less "despotic" and that the symbolic apparatus connected with the office should correspond with that notion. His behavior clearly drew on an amalgam of different forces that came from both England and the local environment, from books, from informants, and from examples set by other actors in this field of reference.

Another strategy aimed at removing the use of violence from the lower levels of the state structure involved jettisoning the idea of the Palayakkars altogether. This was suggested by a collector named Greenway, a successor of Place. He felt that most Palayakkars should be pensioned off and their fees devoted to the new police. He also believed that the whole conception of the system and the name should be changed; this process involved abolishing the name "Palayakkar" or "poligar." To his way of thinking, the name "signified rather the leader of a banditti than an officer of police." The goal of his strategy would be to "destroy all hope of the old system being revived."[66] He wanted to empty the signification of the Palayakkar in the face of the new signifiers—that is, British juridical control—and in its place insert the new definition of the state created by the Company. The negotiated behaviors and institutions related to the historical tasks in which Place and many others were involved, then, meant the removal of violence from lower levels and the use of the "Asiatic depot" model as part of that activity.

One way in which state officials participated in this emptying process involved the writing of texts; one such text was the official *Chingleput Manual* penned by Crole. Prior to the siege of Madras by the French commander Lally in January 1759, Crole, in the *Chingleput Manual,* had said:

> The condition of the district was, in all corners, one of unrest and disorder. The vain-glorious boastings of the French regarding their approaching conquest of the whole of the English possessions, incited the small robber chiefs, or Poligars, who lived in the uncultivated tracts, covered with palmyras [palm trees] and scrub jungle with which the district abounded, to rear the head of insolent regard of authority.

Crole wrote that these Palayakkars lived by hunting "when plunder was not to be had." When both the Nawab and the British began to withdraw their troops from "outlying stations," the Palayakkars became more and more interested in plunder. Two of them in particular, Rangappa Nayak and Vartappa Nayak, "lived in two jungles, between which lay the fort of Tripassore [Tirupaccur]." At this point, wrote Crole, Vartappa Nayak and Rangappa Nayak became "regular pests" in the area around Tirupaccur and even began to plunder grain and cattle from the villages near Poonamallee soon after Ensign Crowley's force withdrew. He also noted that four companies of sepoys under an Indian commander, Jemal Saheb, had to be used to subdue them.[67] Ultimately, the Tirupaccur Palayakkars agreed to pay rupees 14,000 (about pagodas 421) as tribute to the Nawab of Arcot until the war of 1780.[68]

After the retreat of French Commander Lally from Madras in 1759, the British took over Tirupaccur and Poonamallee. Crole said that neither of the Palayakkars expected such a turn of events:

> The English stronger than ever, chas[ed] . . . before them the foes who had seemed certain, a couple of months before, to swallow them up. They [the Palayakkars Rangappa Nayak and Vartappa Nayak] now quaked in anticipation of the vengeance, which seemed certain to overtake them for the robberies and barbarities, committed on the helpless villagers during the dark hours of the siege.

But, wrote Crole, at that point the Company sought conciliation. Both of these men then submitted themselves to the British on the condition that they "place themselves and their forces at the disposal of the commanders of the two forts of Tripassore and Madras."[69] Crole, like Greenway, sought to empty the signification of "poligar" to perform a new and imperative historical task—the creation of a unified state with a sedentary population that was embedded and increasingly interdependent. To accomplish this goal, it was necessary to formulate the past in such a way as to create the future.

Another aspect of the interdependent society sought by Place and others was a self-regulating political economy. In particular, Place sought to invoke the ideas of Adam Smith to prevent state control over prices for the markets in Madras. In May 1798, he wrote to the committee of police:

> My practice founded upon a principle of sound policy has always been to leave the market free and unrestrained, to guard against imposition by forstalling, engrossing or monopolizing, but to leave the prices of all articles whatsoever to the natural course of demand, by which competition is excited, and they will at all times sell at the lowest possible rates.[70]

He criticized the new arrangements made with fishermen in nearby villages, noting that "for the exclusive obligation they are under has been made an excuse for their demurring to supply my own table with the little I require, it therefore has all the operation of a monopoly."[71]

Taken together, then, a variety of strategies shaped new behaviors to both create and express altered political circumstances. Instead of controlled prices to benefit Madras town, Place attempted to create a new kind of political economy in which the rituals and granting of temple honors would exercise a new signification to serve a new set of political requirements. The goal of religion would become less and less to confine the sacred to a given place or individual and more to dissipate the sacred among all individuals, thus making them useful, cooperative, productive citizens.[72] Similarly, violence would no longer be in the hands of the Palayakkars but would be at the disposal of the state, which would gradually abandon its use to control its citizens. At the same time, Place wanted the market to operate invisibly so that the economy would regulate itself without state intervention. To use the words expressing the utopian views of the "native revenue officer" quoted in the Introduction, this would be a society in which rights would be mutually respected and breaches regulated without the "interference of Government."

Creating New Ideas of Leadership and Sacrality

South Indian historiography is marked by pronounced debate regarding roles played by temples and by rulers of "the little kingdoms" of the region. This debate has attempted to uncover the source and power of new leadership and new conceptions regarding sacrality. Nicholas Dirks has argued the centrality of "the little kingdom" in contrast to the Appadurai-Breckenridge formulation in which, in Dirks' words, "sovereignty is essentially procured in temples, where the deity is the paradigmatic sovereign. Further, [in this model] all endowments are equal at the level at which they are dependent on particular endowments for their status within the temple."

In Dirks' view, the Appadurai-Breckenridge analysis puts "too much stress on the autonomy of temples and temple honors." Rather, says Dirks, "the kinds of honors that constituted authority in the old regime were those received as shares of worship in local temples as well as those granted as emblems and titles (pirutus) by kings." Temple ceremony or puja was "a root metaphor for political relations."[73] Dirks concludes that, "like religion itself, the temple was reinvented in an attempt by the colonial state to appear as the protector of all that was good and inviolable in Indian culture and life force that had pulsed through them in the old regime."[74]

In contrast to these characterizations, I would argue that temples and religion were not reinvented by the colonial state but were produced dialogically by the British and local individuals in the nineteenth and twentieth centuries as a way to redefine the sacred and to disaggregate it into all individuals. The example of Place's relation with the Varadaraja temple in Kanchi provides evidence that a "new pulse" was being created through a new competition between local knowledges that involved persons from the area as well as the British. This invocation to create knowledge focused attention on temples, sacrality, and religion per se. Place and his local participants involved in the distribution of temple honors thus incited construction of a new kind of useful, productive religion. Indeed, the definition of what came to be Hinduism or the temple was not imposed or reinvented by the British or by the Indo-British "state." The complicated process of redefining religion included not only activity around the temple itself but also the act of disconnecting the political from the religious and the related process of placing the monopoly of violence in the hands of the state. Given the complexity of the process, we cannot attribute these cultural products to Europeans or to the colonial state alone in a top-down fashion; we must include in that new productive process the many, many individuals from the whole subcontinent who participated.

The extent to which these dialogically produced religious and political mechanisms became important in South India has been well articulated recently in work by Mattison Mines and Vijayalakshmi Gourishankar. Mines and Gourishankar argue that individuality and leadership do exist in the South Asian and South Indian contexts. In their view, the South Indian "Periyār" or big man "lacks the characterizing values of liberty and equality [Louis] Dumont . . . associates with Western individualism, which concurs with the sense, if not the reality, of personal freedom and of individuals as equals."[75] Instead, leadership in South Asia refers to the "galactic" leadership idea of Stanley Tambiah, which includes "social identity marked by eminence, achieved identity associated with deliberate striving after positions that confer honor and establish a status of dominance, charisma, public recognition of the instrumental role played by unique persons in groups, and autonomy defined by responsibility for what one does."[76] Mines and Gourishankar note that while temporal sources of dominance such as land can be shared, temple honors cannot. The use of temple honors by these important persons, they say, explains "a great deal about the relationship between politics and religion . . . because they distinguish *individuals* [emphasis in original]."⁷⁷

Dirks has also argued, as Mines and Gourishankar note, that "colonial rule removed issues of [juridical] power from local political struggles, so that in a sense struggles over symbolic markers of status were all that was left to politics," or "the hollow crown."⁷⁸ The evidence provided by the interaction of Place and the local population of Kanchipuram (along with the definition of individuality and leadership to which Mines and Gourishankar refer) indicates the development of a cultural formation of individuality based on the need for more and more interdependence in a new civil society. In this environment, there would not necessarily be more equality. Rather, as Stephen Mennell has written, "Interdependence does not mean equal interdependence: those who are less dependent on others than others are on them remain more [juridically] powerful. But the web of interdependence increasingly constrains all—the more powerful and the less powerful. And this has long-term effects on their feelings and behavior."⁷⁹ The previous relation of temporal power to religion in the distribution of temple honors was therefore put at risk by Place's taking over the function of distributor of these honors. Place's behavior represented a set of historical relationships that sought to reproduce traditional categories or gave them new significations relative to the new historical requirements. The significations privileged by this late eighteenth-century dialogism were selected to fill the specific need for a more interdependent and more restrained civil society.

Place, like many local persons, as well as Englishmen and other Europeans before and after him, sought to "take the role of the other" in order to innovate in this cultural realm. Place situated his actions, in granting temple honors to a large variety of individuals, at the Varadarajaswami temple in Kanchipuram on the basis of his understanding of the role of Tamil king or "Asiatic despot." He also brought to this activity a strong sense that religion ought to make one prosperous, happy, and cooperative in a society that would run by itself. There is also much evidence that his ideas were put into operation with the assumption that exchange and obligation provided the motive forces necessary to run a political structure. We know, for instance, that when he was in the process of introducing his "new system" of tax assessment into the Jagir he was forced to employ a large number of unusual methods to attain his goal. One strategy we have already identified brought in tenants or Payirkkaris to take over as Mirasidars to cooperate with him.[80]

This creation of special ties was repeated in hundreds of other contexts. For instance, Place obtained special rewards for his office staff in exchange for their loyalty. When the Board of Revenue resisted granting these benefits in March 1796, he wrote that though he sought the assistance of the government in punishing certain individuals such as the "artful, designing, and culpable part of the inhabitants let me not be deprived of the superior gratification of distributing rewards to the meritorious." He also said that "with regard to my own servants [staff in the cacceri or office] I almost stand in the predicament of having professed my promise, under an expectation that they would receive their well earned reward, I have exercised a rigour over them which without it will leave an everlasting reproach upon me."[81] Their responsibilities, he felt, had increased enormously and they should be remunerated. Place, of course, sought to wean the tax officials away from a dependence on the Dubashes to make them more dependent on the Company. In many ways, he was seeking to create a staff that was gelded, that is, a group not subject to the pressures of a local kinship system who could then spend more effort on public service. But he also emphasized his reliance on his own staff when he told his "servants," during the "distribution" of these monies to the amildars on 10 November 1796, that if they performed well they would continue to receive rewards from the Company in the future. The Board could well understand, then, he said, "what must be my situation, if whilst in charge of an important office, where my word should be inviolate, I were to disappoint those who have every claim to my approbation and appear to have deluded them into a dependence upon the assurances hereby given which I was neither sincere in making nor able to fulfill." Equally, Place could argue that this investment by the Company produced loyal servants who could be relied on to work independently in the Company's interest. By contrast, if he were forced to personally superintend his staff members, it would detract from his main assignment and the loss to the state, in fact, "might be much greater." Essentially, Place argued that to increase revenue the government would have to pay more for its employees—for their labor and their loyalty. The Company was as dependent on these men as was Place.

To convince the government, Place referred to the service performed by his staff in increasing the tax collections in the Jagir:

> I am aware how little the necessities of Government at this Juncture admit of liberality or profusion, but with pleasure, I appeal to its candour to say how much greater they might have been, but for the opportune surplus which they received from the Jagheer, and how much they have therefore been relieved by an abundant and punctual revenue which the Jagheer was at no former period, even the most prosperous, thought capable of yielding.[82]

Though Place succeeded in winning these rewards only for the office staff in charge of confidential documents, he still sustained his function as a distributor of royal rewards. His dependence on the loyalty of his staff and the interaction between them illustrates in many ways the processual nature of Place's presumptions, as an individual who operated in a patrimonial or kingly environment (as opposed to one who was attached to a bureaucratic system). Place, despite his bureaucratic interest in accounting and fiscal responsibility, wanted to build a system in which he would be a king, making progresses through the district to receive petitions and give out rewards and honors in person to those of "his kingdom." Place's hopes for the revival of the Jagir were expressed in his desire to reward people who responded to his appeals to values that themselves were in the process of altering.

The goal of ritual thus began changing to one focused more and more on usefulness and productivity. For instance, in May 1797, he requested permission to grant a reward to a person named Swami Mudali, "whose merits and assiduity in the repair of Madurantakam tank [reservoir] and several other works, I do not think have ever been equalled."[83] Here, it appears that Place was trying to formulate what was in fact a heteroglot conception of the past (the creation of ancient cities, waterworks, temples, roads) through a system of rewards to make people and their religion more productive and useful. Swami Mudali apparently was one of the people who responded to Place's hopes and invocation.

Swami Mudali and hundreds of others who were a part of Place's gift-giving and other ritual activities saw recognizable aspects of their own culture being enacted around them. Place could have no idea how he was being construed, or the extent to which previous meanings of Tamil or other local kingship came into doubt. These alterations did not emerge solely from Place's actions, however; they resulted from a much larger process in which he played only a small part.

Therefore, like the Sankarachariyar (Mines and Gourishankar's example), Place acted as an efficient administrator. To use the words of Mines and Gourishankar as applied to contemporary Tamil society,

Place served as a "focal officeholder of a powerful organization" and
was "a charismatic public leader who claims and uses a wide variety of
symbols of kingship." Like the Shankarachariyar, Place also set up special mechanisms to "fund the daily rituals of the temple and finance
temple projects aimed at entertaining the public with grand and opulent
displays."[84] But, at the same time, Place's behavior and that of thousands
of others who participated in his project put the previous meanings of
the Tamil king in doubt. Although inequities remained, as the division
of labor became more complex and an embedded society began to develop, people came gradually to be far more connected with one another.
These increasingly powerful relationships tended to restrict the behavior
of all elements of the population.

At the same time, it is problematic to relate these Tamil leaders, as
Mines and Gourishankar have done, to David Shulman's description
of warrior-heroes of ancient Cangam or Sangam times, who often
"achieve, in the compositions of their poets, a winning individuality
conveyed by unique dramatic results."[85] In this development of the relationship of the individual to the sacred, we are seeking to describe a
general process whose aspects are directly associated with contingent
historical requirements. It is very important for us therefore not to collapse the historical dimension of the process in order to prescribe it. If
we lose sight of the historical dimension, we invoke the same techniques
as Place himself conjured up.

Place accomplished his tasks with the assistance of local Tamil and
Sanskrit ideas about both cosmology and the presumed ethnography of
the local territory. Like the Rabelaisian laughter of the marketplace,
these actions came from no one in particular. Although they were aimed
by individuals at particular audiences, taken together they constituted a
construction independent of the specific contributions of these individuals. The actions, in turn, were immediately used and changed by their
audiences to carry yet a further elaboration into the next interaction.

Making the Jagir into a Garden as a Way
to Connect the British to the Future

Historians have argued that the only reason the British invested so much
money and energy into artificially created reservoirs and other mechanisms for storing and using water, in an environment where water was
particularly valuable, was simply to increase agricultural productivity.
There is no question that this was indeed an important concern. Even

Place had a clause inserted in agreements signed by land controllers to the effect that, "if our tank or tanks should undergo a compleat repair, then this muchilka [agreement] shall be void and we shall be ready to enter into a new settlement [tax assessment] for our said village according as the Circar may desire."[86] Though it is not possible to discount this fact, given the desire for a greater tax base, there is also evidence to show that the British pursued this strategy for other reasons as well. In a report on three subdivisions of the Jagir (Madurantakam, Tirupaccur, and Kanchipuram) written by Place in October 1795, he made a plea to build up the two towns of Madurantakam and Uttiramerur, about forty-five miles to the south and southwest, respectively, of Madras town. He was struck by the fact that the population of the Jagir was attracted by water. "For I can discover no other reason why they should formerly have contained such a number of Inhabitants as they plainly have done, being not more favorably situated than any other spots for any kind of trade."[87] Madurantakam in the mid-1790s, he believed, provided an example of the difficulties in inducing a population to return to an area without the attraction of water. "The tank [of Madurantakam]," he wrote, "broke many years antecedent to the War of 1780, [the Second Anglo-Mysore war]." Though Madurantakam was located on the "high southern road" from Madras, that alone did not appear to offer any great attraction to people. After all, he said, Madurantakam had in 1795 only 250 houses, whereas Place believed that the town had had "some thousands of houses before the War [of 1780]." Likewise, he believed that Uttiramerur toward the north and the west "seems to have been as extensive" as was Madurantakam since it bore vestiges of "much more opulence in the remains of numerous Pagodas [temples] and Chaultries [rest houses for pilgrims] but [now] contains very few more than 300 houses."

Place plainly felt that there were several ways by which the population of these and other towns could be brought back, including the rebuilding of people's houses for them, the reconstructing of their temples, and even more conclusively the repairing of the Jagir tanks or reservoirs. Place said that "if but some of the principal tanks are put into thorough repair, and a uniform system established, capable of yielding a much larger revenue than I have been attempting to settle, that in value it may be made to equal the richest spot in India of the same extent, and that the happiness of the people shall rise in a proportional degree."[88] The accounts of the Nawab of Arcot projected another part of this perception of the Jagir as the potential garden of the subcontinent when they characterized the Jagir as the "*choicest part of my country* [emphasis in original]" when he gave it to the Company.[89] Place pursued the task of repairing the tanks in what could almost be described as a religious fervor. Irrigation became a cultural solution. Place devoted a total of pagodas 150,000 to repairing these artificial reservoirs, an amount that exceeded the entire yearly tax income from the Jagir in the early 1790s before he became collector. He felt that "when completed the Tanks will for many years be monument[s] of British Dominion in India and it would be a pity that the same spirit of liberality should not be extended to other objects [such as temples, roads, and the like], united to accomplish the same public benefit."[90] This activity aimed, therefore, partly to increase wealth but also to extend and communicate the sense of a commanding British presence in the environment.

Formulating the Agricultural Past of Tondaimandalam

If the British used efforts to reshape, repopulate, and rejuvenate the environment as a way to establish their firm connection with the Jagir (to naturalize and place themselves, as it were), various local actors asserted similar connections. Tamils regarded the region around Madras as the center of a cultural region called Toṇḍaimaṇḍalam, one of five such clusters in this language area. Further claims to the area were pressed by the Tondaimandala vellalas, who told British and other investigators that they were the original agricultural settlers in the region. They supported this claim by reference to considerable oral folk material. Other subcastes formed a substantial proportion of the population of the area. These included the paraiyars, who served generally as the Padiyals and Pannaiyals of the vellala Mirasidars, performing the tasks of plowing, transplanting, weeding, and harvesting the crops; the pallis, known as vanikula kshatriyas in the late nineteenth and early twentieth centuries; and the Telugu peasant subcastes originally from the north. According to the 1871 census, in the British administrative area called Chingleput District—which also served as the center of the Tondai cultural area—by far the largest proportion of the inhabitants were vellalas. They amounted to 62 percent of the population, while the paraiyars were 24.3 percent, and the pallis 19 percent. Brahmans, who had palli (not paraiyar) Padiyals and Pannaiyals, were only 3.6 percent of the total.[91]

Thus, local claims to dominance in the area required certain constructions of the past as well as manipulation of dialogically produced documentation techniques such as the census. Formulations of the past necessarily became interactive projects. For instance, from the last decade of the eighteenth century the British sought to document the relationship of these populations to the Tondai country. In the early years of the nineteenth century, Colonel Colin Mackenzie, originally a military engineer, gathered large collections of local oral materials. Some of those oral histories, "transcribed" by Mackenzie's local assistants, illustrated the story or the "history" of the entry of the agriculturalist vellalas into the Tondai country and their battles with the local "forest people" called the kurumbar.[92] In addition, the remains of what were conceived to be the mud forts of the kurumbar, coupled with the oral history, caught the attention of British officials in the late eighteenth and early nineteenth centuries.

Thus, documentary projects, although identified with the names of British administrators, were often dominated by local inhabitants and local physical evidence. A prime example of this is the collaboration between Shankarayya and Ellis. Of all the British responsible for helping to document the past of the Tamil region, perhaps Francis Whyte Ellis, who died of cholera in Ramnad in 1819, is the best known. During his tenure as collector of Madras, he tried to describe the land system of this Tamil cultural region. In 1814, he wrote an extended account of the proprietary system of this region that took the form of comments on the mirasi land controlling system still operating with some force in the Tondai region. Ellis's account of the Tondai country, even more than that produced by Place, formed part of an intensely interactive formulation of local Tamil culture. One educated individual named Shankarayya was very important in this process, although he died before Ellis's manuscript was published. It was Shankarayya's answers to a series of questions on mirasi that formed the basis of the material on which Ellis wrote his comments (referred to in this discussion as the Appendix). Shankarayya had held many posts in the Company's revenue and judicial departments and was assigned to both the northern and southern districts of what became the Madras presidency (the "northern districts" were the largely Telugu ones and "southern districts" largely Tamil). He then obtained an appointment as head of Fort St. George College.[93]

Although Shankarayya's specific answers provided a strong basis for Ellis's construction of the Tondai past, even Ellis argued that these ideas arose from a diffuse authorship. By way of mounting a case to authenticate his work on mirasi, Ellis wrote:

> The facts respecting Mi'ra'si and it's privileges are not matters of speculation, they are known to every inhabitant of the country where they exist, who are brought up in the habitual exercise and observation of them;—the

terms which express them they have received from the lips of their mothers, they have formed the prattling of their infancy, and they remain indelible in their minds and on their tongues.[94]

Ellis could make these assertions, of course, because he could find additional evidence to support Shankarayya's insights. An unusually able linguist, he could read Telugu, Tamil, Kanarese, Malayalam, Sanskrit (in Grantha script), Hebrew, and apparently some Arabic and Persian. This gave him access to a wide variety of written texts not available to most members of the British bureaucracy in Madras. Indeed, the importance of access to language for this project is underscored by one part of Ellis's task in the Appendix, which was to provide a large glossary of words then in use by Tamils in connection with the tax-gathering process for the Company. The way in which this glossary was itself constructed from a great variety of languages as well as written and oral traditions illustrates how heteroglot were these conceptions.

Part of Ellis's self-assignment—encouraged, later, by his superiors, the Board of Revenue and the governor and his council in Madras— involved discerning whether an individual who was a Mirasidar (a person who had a share in what was a coparcenary proprietary system) could alienate that share. That is, Ellis wanted to know whether mirasi constituted a kind of real property so that the British could in turn apply their own legal apparatus to these transactions. Also, Ellis sought to write a history of the Tondai country to show that it was possible to use Tamil literary sources (such as the *Kānchi Purāṇam*) to illustrate the origin of the land system and caste groups who created it. Within this latter task, one of his main goals was to identify with considerable precision not only the extent of the Tondai area but also the actual number of the inhabitants who lived there when it was first settled by agriculturalists (as compared with the late eighteenth century, when Place first gave it centrality by his descriptions). Ellis contended that, for instance:

> the extent and boundaries of the [Tondai] country thus settled, the number of the settlers and its variation in population and property in later times are to be traced, not by vague tradition only, as is too commonly conceived to be the case with respect to the remains of Indian History, but in writings of different periods, as substantially authentic, probably, though intermixed with undisguised fable, as the records of most other countries.[95]

Both Ellis and his superiors, the government of Madras and the Madras Board of Revenue, agreed to believe that it was possible to identify with extraordinary precision the exact boundaries of Tondaimandalam and the ancient subdivisions within it. Indeed, when the government of Madras published Ellis's Appendix in 1818, the Appendix included the sentiments of the governor and his council regarding the possibility of precision noting, for instance, the fact that the map of the "country known to the Natives by the name of Tondamandalam . . . [had been prepared] under the directions of the Officer in charge of the Survey Department" of the Madras government. Information on this map had been contributed by a variety of sources. Ellis found that the indigenous predecessors of the vellalas and the British—the kurumbars—had a series of territorial subdivisions called kōṭṭams improved on by the agriculturalist vellalas who introduced other subdivisions called nātus (or, as it is written in English, "nadus"). The government of Madras noted that although Thomas Barnard's 1770s map of the Jagir did not mention these kottams and nadus, Place's 1799 report did so. Thus, although the subdivision had been bureaucratically documented rather late, the governor's council argued the age-old authenticity of this spatial organization and asserted that for the Tamils living in the area in 1818 all these territorial subdivisions still had great contemporary meaning:

> To the people, however, these divisions, in detail at least, are still well known and, as frequently instanced in the following pages, are always referred to in deeds drawn up according to the old form. It could be easy, therefore, by enquiry on the spot to ascertain if not the precise boundary, the relative situations and general extent, not only of every Cottam, but of every Na'du, throughout that part of the province which remains in possession of the original Tamil settlers, and they may, possibly be traced, even in those parts from which they have been expelled by the encroachments of their Telugu and Cannadiya neighbours.[96]

By reducing all his oral material and other received versions to governmentally approved texts with maps produced by the survey department, Ellis gave to much of the system a monologic quality and a rigidity that it had not had. Momentarily, the mirasi system had become involved in the production of a centripetal project to create an authoritative "knowledge."

The following outline of the centripetal project will illustrate how it worked. As noted, Ellis sought to show that the original agricultural settlers called the vellalas (supported by Chola kings from the south) had overcome a group of forest people called the kurumbar who built mud forts. These mud forts, he felt, were maintained by the Cholas long after they conquered the region, "for the sites of many, marked by high mounds and deep hollows . . . are still pointed out."

From this original base of society, Ellis then attempted to show the extent of certain areas to the north (where Telugu was spoken) as the region where warrior groups had taken over from the Tamil vellalas. He also wanted to document the fact that there was still a substantial region in the lower Tondai area (a Tamil-speaking zone) in the hands of the descendants of the "original" agricultural settlers of the region. Though a population who were not vellalas held a "considerable portion of the whole mirasi right . . . the institutions of the ancient Tamil Government, notwithstanding the innovations of recent times, remain in a great degree in force." He also found, for instance, that in 1797–98, when a survey was undertaken by Place, the proportion of the Mirasidars (coparceners) to the rest of the population had a ratio of 1 to 6.5, or were about 16.5 percent of the total population.[97] By contrast, at the time of their first agricultural settlement, he claimed that the vellala Mirasidars had represented 20 percent of the entire population. He noted that, until the "termination of the Tamil government by the invading Telugus and Muslims[,] none but the Vellalar possessed or were qualified to possess landed property in the ground." Moreover, as the proprietary system called kaniyatci (a Tamil word) or mirasi (a later Arabic term adopted into Urdu and Tamil) developed, not only was it impossible for any person except a vellala to have a share in the product of the land, but the right of even allowing a vellala to become a member (Mirasidar or Kaniyatcikkarar) of this coparcenary group could only be granted by vellalas. In this construction, then, Ellis interwove linguistic culture, region, conquest, and land-controlling systems together in a political project that could be linked directly to the polity that British officials and others wanted to create for the future. This helped to unite culture to land.

The concept of a cultural region played an important part in the project whose outline we are tracing. The Tamil countryside was considered to consist of five socio-emotive regions called tinais. Each of these tinais (mountains, forest or pasture, countryside, seashore, and wasteland) had its own character. In addition, the Tamil country consisted of five cultural regions called Tondainadu or Tondaimandalam, Cholanadu or Cholamandalam, Pandyanadu, Kongunadu, and Cheranadu. In his Appendix, Ellis proceeded to show by extracts from the *Kuvattu Puranam* the exact extent of what he conceived to be the Tondai country. This region, which Tamils identified with the present-day area encompassing the administrative divisions of South Arcot, North Arcot, and the Chingleput districts, he delineated as encompassing

16,645 square miles.[98] Upper Tondai, largely located in what was then the "native state" of Mysore, contained 5,168 square miles. He concluded that "the best features of ancient polity are now obliterated" but that at the same time "enough remains . . . of former institutions to prove that they were the same as other countries, swayed originally by the sceptre of the Tamil Princes." One of the ways he indicated the extent to which ancient practices still obtained was to point to the fact that the paraiyar laborers still possessed "their original mirasi offices," which indicated that they were still part of an "original polity." Furthermore, he noted that the pallis (who were also sometimes Padiyals and Pannaiyals of the brahman Mirasidars) and the kaikolar or sengunthar weavers "retain the Tamil language." What is of interest for us is that the sengunthars were part of the left-caste division who had very broad spatial ideas, in contrast to the vellalas whose self-conception as a right caste was one of extreme localism. The sengunthars throughout the pre-European period considered the propagation of Tamil an almost sacred responsibility. We know that it was the sengunthars who were responsible for spreading a version of the famous Tamil epic by Kamban from the Tamil into the Malayalam area to the west.[99] We will see in the Conclusion of this work that in the twentieth century the sengunthars as left subcastes (many associated with temples and the performing arts) came to play an important role in spreading Tamil as part of a large-scale political movement. Therefore, long before the British arrival, mechanisms both spatial and cultural were at work in the Tamil region to connect large areas through the spread of Tamil. This activity was an essential ingredient in uniting what was considered Tamil culture and territory. Moreover, the policy of reducing spatial mobility during the course of the nineteenth century ultimately aided in identifying and fixing the constituent elements or villages to a large spatial regime considered quintessentially Tamil. The project of cultural "restoration," then, brought even greater benefits to the left and right castes who participated in the dialogic process than it did to British administrators.

Another essential aspect of the project was the recognition that members of the Tondaimandala vellala subcastes considered themselves to be the original agricultural settlers of the area. Moreover, even though various groups, the most important of whom were the brahmans, had deprived many vellala of their rights to the mirasi, in 1797–98 the vellalas still comprised 53 percent of the Mirasidars in the Jagir or 14,757 of the total population of about a quarter of a million persons, followed in proportion by the brahman Mirasidars at 20 percent and Mirasidars of all the other subcastes at 27 percent. According to Ellis, not only had the number of vellala villages in the Tondai country decreased over the years, but the total number of vellala proprietors themselves had decreased as well. Some of the other castes had acquired rights to the mirasi or joint proprietorship by initially securing positions as Payirkkaris or Payirkkudis, tenants who were considered to be "strangers" or "outsiders" by the Mirasidars.[100] Ellis also stated that it was his intention to show that it was possible to derive information

> not perhaps precisely accurate nor very extensive, but more considerably than is generally supposed to exist, thereby to establish that there remain the means to tracing the right of landed property . . . which is claimed and in part enjoyed by the cultivators of the soil in that part of Tondaimandalam still in the possession of the Tamil Aborigines [the Tondaimandala vellalas] to a more remote antiquity than can justly be attributed to the generality of human institutions now existing.

He therefore placed "Tamil indigenous institutions" in an antique light, an important characteristic of the authoritative and monologic reconstruction of the past. How Ellis established his line of argument regarding the migration of the vellalas and their extermination of the kurumbar suggests how perilous was this process. One kind of source used by Ellis may have been a collection of Sanskrit manuscripts found at Pondicherry on the coast south of Madras.[101] These, Ellis tried to prove, were manuscript compositions by Roberto di Nobili, a seventeenth-century Jesuit missionary who created a group of materials under the title "Vedas." Ellis's biographer described these materials as joining together expositions of Jesuit religious doctrines with much legendary history in classical Sanskrit verse "with a view to palming them off on the natives of the Dekkan as the work of the Rishis and Munis, the inspired authors of their scriptures."[102] However, Ellis probably based the dating of the vellalar conquest of the Tondai country, among other things, on another "history" that related the kurumbar to the coming of St. Thomas (traditionally Thomas is considered to have arrived at Mylapore, south of Madras town). This latter manuscript is noted as having been translated from Latin by a certain Ñānapirakāsa Piḷḷai. Describing Thomas being appointed to supervise the propagation of Christianity in the area where the kurumbar king, Kantappa Rāja, ruled, the story seeks to show how Thomas defeated local brahmans by doing miracles and converting many people to Christianity.[103] Interestingly, although Ellis rejected the Jesuits' use of textual materials from the area to legitimize their ideas, he nevertheless used Christian dating and archaicized these sources as a means for making Tamil cultural material ancient and therefore usable in the new historical setting. Moreover, the historical imperatives associated with his work on mirasi required that he archaicize his constructions in much the same way as he accused Nobili of doing.

It is significant in our delineation of this project to note that, in an environment of heteroglossia involving a number of different interpretations that could be put on the "pasts" of the region, Ellis had decided to place it not in the local or regional antique past of the Chola. Instead he placed it precisely at the time of Christ, a way of reckoning time that was not only Western but associated with the reckoning of those who had juridical power. This was his technique for appealing to the ideas of other times and other places, as well as for suggesting a development synchronized with the history of the West. In this, at least, Ellis's British audience was significant; as we know, however, Hindus believed that simply reckoning things by Christian ideas was shallow by comparison with Hindu notions, whose era stretched back much farther into antiquity. In this new construction, placing vellala entrance into the Tondai area for Ellis proved to be the beginning of a "new age," a new millennium that was related to the West and western culture generally. Ellis's contribution, like that made by any novelist, operated in a heteroglot environment. This was an arena in which a number of local and relatively autonomous voices or interpretations from different epochs could be invoked and in which a large number of meanings could be employed for a unified text. Those elements addressing a British audience existed side-by-side and interacted with elements of great meaning to other actors involved in the project. At the same time, Ellis engaged in dialogic activity in which he dealt with elements of the past, the present, and the future simultaneously; these heterogenous elements were even contradictory in their nature. Not surprisingly, the results were not homogenous intellectual structures.

Ellis's argument, then, emphasized that the proprietary institutions of the Tamil-speaking part of the subcontinent retained many usages that were more ancient than other areas of the world. Though this was a decision to privilege one interpretation over another, it played a part in a general discourse involving the Tondaimandala vellalas, the Payirkkari tenants, and the paraiyar and palli Pannaiyals and Padiyals, all of whom invested a great deal in these emerging interpretations. It was also a system in which Ellis sought to connect this part of the subcontinent with the rest of the world and to connect the present with the past.

However, by proclaiming the great antiquity (at least in Christian terms) of these institutions, he was also speaking about the value of these institutions for a more interdependent future. Ellis obviously intended to demonstrate the great similarities between the political, social, and proprietary institutions of the Tamil country and those of Britain. In that sense, he was fulfilling his historical function. At the same time, Ellis simply formed part of a large authoring process, the product of which addressed far more than Ellis's avowed goals for the Company.

It was clear that the British and others from the area used the spatial fixing of the vellalas in the Tondai region as a way to prescribe sedentary villages for the area even though earlier evidence suggested that villagers moved about a great deal. Indeed, the emphasis on sedentary society certainly predated Ellis and his work. Prior to Ellis's account of the mirasi proprietary land system in 1814, Place had outlined many of the same facts and ideas, drawn from his own Tamil, Telugu, and other informants. In a large report written in late 1798 and early 1799, Place had noted that the Chola Raja collected the "whole of the Mudali tribe called the Vellalars who were sent to settle Tondaimandalam."[104] Place also wrote that the country had been divided into territorial domains called kottams, a reference to kurumbar policies. He quoted a story about the meaning of the term "kaniyatci," the older Tamil term for mirasi. According to Place and his local informants, the story indicated that the Chola king from the south had fixed the affections of the vellalas on the soil of the Tondai country "so strongly" that they could not even harbor a wish to leave.[105] Thus, Place could argue that the spatialization of the vellalas in the villages of the Tondai country had begun long before the British arrived. At the same time, Place participated in the expansion of the idea of "vellala," arguing that a person was considered a vellala if he had ever possessed the mirasi or kaniyatci right.[106]

In other Company documents of the late eighteenth century, considerable information emerged to indicate that Company servants knew much about vellala self-ascription as the original agricultural settlers of the area. One document composed by the Board of Revenue focused on the value of the vellalas as sedentarizing agents. In an analysis of mirasi rights of early 1796, the Madras Board of Revenue noted that the right to kaniyatci or mirasi was originally conferred "in compensation for clearing lands . . . to fix the people to their respective villages."[107] All of this helps us understand to some degree the attitude that the British had about the function of the mirasi system and the place that the British believed the vellalas had in the Jagir in the late eighteenth and early nineteenth centuries. What it also illustrates quite clearly is that vellala self-ascriptions contributed to the general process that characterized the society of the Tondai region as both unchanging and composed of certain villages whose populations hardly ever moved. To achieve this result, both the vellalas and the British appealed to "normative" descriptions of other places and other times. In contrast, evidence suggests that at the end of the eighteenth century only slightly more than half of the Mirasidars of the Jagir were vellalas. What is more important, we know that the population moved continually because of trade, war, famine, searches for sufficient water resources, and work.[108] Similarly, the material surrounding the repopulation of the Tondai region after the departure of Hyder's armies provides another vivid example of this movement. Thus, interactional formulations about the "eternal unchanging villages of the Tondai country" primarily related to what local individuals and the British believed and served as projections of future social and political requirements. On the basis of these interactions among Ellis, Place, many other English employees of the Company, and thousands of local individuals, a social utopia constructed from the past was used to invoke a future cooperative and interdependent civil society. These utopian visions of progress and history provided the foundation for the dialogic construction not only of land but also of the future political order.

The Interactive Production of the Mirasi System

According to Ellis, the number of shares in the produce of the Tondai villages, as represented by those in the Jagir, had remained the same for many millennia since the village itself was founded. Moreover, Ellis believed that in each mirasi village the Mirasidars had rights called maniyams. These maniyams belonged to the Mirasidars and could not be taxed by the state under any condition; they constituted private property. If they were confiscated from a Mirasidar, Ellis wrote, the result would be "nothing short of tyranny and oppression"; when these expressions of "exaggerated authority" occurred there would be no room for resistance.[109]

Ellis especially sought to examine the effect of the introduction of the Permanent Settlement in 1800 and 1801 into the area called the Madras district, an area encompassing both the town and its rural hinterland. The Permanent Settlement was a tax assessment system introduced into the Chingleput district in 1802 that fixed the level of the land tax per-

manently and contracted for collection purposes with large land controllers (rather than with individual cultivators or proprietors). According to Ellis, the Permanent Settlement enabled Mirasidars to keep their
maniyam lands free of any kind of state tax but also facilitated their
ability to transfer these rights to any person by sale, a right they previously had lacked.[110] Ellis also argued that under this settlement not only
had the pasankarai villages become arutikarai—from "several possession" to "individual possession"—but also another major alteration had
occurred in rural relations involving the abandonment of a process of
periodical redistribution of land. Though lands were not held in common and were not redistributed any longer after the early years of the
century, the Permanent Settlement nonetheless did not greatly alter the
unified character of mirasi villages in the Chingleput district. Moreover,
transfers of land for which grants and certificates had been issued were
no longer transfers of mirasi but of specific geographically defined "portions of land." The creation of rights attached to specific plots held
permanently was bound to affect the mirasi system. Though no right
had been directly affected by the issue of certificates, the fact is that the
process, Ellis believed, "must progressively lead to the entire extinction
of mirasi."[111]

Obviously, Ellis believed that great damage had been done already
to the previously pristine Tamil proprietary system in the Tondai country. He also believed that every attempt had to be made to put the Mirasidars in charge of their villages so that their rights to tax-free land
such as maniyams would not be abridged. To accomplish the state's
goal, the Mirasidars themselves would be given the right to grant certificates to occupancy tenants and tenants-at-will. He based all these
ideas on the presumption that this was "the original system," hallowed
by virtue of its antiquity and its connection with one of the seats of
Tamil culture in the Tondai country. In his comments on proprietary
forms, Ellis made primary reference not to British divisions of the territory such as districts but to what he conceived to be Tamil cultural
divisions such as Tondaimandalam and Cholamandalam (Tamil "Cō-
lamaṇḍalam"). What this indicates is that his primary intention was to
privilege what interactively had been constructed as "indigenous Tamil"
cultural ideas of land control. Those who sought to "understand" these
spatial ideas necessarily altered and recreated them. Both Bundla Ramaswami Naidu's attempts to "understand" the Christian chronological
system and Ellis's attempt to "understand" the Tamil spatial system
became active behaviors. Both attempts were directed at epistemic are-

nas that were tension-filled and highly contested. Each had to construct his statements on what was alien ground, against another apperceptive environment.

Since Ellis's ideas became monologic dogma by the middle of the century, it is of some interest to examine the kind of opposition that developed to them. In the second decade of the nineteenth century, another tax assessment practice was introduced into Chingleput and other districts called the ryotwari system.[112] The ryotwari system assessed each individual (ryot), who was held responsible for paying the taxes on a given piece of land, and put in motion a process of tax reassessment every thirty years. Moreover, several years after the ryotwari system had been introduced, the Madras government began altering the way in which taxes were to be collected in the Madras presidency. In a letter to the "President and members of the Board of Revenue" written in August 1814, the secretary of the Revenue Department noted:

> In preparing a final reply to the letter from the Honourable the Court of Directors in the Revenue Department, dated the 16th of December, 1812, the Honourable the Governor in Council has found that the information before the Government on particular points concerning the practical introduction of the decennial village-lease settlement, the usage in former revenue settlement, and the nature of landed tenure, is less precise and complete than the Governor in Council and the Honourable Court would wish to possess. I have, therefore been instructed to frame the annexed queries, and to desire that they may be circulated for answers to the collectors of the several districts into which the decennial village-lease settlement has been introduced.[113]

Various collectors were then sent a set of questions on proprietary forms. According to our evidence, the only person who responded to these queries was Ellis himself. A. D. Campbell said in 1817 that Ellis's comments on mirasi rights were in response to certain questions of mirasi posed by the Board of Revenue on 2 August 1814: "The information they contain [Campbell wrote] is generally so correct and important that they [the Board of Revenue] beg leave to recommend that the enclosures of Mr. Ellis' letter be printed for the use of the service at large."[114] By September 1817, the Board of Revenue wrote to Ellis saying that they wanted to print two hundred copies of his answers to the questions on mirasi and asked him to supervise the entire operation.[115]

However, when the Court of Directors heard that Ellis's Appendix on mirasi had been printed, it wrote back to Madras seeking to discount the importance that the Board had placed on Ellis's interpretations:

> We are surprised [that] the replies of Mr. Ellis [who had meanwhile died in 1819 in Ramnad] are the only replies we hear of on this occasion. The queries were general. It is expedient that a question of this sort would be decided, not upon one man's opinions, but by a consideration of all the information which can be obtained. . . . We disapprove of this printing and circulating of Mr. Ellis's opinions alone, upon the ground that it must, to a great degree, have the effect of imposing upon the service the opinions of Mr. Ellis as the authoritative conclusions of the Government. At that time, however, the Government were without those means of forming a conclusion which they themselves had called for, namely, the replies of the several collectors. That the opinions of Mr. Ellis happened to coincide with the preconceived opinions of the Board of Revenue was only an additional reason for caution on your part, in order that a question of this magnitude might be decided, not on authority only, but on deliberate inquiry and full information.[116]

The Court of Directors was calling for a more dialogic production of meaning about proprietary relations in the Tamil area, possibly so that they or Company employees could select and shape from these an authoritative (and momentarily monologic) statement.

More vigorous than even that of the Court of Directors was the resistance voiced by Thomas Munro, who by 1824 was a person of considerable stature and authority.[117] Munro wrote his minute on mirasi about three years after the protest from the Court of Directors, aware that he spoke against monologic formulations already strongly held by the Board of Revenue:

> The Board of Revenue seem to have considered the mirasidars of the village were granted on the original settlement [of the village]. They say that on the original establishment of every Tamil village, the hereditary right to all the lands was vested in all the occupants. They speak of this original settlement as a thing that was perfectly certain. But all this is assumed without the least proof, and is altogether incredible. The account given by Mr. Ellis is not more satisfactory. He supposes that the Carnatic was chiefly forest until Ananda Chuckravorti, sovereign of Canara, whose capital was Banawassi, settled three hundred thousand colonists, of whom one-fifth were vellalers, in Tondumandalam. This is evidently fabulous. No prince ever planted such a colony; no country could have supplied the drain. The number of deaths from casualties in such an undertaking would have been as great as that of the surviving colonists. New settlers brought from Canara and Banawassi would die very fast in the Carnatic, even now when it is cleared. We are not told how three hundred thousand colonists were to maintain themselves among jungles to be cleared away, when we know that, even at this day, such a population could not be maintained without the aid of numerous tanks and water courses for the cultivation of the lands, which would be otherwise very unproductive. It is much more likely that the mirassi tenure,

with all its incidents, as described by Mr. Ellis, was the gradual growth of a country long peopled and cultivated than that it was created at once by a grant to a particular tribe of Hindu cultivator, Vellalers, on their first settling in Arcot [the Tondai country], and that province was then an uncultivated forest. It probably originated in local circumstances, and perhaps more in the great number of tanks and water-courses constructed at the public expense, than in any other.

Munro's remarks simply provided another element in the creation of the mirasi system.

However, in the quarter century that followed, the formulations made by Ellis came to be more and more usable as a way to conceive of the requirements of the future. In this period, the primary goal was to produce a population immobilized, who managed permanent villages. For instance, the example provided by many Parakkudis (tenants without the right to retain their leases from year to year) in the Baramahal to the southwest was contrary to the goal of sedentarization. In the Baramahal area of Tamil Nadu, Parakkudis moved around in the period right before the monsoon, "especially during the months of March and April, the period at which the *ryots* from motives of caprice, superstition, or other causes migrate from one village to another, and that at which they received their cowle [agreement] for the year from the renters."[118] Ellis's ideas about the pasts of Tondaimandalam came to strengthen those resolves to build a sedentary rural structure in the Chingleput district in order to fix in place a relationship of tenant and a particular parcel of land, the tax potential of which could be firmly determined by the state. The past thus became important for building a more embedded and cooperative rural society for the future.

By mid-century, Ellis's ideas came to be inscribed in the semiofficial dictionary of Indian revenue and judicial terms compiled by the famous Orientalist H. H. Wilson. For instance, under the entry "Tondaiman-dalam" is the comment that "Mr. Ellis supposes it to have derived its appellation from tondama'n, a prince so named, who conquered the country probably before the era of Christianity, and granted peculiar privileges to the first settlers."[119] In 1893, B. H. Baden-Powell in his *Land Systems of British India* said that "Sir T. Munro wrote a minute, in 1824, which does not exhibit his usual insight into facts. He there questions the Vellalar immigration of Chingleput, and makes other more questionable statements. No one now doubts the historical truth of the immigration."[120] In the same context, he calls the mirasi system "the old Dravidian form of village."[121] That the validity of Ellis's views on mirasi were accurate, said Baden-Powell, was proved by "its absolute concordance with what is observed in other parts of Madras."[122] The definitiveness and monologic quality of Ellis's ideas proved convincing not only to British administrators but to the local actors who had interacted with him. That is, Mirasidars, and later even those who argued the case of Dravidianism in the late nineteenth and the early twentieth centuries, depended on this construction of the past. Finally, it has even been accepted by a modern economic historian of the Tamil region (see Conclusion).

To summarize my analysis, then, we see that in the period between 1790 and 1820 a series of intensive interactions between local populations and the Company employees in the Jagir focused on formulations of the past. These interactions may be characterized as positive, creative activities that did not destroy local culture. They were not exercises in which local institutions were reinvented by the British. Rather, local and autonomous voices produced new, historically derived and functional knowledge. Though some of these formulations, such as that about the mirasi system, were not officially adopted as monologic "truth" until midcentury, we will see that it was embraced by the Mirasidars, Payirkkaris, and paraiyar and palli Pannaiyals much earlier. Finally, this knowledge about the Mirasidar system was useful as a way to create a more sedentary, interdependent society whose behavior gradually became more and more restrained by the growth of the division of labor and consequently by embeddedness. Embeddedness, in turn, helped to shape notions of a Tamil culture that was geographically rooted in a particular place and socially expressive of certain sedentary relationships.

CHAPTER 3

The Rise and Consolidation of the Chingleput Mirasidars

Contention marked Chingleput rural society during much of the nineteenth century. In the early years, tussles occurred between the Mirasidars and those individuals who became the "Mutahdars" or "Zamindars" under the land-tax assessment system known as the Permanent Settlement. This group of land controllers, defined by the fact that they were the fifty-seven individuals who had purchased the divisions of the district called mutahs, constituted a taxation overlay on top of the mirasi and other villages in the district. During the second decade of the century, however, a new assessment system called the ryotwari land tax assessment system was introduced. That structure eliminated the Mutahdars and involved a periodic reassessment of the tax demand, payable in cash and not in kind. As part of that new system, the East India Company government made tax agreements with thousands of Mirasidars and other landowners of the district. In many ways, the contentions arising from the introduction of the ryotwari system between the Mirasidars and British officials expressed themselves in attempts by the Mirasidars to gradually reduce the taxes on the area by reducing productivity. However, as we will see, the effect of these conflicts momentarily enhanced the position of the Mirasidars while at the same time reducing both the amount of land cultivated and the taxes collected.

From the point of view of the Mirasidars, who were often able to exclude occupancy tenants and the state, decreasing productivity made good sense. This helps us to understand how the tax system operated.

It also helps us to see how the idea of a decaying agrarian countryside and the need for a future-oriented utopia arose in this period. This heteroglot construction of a utopia looked on the past as essentially crude and barbarian and consequently switched the utopia to a future that was fitted to new political and social requirements. These formulations also intensified the sedentary aspect of Chingleput villages and helped to develop a more embedded society. All of these aspects, of course, informed the overall project of constructing a new colonial society in South India and thus may stand as another key moment illuminating the heteroglossia of South Indian history. Let us examine the practical working out of these dialogic formulations in the relation between the mirasi taxation system and its cultural basis in the nineteenth century.

Creating Utopian Visions of Future Tax Revenues from the Jagir

British optimistic expectations regarding the taxes they could collect from the Jagir resulted from their historical experience. For these hopes to be achieved, however, a place had to be made in local society for the British. Compared, of course, to the land controllers of the area—the vellalas, Brahmans, pallis, and others—they stood as newcomers who had to fit into the proprietary system as it operated in the area. In the generation between 1790 and 1820, construction of this proprietary system into an ineffably ancient and unchanging one was shaped by the British, land controllers, and many others lower in the social and economic hierarchy. In this case, the interaction often focused on the level of tax collected from the Jagir (or after 1802, the Chingleput district). During the nineteenth century, a great debate had arisen, for the Jagir's tax figures helped focus controversy on the fact that the Jagir had much wet paddy land, the tax value of which appeared to have declined rather than increased in value. The Nawab of Arcot, Sadat Ali (d. 1732), provided the earliest tax figures; he seems to have extracted pagodas 384,190 in taxes.[1] Moreover, between the time when the Company gained control of this area until 1783 (which included the period of the war of 1780, the second Anglo-Mysore war), another Nawab of Arcot, Muhammad Ali (d. 1795), paid the Company pagodas 368,350 as the rent of the Jagir. The Company did not gain full control of the Jagir until 1783. Between 1783 and 1793, the Company made successive attempts through tax farmers to increase the income from the area, but the net yearly receipts garnered by the Company from the Jagir did not exceed much more than one-quarter the amount derived from the same area while it was rented to the Nawab.[2] Faced with this dilemma, the Company employee in charge of the Jagir, called the superintendent and later the collector, tried to enlarge the government share of the harvest between 1785 and 1790. It is clear that the dilemma arose because the government share (called melvaram in the crop-sharing system that was used in the Jagir) had been successfully reduced by the Mirasidars before the Company attempted to impose itself on the area. Given the great opposition raised by the Mirasidars, the tax farmers ultimately found it easier to return to the old share division (disadvantageous to both the renters and, of course, the Company); in 1790, the new revised varam or harvest share distribution that the Company had tried to impose was annulled.[3] The continued low amounts of tax that the Jagir produced reflected a clear defeat suffered by the Company government.

By the early 1790s, the Company Board of Revenue in Madras felt strongly that the Jagir should be made to yield the taxes that it believed were possible taking into consideration the amounts supposedly gathered by the Nawabs. Though the assessments or settlements of 1791–92 produced a surplus over what had been collected the year before, the total still fell far below the amount (pagodas 368,350) paid by the Nawab as renter. In 1783, the committee of assigned revenue, the supervising agency for the Jagir at the time, had set the figure of pagodas 400,000 as the potential tax productivity of the Jagir after projected improvements were made over the next decade. That this figure formed part of the unstated expectations that the Board of Revenue held for the Jagir in the 1790s is attested to by the fact that in 1799 Collector Lionel Place said, "By the fairest and most liberal deductions I have shown it [the Jagir] capable of yielding a Revenue of 4 Lacks [400,000] of Pagodas per Annum."[4] In the months between December 1798 and October 1799, no rain fell in the area, and the drought momentarily reduced British expectations. Place's successor, Hodgson, in 1799 carried out a village settlement or a tax assessment in which each village was asked to pay a lump sum. The division among the cultivators at the village level was left to the Mirasidars and other taxpayers themselves based on "an estimate of the actual produce of each village" to pagodas 324,045 in 1799–1800 (12 July to 11 July, the official revenue or tax year).[5] Together with the money collected from the French and Dutch settlements, the tax collections came to pagodas 346,571, a figure that pleased the Board of Revenue immensely.[6] Edward Greenway, who was responsible for introducing the Permanent Settlement into the Chingleput district in 1802 (to assess the taxes of the area in perpetuity) reported in May 1801 that the result of his jammabandi or tax collections in the Jagir was pagodas 373,800. He also said that if he were to add the amount of money repaid by Mirasidars to the Company for loans made toward cultivation costs (called taccavi), the total figure would come to pagodas 398,795. This would thereby give "an advantage over Mr. Place's [average] Gross collections [between 1795 and 1798] of Pagodas 11,700."[7] In these years, the economic expectations from the Jagir (which were, in many ways, perpetuated throughout the nineteenth century as well) helped to consistently fuel a sense of frustration by British administrators over their inability to bring prosperity to and derive taxes from this area.

As we have seen, one of the main events of Place's collectorship was an analysis of the landholding system as it existed in the Jagir. During this inquiry, Place continually compared his performance to that of Alexander Read, collector of the Baramahal southwest of Madras, an area from which substantial taxes had been derived. He tried on many occasions to match the Jagir's tax revenues with those of the Baramahal, even using this incentive to extract as much as he could through what he felt were the "indigenous" proprietary systems.

Many historians have regarded this tax revenue context as the setting of the interaction between rulers and ruled in the Jagir. If we focus instead on the ways in which a dialogic construction of South Indian colonial society affected the Mirasidars, we find that the process of defining society, particularly the relationship between state and sedentary village communities, is of greater importance. The first point to explore for this purpose relates to the sedentarization process to which we referred earlier. The combined effect of the court system introduced in the early part of the nineteenth century, the Permanent Settlement introduced after 1802, and the ryotwari tax collection system introduced after 1820 served to associate particular geographically specified pieces of land with specific individuals and families.[8]

Our story begins, once again, with Lionel Place. In 1802, the Company decided to introduce the Permanent Settlement into the Chingleput district. Place had by then been named to the Board of Revenue, although he soon came to feel that the environment of the Board was unbearable. Perhaps more important, he also became convinced that the land assessment system being introduced into the Chingleput district in place of the village system of tax collecting was totally unacceptable. He knew that this new assessment would divide the district up into a series of lots called mutahs to be sold to individuals at an auction. When in 1802 Place wrote an account of his struggles while on the Board of Revenue, he situated himself firmly as the protector of the Mirasidars of the Jagir. Given his early efforts to defeat Mirasidar influence in the countryside, this position is certainly ironic. Indeed, he only began to support these Mirasidars in 1799.

Tenant-Mirasidar Disputes during the Permanent Settlement

Place, feeling that he had few alternatives, resigned from the Board of Revenue in 1802, arguing that the special commission for introducing the Permanent Settlement had appropriated many of the functions of the Board of Revenue when it was introduced into the Jagir. Moreover, he resigned because he believed that the Mirasidars of Chingleput would no longer possess an idealistic champion in the face of the proposed changes that the special commission sought to introduce into the Jagir with the Permanent Settlement. In this context, Place wrote in 1802 that he felt particularly grieved because, although he had tried to reform the proprietary relations in the Jagir, he was now being excluded from an activity for which he possessed special knowledge.[9] The fundamental argument Place advanced was that the tax assessment should not be made with the Zamindars or Mutahdars but rather with the Mirasidars of their respective villages. Otherwise, "the hereditary proprietors of the land are bereft of all interest in it." Unfortunately, Place said, the Mirasidars had "no advocate to represent their situation."[10] Reversing his earlier attacks on the mirasi system, Place began in 1799 to invoke knowledge constructed interactively with other Company employees, with his Tamil and other informants, with the Mirasidars themselves, with the tenants, and with laborers. The ideas that he articulated drew on local Tamil and Sanskrit ideas mixed with ideas brought from England regarding cultural renewal. That is, his opposition to the special commission led him to participate in the process by which the mirasi system was constructed into an essentialized, monologic "original" Tamil proprietary form.

Both the proposals and actions of the special commission and the work of Edward Greenway, the collector responsible for introducing the Permanent Settlement, followed the system introduced in Bengal as a strategy for lessening the weight of government on the countryside. The Jagir was divided up into a set of mutahs or tax subdivisions; these fifty-seven mutahs were auctioned as units, purchased by individuals called Zamindars or Mutahdars. Under the terms of the Permanent Settlement tax system introduced in the Jagir, the Zamindars who purchased their mutahs or zamindaris at auction in June 1802 were permitted to alienate their holdings. The assessment aimed, among other things, to assign the task of "governing" the countryside to the Mutahdars, who could then presumably derive the benefits from the increasing value of the land. That is, the Company presumed that the Zamindars would absorb the costs of tax collection and thus the Company would be saved both expense and trouble. At the same time, the Company would be assured of uninterrupted income from the Jagir.[11]

The mutahs or estates included a large number of Mirasidari and non-Mirasidari villages, whose fate did not dramatically alter with this new arrangement. Under the Permanent Settlement, the strength of the Mirasidars in individual villages, however, remained largely untouched and it may even have been to some degree augmented by this tax settlement. Moreover, under the Permanent Settlement, with some exceptions, settlements with individual villages continued. The Zamindar's tax assistants made agreements with village Mirasidars for the next year's tax. Zamindars or Mutahdars themselves remained responsible for the payment of a set of permanently set tax demands, sums that had been set by Greenway in consultation with the special commission whose job it had been to oversee the implementation of this tax assessment system in the Jagir. In addition, the settlement only applied to 1,881 villages of the 2,246 in the Jagir. The remaining 365 villages had been already alienated to various individuals who previously had been a part of the previous tax-collecting or "watching" system of the Jagir in the late eighteenth century; these included the Nattars and the Palayakkars.[12] Thus, during the period of the Permanent Settlement, the Zamindar or Mutahdar, though he had purchased his mutah and had the right to alienate it, simply became an individual placed at the top of a large number of villages controlled by Mirasidars.

One of the most important effects of this tax assessment was to change the Jagir pasankarai villages (those held in joint possession) into arutikarai villages (those held in separate possession). Ellis described how this process was accomplished: the inhabitants or Mirasidars of pasankarai villages came together to draw lots "in the usual manner, but under condition that they should hold permanently the several portions of land included in the lots that fell to them and for which they afterwards applied to the Collector for certificates."[13] In other words, the redistribution system that had operated from time to time in years past would cease altogether from that time onward. The tenants-at-will or Parakkudis under the Mirasidars were, for the first time, often given certificates indicating this position. However, the opposition of the Mirasidars usually prevented the occupancy tenants or Ulkkudis from acquiring certificates. The state supported the Mirasidars in the expression of juridical power, Ellis arguing that it should be the Mirasidars who had the sole right to grant the certificates to the Ulkkudis or occupancy tenants, since this right would place the Mirasidars "in the situation to which they consider themselves exclusively entitled." From the state's perspective, giving the Mirasidars the piravēttikam or general management of the village aligned the interests of the Mirasidars and the state. This consolidation of interest would "prevent the meddling and vexations [vexatious] interference of the Sircar [state] officers." Alternatively, were the state to exercise the responsibility of granting the deeds, said Ellis, a wedge would be driven between the government and the people, while the Mirasidars would be jealous of the independence of the tenants (especially if these tenants were supported by state tax employees).[14] In his view, the state should have given over the right of dealing with the tenants entirely to the Mirasidars. In this way, the mirasi system and the Permanent Settlement could be construed as complementary, with mutual benefits going to many authors of this dialogic process.

Not all actors benefited, however. Both during Place's tenure in the 1790s and when Ellis wrote in 1814, one of the major dynamics in the Jagir had become a power struggle waged between the Mirasidars and the tenants (particularly the occupancy tenants or Ulkkudis). During the desertions of 1796, for instance, Place said that although some Mirasidars deserted from Karanguli, they did so before they made any agreements for the payment of the taxes on their villages, while others did so even after they had agreed to pay a given tax.[15] However, some 118 people from this Karanguli area petitioned the Board of Revenue in June 1796, complaining that "the inheritance of some of our villages were given in writing to the inferior inhabitants and Poycarys [Ulkkudi Payirkkaris or occupancy tenants]."[16] Another mirasi petition from the Karanguli area to the Madras board complained of "our villages [being] rented to Poyakers [Ulkkudis or occupancy tenants] or Strangers on whom our Meerassees have likewise been bestowed."[17] The Mirasidars of Perumbedu in the present-day Ponneri taluk north of Madras deliberately neglected the cultivation and would not make agreements with Place. He noted that not only did the Mirasidars possess the best lands but that those lands were now "overrun with weeds and yielded not even half of what they would have done." However

> what appeared most unaccountable was that not withstanding a short cultivation and the advantage . . . of the water course from the [Kortiliar] River, almost the . . . whole stock of water in the tank had suddenly disappeared or been drained off in little more than two months. . . . It appeared the Inhabitants [Mirasidars] had willfully, but secretly let off from their fields in the night, what they had let into them in the daytime; and by thus shamefully exhausting it, put it equally out of their power as that the Circar [the state], to carry on any further cultivation.[18]

In other words, the Mirasidars had tried to make water unavailable in the likelihood that their lands would be given to the Perumbedu occupancy tenants to cultivate. By contrast, the occupancy tenants who had been brought into Perumbedu by Place had agreed to every request and then done everything they had agreed to. As a result, the taxes collected from Perumbedu were mainly from occupancy tenants, not from Mirasidars.[19]

During his time as collector, Place tried to manipulate the uncooperative Mirasidars by getting occupancy tenants to undertake agrarian projects and tillage that the Mirasidars were unwilling to do. It was the produce of just such tenant labor that enabled Place to bring in such considerable amounts of tax revenue in 1796–97. Crole, writing in 1875, noted that Place had found no less than 1,827 out of 17,821 shares to be held by "such persons [occupancy tenants] who were called 'kani kudis [Tamil "kāṇi kuṭi"].' "[20] What complicated this finding was that Place originally believed that he was within his rights to replace Mirasidars if they did not cooperate and especially after they deserted the Jagir for the Nawab's territory. As we have seen, Place changed his mind in 1799 and ultimately came to believe that Mirasidars could not be removed by government fiat. Nonetheless, the crisis in the Jagir between 1795 and 1799 helped to fuel the fights between Mirasidars and occupancy tenants. It was to obviate this problem, which was also to some extent exacerbated by the Permanent Settlement, that Ellis sought to prevent the government from having the right to issue certificates to tenants and instead to direct interactions specifically to the Mirasidars.

The discussion about what was mirasi and what was not arose precisely because of the great tension that existed between occupancy tenants and Mirasidars. The Mirasidars sought to use the state's dialogically produced definition of mirasi to exclude the occupancy tenants, while the occupancy tenants tried to use the state's requirement for more taxes as a way to be included in the mirasi system. The competition over both the definition of the mirasi system and the land itself helped to intensify the sedentarization project engaged in by Company employees and the local population (whether they were Mirasidars, tenants, or Pannaiyals). The discussion over mirasi—which one historian has termed "massively irrelevant"—therefore became a central activity for everybody concerned.[21]

This tension between the Mirasidars and the occupancy tenants continued to grow throughout the century following the time of Ellis. In midcentury, a dispute arose over the practice of a collector named Cochrane, who had been in the habit of entering the names of the occupancy tenants or Payirkkaris in the 1853 cultivation accounts of Nanjepuram and Tallavarampundy (both located in the present-day Kanchipuram taluk).[22] Later, Collector Smollett decided that, since the practice had led to much contention, and since the interest of the Payirkkaris could best be supported by a strict enforcement of their engagements with the Mirasidars when complaints were made, the system would be abandoned that year. "It was well intentioned but has not given satisfaction to the meerasidars."[23] By that time, the struggle of the Mirasidars to resist the invasion of the occupancy tenants into mirasi land was so strong that the government had begun measuring the losses incurred. The tax value of the land left deliberately uncultivated by the Mirasidars to prevent the tenants occupying it was being represented in monetary terms by the state.[24] This measurement had been undertaken to indicate how much money the state was losing specifically due to the intransigence of the Mirasidars in refusing to take on tenants who would widen the scope of their cultivation.

Evoking a Decayed Present; Conciliating and Mediating

With such measurements confronting them, the notion of moral and economic decay became a prevailing idea that developed from the 1780s onward, first in the Jagir and later in the Chingleput district. That is, the concept of "decay" implied that the present situation of the district was being compared to a better state—either what it had been (or what it was conceived to have been) in the past. A discussion of the nature of the distant past of this territory fueled this debate. As we have seen, this discussion, which particularly concerned the way in which the area was first settled and how mirasi came to evolve—as introduced by Place, his Tamil and other informants, and the Board of Revenue and elaborated

by Ellis, Shankarayya, the Mirasidars, the Ulkkudis, and the Pannaiyals—continued after Ellis's death in 1819. Edward Smalley, collector
of the district immediately after Ellis, wrote:

> The Royajee, the Dewan of the Nawab of the Carnatic purchased it [some
> mirasi land] in order to present it to some Bramins. The tradition of the
> country is that a son of Nulla Chakravarty Rajah of Cholah Daysom having
> heard that some shepherds and cowherds were cultivating a little land in
> Tondamandalam (which included the Chingleput zillah), a province em-
> braced in Cholah Daysem, conceived the idea of clearing the lands of jungle
> and bringing them into a state of cultivation. In order to do this he conferred
> the cawneyatchee [kaniyatci] on the Vellalers who he invited from Cholah
> Daysam. The whole of Tondamandulum was then divided into 24 cottums,
> these cottums into 66 nauds, and the latter into 1,999 nuttams [village sites].
> The land and ownership were both originally Pasoncary. In course of time,
> the Rajahs to gratify the Bramins gave them many villages having . . . pur-
> chased the cawneyatchee from the Vellalers.[25]

However, the rise of the town of Madras and the requirements of the
British administration for tax income had irreparably altered all of that:

> The profits of trade at the Presidency [the town of Madras] are so much
> higher than the rent of land in this district that a great number of cultivators
> have neglected their lands and taken their stock thither. There are some other
> local circumstances which have proved disadvantageous to the district. As
> the high roads on each side of Madras pass through the District there is a
> constant demand for coolies which are supplied from the neighbouring vil-
> lages by the Auminjie as they are called that the village labourers who are
> called from their proper duty to bear loads. I do not mean to dwell upon this
> subject as I do not know that there is any remedy. The neighbourhood of
> the Presidency whilst it is thus advantageous does not afford the benefit of a
> good market to compensate because the supply of provision [for Madras] is
> in great measure brought to Madras by sea. I do not mean that a large quan-
> tity of grain is not exported to Madras, but that it is not a particularly ad-
> vantageous market in consequence of its situation on the coast. A view of
> the revenue of the district shows that it was either formerly in much better
> condition or that a large[r] revenue was drawn from it than its resources
> would admit, the consequence of which is its present deteriorated state. I do
> not much trust in the [Mughal] Caumul Bareez for the reasons stated in . . .
> [Greenway's] report on the Permanent Settlement. The Collections during
> Mr. Place's management were large but they were made at the expense of
> the land owners. The rents [taxes] were so high that a large number of meer-
> asidars quitted the District. I should rather think that the present state of the
> revenue is accounted for by the former high rents [taxes] having exhausted
> the stock of the cultivators and by the zemindars who very generally resorted
> to temporary expedients for the collection of money without any regard to
> the future welfare of the country. An estate [mutah or zamindari] is rarely

purchased by Government on account of a defaulting zemindar [or Mutah-
dar] but it is found in the worst condition. The Permanent Settlement was
certainly moderate and if it had been made direct with the cultivators it would
not, I think, have failed. All that the zemindars could scrape from their lands,
they wasted at Madras. Had a settlement to the extent of the Permanent
Bariz [tax demand] been made with each landowner [Mirasidar] for the cultivated land twenty years ago, it is probable that the District would have
been in an improved and improving condition with much of the waste cultivated, and paying an additional revenue.[26]

That is, the very impact of colonial rule had itself led to decay by si-
phoning off labor and excess produce, by exacting too harsh a revenue
demand, and by creating an extra layer of absentee landlords uninter-
ested in improving cultivation. In this context, even wasteland was conceived of as a sign of moral decay. Indeed, in this construction of the
recent colonial past an intimate connection was being established between colonial administrative decisions and decay. This connection had
a number of repercussions, not the least of which was a decline in status
of the Company's official representative with local knowledge. There is
evidence, for instance, that as the district's taxes dwindled in the early
part of the nineteenth century, the collector's position in the hierarchy
of Company politics also diminished.

In an interesting case that well illustrates this point, the collector of
Chingleput protested the possible transfer of the Vullur salt production
pans from his jurisdiction to that of the Madras collector's. These salt
pans produced a considerable income for the government—and commission for whichever collector possessed jurisdiction over the pans.
Because the production and sale of salt was a government monopoly,
Collector J. Babbington argued that the difference in the cost of production and the price at which the salt was sold to the consumer was so
great that it was very difficult to protect it from "fraud" or "peculation."
Babbington listed a large number of reasons why the collector of Chingleput could sell the salt and provide the necessary surveillance better
than his colleague, the collector of Madras. He wrote, "That authority
however which has the best means of superintendence, and of preventing
frauds and peculation in the salt, will be . . . the most likely to realize a
high revenue [from its sale]."[27] Moreover, he said that the Board of
Revenue had to be aware that

> a part of the emoluments of the Collector consists of a commission on the
> net revenue from the sale of salt, and even if you should think the duty would
> be conducted equally advantageously for Government by either officer [either
> the Collector of Chingleput or the Collector of Madras] you may not deem

it proper to sanction any arrangement which whilst it renders the receipts of an officer holding an inferior collectorship takes out of his hands a branch of revenue in his own district to swell the allowances of that [of the Collector of Madras] which is already the highest in the service.[28]

Even more important than the temporary loss of personal income to a collector was the substantial loss of district tax income from land in the early years of the nineteenth century. The loss during the period of the Permanent Settlement (1802–20) in the district had been quite significant due to the massive power struggle not only between the Mirasidars and the occupancy tenants but also between the Mirasidars and the Zamindars or Mutahdars. Smalley noted:

> With respect to certain privileges of poracalum ["paraiyar kalavasam" or a portion of the harvest given to the paraiyar and palli Padiyals and Pannaiyals], etc., the inhabitants [Mirasidars] secretly instigated their laborers to dispute with the zemindars and to quit the villages so that the cultivation might be diminished. Besides, the inhabitants [Mirasidars] by trading with Bandies [bullock carts] and Baggage bullocks, etc., were unable to attend to the cultivation. From such bad and unbecoming conduct on the part of the inhabitants as above set forth and also from various other improper acts, loss was sustained by the zemindars. . . . The inhabitants [Mirasidars] in defiance of the Mootahdars [or Zamindars] were very negligent in clearing the River Channels, etc., at the proper seasons. They ploughed the lands only once or twice instead of ten times without doing in the same manner as they had done during the sircar management and were careless in weeding in time. They likewise left some of the saighaul [arable] lands waste without yearly cultivating the whole according to the custom and instead they cultivated the gramma and mauniam [tax-free land] in full and so obtained an increase in the gross produce [of the village from their tax-free lands]. . . . When the zemindars demanded of the inhabitants the reason for their leaving the cultivable lands waste, the inhabitants [Mirasidars] bribed the gomastahs [agents] of the zemindars and pretended that they were obliged to leave them waste. Thus they apologized and escaped further notice. Moreover the inhabitants combined with the Gomastahs [agents] of the zemindars and committed great frauds in the Cundoomodal or actual produce. They brought forward groundless complaints into the court against the zemindars so that loss was sustained in the cultivation, etc. . . . The Meerassee inhabitants with a view of acquiring the privileges of Toonduvaram or Swaumibhogham, [small portions of the harvest paid to the Mirasidars which symbolically indicated their position] etc., more than before, and of having the same privileges created in the villages where none existed, procured the consent of the zemindars and thereby caused unjust exactions upon the Sookawasie inhabitants [occupancy tenants], who cultivate extensively, by which a diminution occurred in the cultivation. The inhabitants who obtained rents under the

zemindars associated with their Gomastahs, committed frauds and became pretended debtors to the zemindars.[29]

As a result of the actions of the Mirasidars, their Padiyals, and the Pannaiyals between 1804–05 and 1822, the state had, according to this formulation, lost pagodas 61,500 or rupees 215,215 every year from this district alone in the Permanent Settlement. The effect of this kind of behavior had been, he said, to reduce the yearly tax income of the district from pagodas 300,000 to pagodas 190,000. If the costs of waterway repair and employee salaries were also deducted (pagodas 38,000), and if the tax loss every year "from the failure of the inhabitants to cultivate as much as they did" when the Permanent Settlement was introduced (pagodas 28,000) was subtracted as well, the total cost to the state was pagodas 66,000. That is, the state received a mere pagodas 124,000 a year from the district during this period, in the face of hopes of pagodas 400,000. This was very similar to the level of income that came into the coffers of the Company before Place became collector in 1794.

How to recover from this state of decay? Smalley believed one way to enhance the productivity of the district at the moment when the ryotwari tax assessment system was introduced into it was to focus more attention on the "most valuable part of the cultivated lands, namely those dependent on rivers and springs." Smalley wanted to create a group of village or revenue "establishment" staff "for clearing the channels of rivers and springs which at present from the constant attention required are too much neglected."[30] What is important about this suggestion is that it had the same structural significance as Place's interest in creating gardens and groves of bamboo in many locations within the district.[31] For both men, hopes to revive the fallen and chaotic state of the district rested on the introduction of a pristine gardenlike environment into what they perceived as an otherwise decayed district. They both used utopian ideas not only to transfigure the past but also as a way to prefigure the future.

At the historical moment when the ryotwari system of land holding was introduced in 1821, Collector Smalley noted that in the previous twelve months there had been three severe storms responsible for destroying cattle, water courses, and crops. "Here," he said, "is a district gradually fallen into decay summing up its losses with adverse seasons." He claimed that the impact of the storm the previous May had been so destructive because the tanks were poorly constructed.[32] However, he maintained that the district had been destroyed not by the storms but mainly by the Mirasidars, asserting that the district "has suffered more by the neglect of the Mirasidars, many of whom employ their time and means at Madras."³³ Like many collectors from Place onwards, Smalley felt that the only thing to do was to replace irresponsible Mirasidars with individuals who were not part of that closed corporation, people who would cooperate both in seeking to extend the amount of cultivation and in willingly paying the required government taxes. He argued, "If the meerassidars will not take their lands for the fixed teerwah [tax demand] the land and its privileges must be given to others."³⁴ "On the other hand," he acknowledged, "strangers [i.e., occupancy tenants] should not be admitted without the Merassidars being first offered the rent of their village."³⁵ In other words, in Smalley's view, the Mirasidars should still have been given first choice if they wanted to assume responsibility for paying the taxes on their village.

Smalley's views, like all dialogic productions, are thus peculiarly contradictory. He wanted to get rid of uncooperative Mirasidars (as Place had wished and had succeeded in doing) while at the same time he did not want to introduce any outsiders or occupancy tenants into Chingleput villages without the Mirasidars' specific endorsement. Ultimately, he was not willing to question the right of the Mirasidars to do what they wanted in the village. However, since the Mirasidars were treated well, and since they were privileged, Smalley felt that they should assist the state in carrying out its tax-gathering activities. Mirasidars should have been forced to play the same role as public servants: "Their chief duty is to attend to the cultivation but in this District they seem to think it no part of their business." Indeed, Smalley wanted the Mirasidars to be more active in cultivating their lands from the very beginning of the growing season. He was convinced that the cultivators should be left free to pursue their economic activities as they wished but at the same time they should be induced to cultivate more land by "making it their interest to do so." It was totally inappropriate to allow the Mirasidars to remain passive at the beginning of the tax year since that would diminish the taxes from the land.³⁶ Smalley also felt that if village accountants and Mirasidars did not show the tenants the duty that they owed the state, cultivation would be neglected and these offices would be reduced to mere sinecures. Simply obtaining the signature of the Mirasidars in order to determine how much land they would cultivate yielded nothing. Rather, the administration must "call upon the Mer-asidars to fulfill their duty of superintendence." This would be critical to the management of the land.

As a result, Smalley decided to invoke the aid of the Mirasidars in gathering the taxes, through agreements struck with each Mirasidar "binding them to cultivate the whole of the lands in their respective villages" at various points in the revenue year, and indicating the amount of wet and dry land they were intending to cultivate.[37] These agreements would also express their willingness "to be extremely careful in carrying on the cultivation at the proper season after carefully clearing the fields." Smalley's proclamation to this effect directed that since the Mirasidars had much tax-free maniyam land, they would also cultivate government land that was taxed through the help of the Payirkkaris or tenants "so as not to leave even an extent of land as a cow's foot uncultivated."[38]

Smalley felt that the problems confronting any person who sought to bring in a new assessment were as vast as those following the original introduction of the ryotwari or individual tax assessment. Both actors faced problems that stemmed from the fact that a knowledge of the taxes of an area in any given year could not assist in predicting the "true" or constructed taxable amount of any given area. Smalley felt, therefore, that the actual collections of taxes of any village were no real guide to its taxation possibilities; it was impossible to know the appropriate taxes for any area. In some villages, the actual tax collections were small

> not from internal defects in the land, or an impossibility of producing a greater [tax revenue], but from mismanagement and where the [tax] assessment was notoriously low. The Meerasidars have for some years been aware of the existing [government] orders to assess according to the Actual [tax] Collections and have done everything in their power to lessen them. If we can shew that the cultivation was neglected not only in extent of land, but in means, and that even the actual produce was not brought to account, the actual collections cannot be considered a fair standard for [making a "correct" tax] assessment.[39]

Thus, at no point would the Mirasidars participate in setting the level of tax except to reduce it to the lowest degree possible. Indian cultivators had never and would never pay their taxes willingly; they would pay only as much as they were forced to. They could not conceive of taxing themselves. "They will never consent, in plain terms, to a fair assessment." He also believed that the "common intercourse" characterizing relations between landlord and tenant that he supposed to exist in England was "quite foreign to the habits and knowledge of Indians."[40] This benign "common intercourse" between English tenant and landlord was, of course, a construction belied by much evidence both from England and many other countries. Smalley needed to believe this construction in order to characterize rural relations in the Chingleput district. He recognized, however, that "should regulations be made which outstep the progress of society they can never be carried into actual operation. The meerasidars of this District will not voluntarily enter into any terms which I as Collector would dare to put forward."[41] Without the support of the Mirasidars, he could do nothing. That is, without a negotiation regarding not only the amount but also the definition of the tax system, it would be impossible for any district officer to collect the taxes.

Nonetheless, Smalley felt that he could understand the productivity of an area partly through persuasion and partly through mediation. This nexus formed a critical activity in shaping the interactions between government and Mirasidars and lies at the heart of the dialogic process itself. Even Place, when he wrote his account of Tirumalisai (the original site of much of the hostility represented in the Poonamallee Petition), referred in 1796 to this strategy as the critical ingredient in enabling the Company to get its tax levels both accepted and collected. Place said that his attempts focused on fostering the interests "of the husbandman, as of the circar, and [on] the most scrutinizing inquiry into what injured or benefitted either the one or the other." Place believed that he easily could have tried to impose on the inhabitants authoritatively a burden that they could not bear "in the spirit of Mahomedan tyranny." In that case, he would not have given them the chance of understanding the "true" taxable value of the village. On the other hand, he said, by leaving a copy of the tīrvai—the government tax demand—he showed himself "solicitous that we should ingeniously and mutually understand the value of the villages, and the terms upon which they were to be rented out."[42] This was heteroglossia at work.

Significantly, then, both Smalley and Place felt that there was a way to get the Mirasidars to come to terms with the state's due tax requirements. This way, said Place, "though not expressed, of ascertaining the just revenue and to which the cultivators virtually assent [still existed]. This is neither more nor less than discussing and regulating the [tax] demand partly by persuasion and partly by mediation."[43] Both Place and Smalley found themselves at an important cultural crossroads, a historical moment at which British and local cultures entered into a series of new and more complex productive epistemic relations. They could see, and they said this clearly, that these were negotiated activities.

Mirasidars Abandon Highly Taxed Land to Impoverish the State

However, no matter what the agents of the state sought to do, they could not eliminate the fact that the Mirasidars continued to cultivate less and less good land and take on more and more poor land. Mirasidars did this to reduce the tax base of the future, which would itself be based on diminished productivity, and thus lead to lower taxes later. However, the Mirasidars took on much of this poor land to deliberately keep Payirkkaris or occupancy tenants out. In this way, they could defeat not only the tenants but also the state.

The establishment of the ryotwari system led the Mirasidars of the area to adopt a strategy they had employed to great effect during the Permanent Settlement. In the Permanent Settlement, the Mirasidars had been confronted by demands from the Mutahdars or Zamindars for higher returns on their land. As we have seen, many Mirasidars handled these demands by cultivating their lands so poorly that they would then be sued by the Zamindar. When sued, the Mirasidar allowed only a small portion of his wealth to be distrained, the Zamindar lost his mutah, and the land reverted to the state. The government had to reduce the tax demand when assessing for the ensuing tax year. Consequently, the Mirasidars could then take up the land again under reduced pressure to levy taxes and a diminished demand from the state.[44]

So the strategy adopted by the Mirasidars under the ryotwari system in the 1820s of abandoning higher assessed land for lower had already begun to be employed under the Permanent Settlement. The goal of the Mirasidars, after all, remained the reduction of the credible basis on which the tax assessment itself was calculated; they did this by using the state's own mechanisms to diminish taxation levels. In their resistance strategies, the Mirasidars invoked the sensibilities and vulnerabilities of the state in order to create new kinds of meaning. They thereby assisted the production of new definitions of the mirasi system, redefining it as a system that was inconvenient or even impoverishing to the state but that was essential to prevent the population from moving around.

Mirasidars clearly decided that by far the most effective way to force this new definition was to start cultivating less fertile lands; evidence suggests that this had begun in the latter part of the eighteenth century.

When Place had his difficulties with the Mirasidars of Tirumalisai, the Board of Revenue told him that he was to make each Mirasidar in the Jagir "declare in writing" the amount of land he was willing to "enter into engagements with the Circar," that is, that he would be willing to cultivate and be taxed on. He was also instructed to tell each Mirasidar that the government intended to "bestow the surplus" land that the Mirasidar could not cultivate on "new meerassidars." Moreover, the collector was held responsible for appointing Mirasidars to any vacant lands where no Mirasidars existed.[45] In 1819, another collector named Cooke noted that most of the waste land taken up was land of poorer quality since the taxes on them were lower.[46] Shortly afterwards in 1821, Smalley also reported that the Mirasidars of the cusba Madurantakam to the south of Madras, "thinking the assessment of the first sort [best quality] of land to be too high have left it uncultivated."[47]

Mirasidars also took on land for the specific purpose of keeping others out. Cooke, for instance, noted that the Mirasidars in Manimangalam just south of Madras had made agreements or muchalkas for carrying on "an extent of cultivation for the purpose of excluding others from the possession of the land." When animosity in a village made one group unwilling to take the land even though they would lose by this "from malevolence," these same Mirasidars often deliberately neglected their cultivation so that production measured only half of what it could. They also intentionally did not cultivate lands that they had agreed to take on "in order that they might thereby ruin the persons who had engaged for the [collective] rent of the village."[48] Thus, despite the construction of the village as "immemorial," at this time there was no such thing as a "cooperative village system" in which Mirasidars worked together to pay the agreed-on tax assessment. The utopian past in which people worked in harmony for the common good of the village was belied. Instead, these utopian goals and visions of British administrators and local commentators alike projected the needs and hopes for a more cooperative village in the future.

Mirasidar and Payirkkari Attempts to Dislodge Each Other

The substantial amount of conflict between Mirasidars and tenants provided another reason for the "backward" state of the district. Cooke, for instance, noted that it was quite common during the second decade of the nineteenth century for Mirasidars to enter into engagements for cultivation beyond their means rather than admit strangers or tenants into their lands. They did this, he said, because they preferred to allow the lands to lie in waste if they could not get tenants to cultivate on their terms "and often . . . [threw] obstacles in the way of pyacarries [Payirkkaris or tenants] who have been procured by the sirkar [government] servants to cultivate. . . . The loss of the merassidars is merely their toonduvaram and coopatum [small symbolic payments made to the Mirasidars to illustrate their position] that vary according to the custom of the village but the loss to the state is very serious." The Mirasidars continued to enjoy the benefits of their tax-free maniam lands, which yielded 50 percent more income than circar or taxed land because of the attention they devoted to it.[49] In effect, the Mirasidars succeeded in their attempts both to prevent tenants from taking up land and to impoverish the state.

These problems remained intractable throughout the century. At midcentury, a collector said that although rupees 3,328 was received from the fields of one village, he found that "their cultivation had been wantonly neglected and was owing to dissensions between pykarries [tenants] and Mirasidars, the latter of whom engaged to cultivate them but omitted doing so."[50]

In 1875, Collector R. W. Barlow wrote an account of the problems arising out of the mirasi system. His particular concern focused on the substantial coercive process that this system engendered, and he searched for ways to alter it.[51] Barlow undertook this examination because the government was about to begin a ryotwari reassessment of the taxes in the Chingleput district. According to Barlow, the cause of the backward state of the district was the large amount of land left uncultivated. That problem, he believed, resulted from a complex set of Mirasidar responses. Before 1856, under what was known as the dittam or plan system, each Mirasidar had been accustomed to cultivating as much or as little as he wanted of the taxed circar lands in his village, but the only lands entered in his paṭṭa or title deed were those he chose to cultivate for that year. The Mirasidars also habitually assigned to Payirkkaris or tenants any portions of the remaining arable land that suited them. Land in the village was classified as either patta land (land included in title deeds), samudāyam (common land), or wasteland (whether arable or nonarable). Samudayam land usually constituted a small proportion of village land, occupying perhaps 3 percent of the total area of arable land. In the period before 1856, the samudayam or common land was made out in the names of the main Mirasidars. Government made no charge for the remaining wasteland, no matter how great it was and even though it resulted from the fact that the Mirasidars had prevented the wasteland from being cultivated. "This state of things though doubtless satisfactory to the mirassidars, was prejudicial to the interests of Government, as a large portion of the assessed land remained annually unutilised."[52]

Under the system introduced in 1856, the Mirasidars had to declare how much of their share (or panku lands) they wanted to have entered in their respective individual pattas or title deeds. They would be responsible for all of these every year unless they resigned them before 15 August of any given revenue year. Furthermore, taxes would be levied on those fields whether the land was cultivated or not. In 1859, more stringent rules were introduced to govern the way in which the collector was permitted to remit or not charge a tax assessment on land, and these laws were more rigidly enforced. Naturally, Mirasidars resented these new rules. However, said Barlow, things might have gone smoothly if the Darkhast Rules—or rules governing the application to take up arable waste land for cultivation—had not been introduced.

By these new Darkhast Rules, the Mirasidars found that their own patta or title deed land could be alienated to occupancy tenants (Ulkkudis) or even tenants-at-will (Parakkudis) if the Mirasidars would not themselves be responsible for these lands and tenants applied to cultivate this land. Once the pattas or title deeds were granted to tenants, they could not be canceled after they were issued, "so the alienation of the land from the mirassidar would be virtually permanent."

The new laws produced a serious emergency because they forced the Mirasidars to increasingly pauperize themselves to keep out the tenants. Every year, the Mirasidars took on more land than they could manage rather than see lands to which they clung go into the hands of tenants. The result was "their gradual impoverishment, and their lands eventually coming to the hammer." Tenants paid what were called swantantrams or what the British called "manor fees," paid to the Mirasidar to indicate his position, when the tenants cultivated either samudayam or Mirasidar patta land (circar taxed land). However, when tenants started to get pattas or title deeds on their own, they no longer willingly paid these swatantrams and "frequently declined to do so at all, causing the mirassidars considerable trouble and expense if they had recourse to the Courts to enforce payment." Barlow considered that these swatantrams formed the main problem between the tenants and the Mirasidars.

Still very influential, the Mirasidars managed to keep large areas of land out of cultivation. These lands could have been usefully cultivated by the tenants and their withdrawal naturally caused much resentment. In 1874, Barlow wrote that land was auctioned by the government for a pittance to "the nearest relative of the last holder. By private arrangement the land then passes to this individual and no one is the worse except the Poyakary [occupancy tenant] who is kept out and the Government that has lost a year's revenue."[53]

Barlow identified the samudayam or non-patta land as the battleground for the conflicts between the Payirkkaris and the Mirasidars. Much of this samudayam land had long been held by the Payirkkaris "or their ancestors ever since the land was first reclaimed by them from the jungle." Therefore, when difficulties arose over the payment of the tax, the government possessed "no account to show whether the Mirasidars who hold the putta, or the Poyakaris who cultivate are at fault." If the revenue officials carried out an inquiry, they had nothing to go on except the interested statements of unpaid monigars who were village servants and usually Mirasidars as well. "Distraining officers themselves have too often a personal bias to one side or the other." After the Mirasidars had received all the charges from the tenants on the samudayam land, they often intentionally did not pay the taxes "in the hope of getting the individual holdings of some of the more obnoxious Poyakaries attached for arrears." In the face of such Mirasidar action, the tenants could only "free their little holdings" by paying the total arrears against the samudayam patta, something that they could never do.

For their part, the tenants also proved aggressive in seeking to embarrass and get rid of Mirasidars. Barlow said that often the tenants banded together to withhold both the tax assessment and the swatantrams or "manor fees" due to the Mirasidars with the hope that "the personal property of some unpopular mirassidars may be attached." The tenants would then be left undisturbed in their holdings. Often, he said, the tenants intrigued with the local tax officials; when they were successful, Barlow noted that the only option available to the Mirasidars was to initiate a rent suit or an expensive court action. "In some villages where these disputes have run high false complaints of trespass, theft, robbery, and even arson are of frequent occurrence," as was reported by the magistracy and the police.

Mirasidar Subversion of State Coercive Strategies

One way to look at the relations within the mirasi system is to look at the conflict that developed between the British administration and the Mirasidars over the collection of taxes. This perspective allows us to understand the institutional mechanisms introduced by the state that aided in the process of defining the mirasi system even further and made the sedentary ideal increasingly critical for the definition of citizenship, not only in Chingleput but on the subcontinent generally. As we have seen, during the first half of the century, the state made tax settlements with the Mirasidars through mediation and consultation. By the 1870s, however, this particular style of inducing the Mirasidars to come to terms with the economic requirements of the state was considered out-moded. In its place, a system of courts, institutionalized coercion, and juridical power was introduced to retrieve what the state conceived to be its appropriate share of the village produce.

Within this context, it is important to note that one of the main characteristics of Chingleput administration, from the beginning of the nineteenth century, had been the considerable amount of annual tax arrears existing at the end of each tax year. For instance, in 1853, Collector J. H. Cochrane showed that between 1841 and 1851–52 the amount of unpaid balance on the tax assessment in the district every year had never fallen below 11 percent of the yearly tax demand. Sometimes it rose to 22 percent and even 35 percent.[54] This general characteristic of the tax-gathering process was common to the entire presidency but was much more exaggerated in Chingleput than elsewhere.[55] Between 1855 and 1873, the number of coercive processes served every year to recover those arrears in Chingleput alone rose from 2,692 to 394,693. During that period, the number of coercive processes in the entire presidency also increased from 273,191 to 2,508,606. That is, although the number of coercive processes increased a little over ninefold in the entire presidency during that period, the number of coercive processes served in Chingleput alone during that period increased by more than 146–fold.[56] The Board of Revenue also discovered that during that period the amount of money realized by the state each year in Chingleput from these coercive processes rose from a mere rupees 485 to rupees 115,772, a 238-fold increase. By comparison, the increase realized by coercive processes in the entire presidency in that period rose from rupees 14,776 to rupees 452,789, only a 30-fold increase (see table 1).

The Board convinced itself that the increase in the number of coercive processes had nothing to do with the enhancement of the tax demand. Yet in 1855–56 the demand in Chingleput had been rupees 1,046,793, whereas by 1872 it had risen to 2,376,276. In the whole presidency during that period, it rose from rupees 37,039,916 to 45,238,597 (see table 2). Moreover, examining the individual situation of Chingleput

TABLE 1

Amount Realized by Coercive Processes in Chingleput
and the Madras Presidency, 1855–73 (in rupees)

	1855–56	1860–61	1865–66	1870–71	1872–73
Chingleput	485	—	—	64,823	115,772
Chingleput and Madras	—	3,237	34,323	—	—
Madras	—	—	—	1,241	4,946
Madras Presidency	14,485	34,040	65,709	304,179	452,789

SOURCE: BORP, 1 April 1874, no. 754, TNSA.

TABLE 2

Amount of Tax Demand in Chingleput and the
Madras Presidency, 1855–73 (in rupees)

	1855–56	1860–61	1865–66	1870–71	1872–73
Chingleput	1,046,793	—	—	2,044,040	2,376,276
Chingleput and Madras	—	1,437,097	1,754,848	—	—
Madras Presidency	37,039,916	38,111,261	40,622,384	45,776,283	45,338,597

SOURCE: BORP, 1 April 1874, no. 754, TNSA.

makes even more apparent its peculiarity. In 1871–72, for example,
though the amount of land revenue and arrears amounted to rupees
1,489,734 in Chingleput, the value of property distrained was rupees
431,490 or 28.9 percent of the entire tax demand for the year. Considered from the point of the entire presidency, the total tax demand for
1871–72 was rupees 44,878,526, whereas the value of property distrained in the entire presidency came only to rupees 1,679,230. This was
only 3.74 percent of the total land revenue demand for the entire presidency (see table 3).

When the Board looked at the way in which the coercive process
operated in the presidency as contrasted with Chingleput, they found
that in all districts except Chingleput, landowners would pay their taxes
before the actual sale. In Chingleput, not a single defaulter paid his taxes

TABLE 3

Comparative Statement of Tax Revenue and Distraint
Proceedings in Chingleput and
the Madras Presidency, 1871–72

	No. of Pattas	Demand (in rupees)	Land Revenue Collections and Arrears
Chingleput	55,095	2,217,474	1,489,734
Madras Presidency	2,445,209	—	44,878,526

	No. of Defaulters	Value of Proceedings Distrained	No. Who Paid without Sale
Chingleput	21,178	431,490	0
Madras Presidency	145,998	1,679,230	77,679

SOURCE: BORP, 1 April 1874, no. 754, TNSA.

before the actual sale of his property. Therefore, the amount distrained
in Chingleput (one of twenty-four districts in the presidency) alone
amounted to slightly more than a quarter (25.6 percent) of the entire
amount distrained in the entire presidency. This was true even though
the number of defaulters in Chingleput was only 14.5 percent of the
total in the presidency.

This new "legal" approach had the effect of increasing the number
of coercive processes in the district far in excess of any other area of the
presidency, although this increase occurred to some extent in the other
districts as well.[57] Significantly, unlike other districts where most or at
least many of the defaulting cultivators paid their taxes before their
lands were auctioned by the government, there is no record in this period
that any Mirasidar in Chingleput paid his taxes before the auction took
place.[58] The Madras administration argued that in the period 1855–73,
"law has been substituted for arbitrary usage, and . . . the people have
become more enlightened and more able to hold their own against officials."[59] Previously, the ability of the state to derive taxes from the
cultivators of Madras presidency had been greatly limited by several
factors. An account by the Board of Revenue said:

The recovery of arrears by coercive processes was [previously] discouraged partly because the sale of land required reference to the Board of Revenue and gave endless trouble to the higher authorities while section 6, Regulation XXVII of 1802 and subsequently Sect. 2 Act XXXIX of 1858 made
it unsafe to attach personal property and partly because it was seen as a sign
of inefficient administration.

During the period prior to the submission of the Torture Commission's
report in 1855, the Tahsildars, the main government tax-gathering officers, typically brought pressure on the cultivators

which [according to the Board] sometimes no doubt amounted to cruelty
and extortion, but more often consisted in the mere presence and importunity
of the tahsildar and his peons. The revelations of the Torture Commission
. . . and the consequent activity of district officers in watching for repressing
anything which had the appearance of being an illegal pressure, put an end
to the old order of things. Land became more saleable in consequence of the
high prices and attachment and sale were made easier by Act XXXIX of
1858.

Then Act II of 1864 made the attachment and sale of property for arrears
comparatively easy and produced a

vast effect not so much because the law was changed as because it was
expressed more clearly and became more widely known than the Act which
it replaced. It soon became manifest not only to the Tahsildars [government
tax employees] but also to the people that the old way in which 'persuasive
methods' of collecting the revenue were used and land resumed and written
off without selling the land for arrears was irregular and even illegal. As soon
as arrears attracted notice in any taluq, the tahsildar was asked not why he
allowed them to increase but why he did not make sufficient use of the coercive processes sanctioned by the law; and when the coercive process was
served, the ryot who received it knew that it entailed no necessary danger to
his property nor pecuniary loss.[60]

The government came to consider the "coercive method" the "correct
method" because it did not involve the arbitrary resumption of land and
the cultivators knew, said the Board, that the new coercive system essentially did not harm their own economic interests. The Board said that
writing off arrears irrecoverable through death, poverty, or desertion
was also reduced. Now it was known, wrote the Board, that trouble
was avoided

and regularity is substituted for irregularity—if the land is sold for arrears,
and that the title of Government to the land can only be legally recovered in
this way—not by summary resumption. The effect of increased enlightenment
and knowledge of the law is shown by the large number of cases, in which

ryots allow a coercive process to be issued, whilst they have the means of paying punctually, and intend to do so before the day of sale arrives.

However, the mirasi system of Chingleput is

> of great importance, and tends to increase the sales for arrears in the district where they are largest. It has constantly attracted attention. . . . Nevertheless the [mirasi] system is strongly rooted in law and immemorial custom. It is there, and must be regarded as in many respects neither more nor less than a ["gigantic" marked out] great but necessary evil.[61]

Therefore, the benefits accrued by sedentarized inhabitants in their villages outweighed the "costs" of the mirasi system, rural conflict and state impoverishment. The phrase characterizing the mirasi system as "rooted in law and immemorial custom" and the assertion that it was "neither more nor less than a great but necessary evil" were repeated in government documents on other occasions. For instance, a report on the paraiyars in September 1892 repeated these phrases to indicate the government's knowledge of the problem in Chingleput but its unwillingness to do anything about it. These phrases illustrate the heteroglot, dialogic system in which truth and knowledge were created. In this case, the changing mirasi system came to be simply a representation of the increasing interdependence in society. That is, the definitions of the mirasi system became knowledge produced to epitomize the increasing division of labor in society at that moment.

Similarly, the rise in the number of coercive cases became simply another way used by the Board to demonstrate the essential rightness of their approach. What Board members did not see was that the legal system merely reflected and strengthened constructed discursive categories. It was not "produced" simply by the state from the top down. Nevertheless, the Board's analysis concluded that the extent to which coercive processes were used was "no sign that the people are oppressed or that they are less able to pay their dues than formerly." They noted that in Chingleput "the land is poor, and the Board do not anticipate that the settlement now in progress will raise the [tax] demand." In 1875, C. S. Crole, author of the *Chingleput Manual,* wrote that in the Chingleput district "the destruction of the cattle produces inability to cultivate, waste, loss of revenue, poverty and backwardness compared with other districts. Moreover, the soil of the district is itself generally of inferior quality and easily exhausted."[62] Thus, the 1790s excitement and interest in the potential of the Jagir as a fertile area had been converted into the characterization of a district with inferior soils. In this altered vision of the district, the large amount of tax defaulting in the area came to be represented as a product of a wasteland, moral decay, and an exhausted soil that was hopelessly unfruitful. Crole noted also that during the tax year 1871–72 in Chingleput, 38 percent of all tax defaulters (whom he referred to as ryots) were Mirasidars. Both here and in many other government documents thereafter, this "backwardness" of the Chingleput district simply became attributed to the unproductivity of the soil. This idea was even inscribed in the answers given in Parliament to questions put by Samuel Smith, a liberal member of Parliament (MP) who participated with Dadabhai Naoroji in a debate on the "condition of India." On 25 June 1891, the under secretary of state for India said that in the inquiry of 1887–88, including the "Condition of the People—Papers laid on the table on 21st June 1889," it was stated that "owing to its infertile soil and to certain accidents of tenure, [the Chingleput district] was among the most backward parts of Madras Presidency."[63]

In this manner, "infertile soil" became part of the knowledge produced interactively by Crole, the Board of Revenue, the Mirasidars, the Payirkkaris, the Pannaiyals, and many other authors to explain why agriculture in the area was so unproductive. Although articulated by Crole in 1875, this characterization was a multiauthored construction advanced to illustrate that the backward state of the district was a given, that since the infertility was innate it was something that could not be altered. The production of the "decayed" description of Chingleput as "truth" resulted from a need to satisfy both British and local Indian requirements. These in turn interacted with local and other appeals to ideals of a former time and another place. For the British employees of the Company and the local inhabitants in the eighteenth and early nineteenth centuries, the Jagir and Chingleput existed in a state of decay. Whether from the Sanskritic or Tamil point of view, contemporary society was in the Dark Age and the "harmonious" past was essential to project new requirements for a more interdependent and embedded future.

Reintroduction of Heteroglot Consultation to Reassess the District

In 1875, when the tax reassessment of Chingleput was about to begin, ideas presented by Barlow analyzing the situation in the district formed one perspective. According to Barlow, one of the main bones of contention was the fact that the Mirasidars always demanded the fees called swatantrams from Payirkkaris cultivating samudayam lands, since this was the only marker by which the Mirasidars could clearly demonstrate that they were Mirasidars. Barlow thought that these payments were sometimes made and sometimes not, although the intention of the Payirkkaris was not to pay them in order to resist the Mirasidars' pretensions. The Mirasidars were then forced to file an expensive civil suit to have these swatantrams paid. Even though the monetary amount derived by the Mirasidars from the swatantrams was small, it had high symbolic value. Naturally, therefore, Barlow believed that the government's only remedy to this situation was to recognize the validity of these swatantrams, or what he called "manor fees," when Payirkkaris applied for samudayam lands. Moreover, he felt that an agreement should be required of each tenant before a patta or title deed was issued in which the "amount and nature of the swatantrams, and his liability [the Payirkkari's] are clearly set forth."[64] He believed that the main issue in contention between these two groups would thereby be eliminated and that the Mirasidars would then allow the tenants to take over arable waste land from the Mirasidar's "already overgrown holding under the burden of which he is gradually becoming impoverished."[65] In other words, in his view, not only would the antagonism between the Mirasidars and the Payirkkaris decrease, but the Mirasidars would then allow arable wasteland to be rented. This would eliminate a critical problem in the district.

R. K. Puckle, a Board of Revenue member, used Barlow's testament regarding the potential effectiveness of legalized swatantrams to make them an integral part of the new tax assessment of the district. He felt that the condition of Chingleput was "most unsatisfactory" and that it had a "greater arrears of revenue [and] . . . a longer list of coercive processes than any other district in the presidency." To find out what the cultivators of Mirasidars of the district "wanted," Puckle went out to villages and talked to them. This activity, considered by Place, Smalley, and others of the first three decades of the nineteenth century to be central to the taxation process, involved consultation and mediation, which by 1875 were considered old-fashioned since they did not employ legal coercion. Puckle said that "for years past, I have been accustomed to consult the villagers and carry them with me at every step of the process." It is this approach of consulting the Mirasidars that formed one part of the intellectual and psychic interaction that took place between the British revenue authorities and the Mirasidars. As we have seen in the case of Read in the Baramahal and Place in the late 1790s, these collectors had adopted local behavior and presented it as being something that was British. However, the way in which accessibility to political authority was used by Read, Place, and now by Puckle was an innovative approach that could no longer be defined as either Indian or British. Here the dialogic activity between Tamil and Telugu Mirasidars and British tax officials expressed itself most powerfully. Puckle noted that the Mirasidars to whom he had talked would not oppose what was called immemorial waste being granted on patta or title deed to a tenant if the Mirasidars could be assured of receiving the swatantrams. Mirasidars vowed that if swatantrams were recognized by the state they would gladly resign some lands on which they had been paying taxes in order to keep others out.

Ideas about the mirasi system—produced by a large number of people who operated around Place, Ellis, and many others, and later accepted by the Madras government—were communicated back to the Mirasidars by Puckle and others like him. Then, by asking the Mirasidars what they wanted as a way to solve this problem, he essentially asked them for a changed, heteroglot definition of the mirasi system, a definition altered from that used in another epistemological arena of the late eighteenth century. That is to say, as part of the operation of heteroglossia, officials (whether Place, Smalley, or Puckle) "consulted" the Mirasidars and thus produced interactive definitions of the mirasi system that were communicated; these in turn were accepted by the Mirasidars as being the "indigenous system." Many voices from many different epochs and social origins contributed to the production.

Under this tax reassessment, the Indo-British administration attempted to increase the tax revenue at the same time that it made it more acceptable to the Mirasidars. Puckle, who sought to assuage the Mirasidars above all else, noted that the "assessed waste land" in Chingleput was 375,000 acres, which he said was probably a substantial overestimate. Nonetheless, he concluded that if that land were cultivated it would yield rupees 468,750 when taxed at the rate of rupees 1-4-0 an acre. The Board of Revenue also recognized that 38 percent of the pattadars or title holders of Chingleput were defaulters between July 1871 and July 1872 and that 19 percent of the tax demand was unrealized until coercive processes were served.[66]

In deciding that the swatantrams would be legalized, the government followed the ideas of Barlow and Puckle. Puckle had said that the Mirasidars were "very generally anxious to divide the common [or samu-

dayam] lands if they were assisted in that process." The Board concluded
that the differences between the Mirasidars and the Payirkkaris would
cease to exist and the "long asserted and much cherished" claims of the
swatantrams would be recognized. This would ensure the "future quiet
of the Chingleput district" since the Mirasidars would "abstain from all
factious opposition to outsiders [i.e., Payirkkaris or tenants]."[67]

The Future as a Social and Economic Utopia

The Board's decision provoked a long analysis in 1875 of the Mirasidar
system as it had grown up under the British. C. S. Crole, a subcollector
of Chingleput under Barlow at the time, undertook this examination.
Crole felt that he could not enforce the payment of the swatantrams by
the tenants to the Mirasidars though the director of revenue settlement
Banbury had said these would "not only . . . secure prompt collection
and prevent arrears, but actually . . . change the face of the district, by
bringing under cultivation a large proportion of the variously estimated
375,000 or 154,000 acres now lying waste for want of sanction to such
a proposal." Crole had no confidence whatever in the utility of the proposal of recognizing the swatantrams as a way to bring this land under
cultivation.

   Tenants, Crole believed, played an essential part in Chingleput's
agrarian society long before the British arrived. Moreover, in his illustrations from the village of Petapur (in Madurantakam Taluk) Crole
pointed out that "there were also a large number [of tenants] in possession of holdings, not being recognized shares or pungus, from time immemorial. The large body has been swelled by continual accretions as
waste was, from time to time, assigned to outsiders owing to its refusal
by the mirasidars."[68] In other words, the Payirkkaris existed in the Chingleput district before the British arrived, an era construed here as "from
time immemorial," and their existence had been documented by Place
in 1796.[69]

   More important, Crole argued, the Payirkkaris, far from being un-
equal contenders, in many ways stood as equals to the Mirasidars of the
district:

> I shall not now stop to discuss the minute differences which Mr. Place
> discovered between these Payikaris and Mirassidars. They have all along
> really been the same in the eye of the Government, but it will be one of the
> effects of Mr. Puckle's proposal to exact from payikaris taking up land in
> future the payment of swatantrams to Mirassidars to put an end to this

equality. I undertake to show clearly that this step, besides being a retrogression from the policy laid down by Government making every class, caste and creed equal, is not required and is founded on a misconception of the mirassi question.

Crole also said that this policy argued against the success of the new assessment. "Mr. Puckle . . . [had] convinced himself from the evidence adduced in his report that the non-payment of these fees [swatantrams] is the sole cause of the backward state of this district and of the large extent of waste." Yet it was unlikely that, for the mere payment of these fees, the fifty-eight Mirasidars of, say, Tirukatchur village in present-day Chingleput Taluk would allow someone from Madras to come to their village, take up wasteland, and cultivate it there simply by paying annas 12 (16 annas equals 1 rupee) every year, the value of the swatantrams there:

> The right over this waste has been truly described as 'much cherished and long contested.' It is futile to believe that the value of such a right can possibly be represented by a sum so paltry as not to suffice to keep the mirassidars in betel and nut. . . . The Government will ere long find itself woefully mistaken if, by the retrograde step of setting up two different classes of cultivators, they expect to see the end of the struggle between Mirassidars and Payikaris and the final security to this district of good cultivation, peace, prosperity and progress. I fearlessly maintain that the mirassidars consulted by Mr. Puckle never really intended to comply with his terms. They are glad of an opportunity of renewing a groundless claim, and they left to the future the decision of what course they would pursue on the attempted introduction of the hateful payikari into the fields of their village; an event staved off from time immemorial by the adoption of the single expedient open to them [of not allowing any tenant to cultivate the land].

This the Mirasidars had been doing in the past and would continue to do for many years in the future.

As part of his explanation, Crole created what he considered an historical account seeking to put the situation into perspective. Though he used Place for his own project, we should remember that Place attributed utopia to the past, while Crole situated it in the future. For this purpose, he described the experience of the Jagir in the 1780s and 1790s. During the war of 1780, most of the Mirasidars of the Jagir moved to Madras town for protection. Repeating some of Place's own words, Crole said, "As regards the remainder that the wars of the Carnatic left little but the bones of its former inhabitants."[70]

Moreover, wrote Crole,

Everything was in a state of chaos. Rights were undefined and the administration in disorder. In reducing this disorder to order, he [Place] recognized
the resident inhabitants [Mirasidars] in their holdings, and the village system
being then the one institution which had survived the storm of anarchy and
misrule, each village was treated with fiscally in the light of a little close
republic, as it was. I may remark that the mass of the cultivators were either
Vellalas or Brahmins and I need hardly remind you, that these two castes
represent two historical facts—the first a gradual and peaceful colonization,
the second a victorious eruption—and that both belong to ages whose history
can now be traced only by reading the semi-religious fables still extant by
the light of the occasional gleams shed on them by living facts.

On the basis of Place's comments, said Crole, it was "clear as noon-day
. . . that the mirassi system and a gross rental are inseparable parts of
the system [i.e., the village system] he exhumed and introduced." In
other words, Place—to deal with the requirements of the situation in
which he found himself—accorded validity to the "village community,"
which had existed in a very much more ambivalent form when people
frequently moved around. Moreover, at least according to Crole, Place
sought to "create" the village in a form that enabled him to collect the
taxes but simultaneously had to be brought back from decay; this form
was proffered as "truth." Historical requirements thus determined the
kind of knowledge about the village that was needed. Again, the main
goal at the time was to collect the maximum taxes in a way that helped
to create a sedentary, embedded village society. Such knowledge enabled
Indo-British administrators to be rulers over a land filled with villages,
and village inhabitants, who always replicated themselves and who
acted cooperatively to pay their taxes. The conception of the village
system was constructed to address the purposes for the present and for
the future:

Each village was divided into so many shares. The holders of these shares
cultivated each year as much of the village lands belonging to their Pungus
[or shares of the village product], as they were able, or as the season permitted. For this purpose they employed farm laborers (Padiyals), or contracted with subtenants (Payikaris or Sukavasis). The shareholders were held
responsible for the realization of a fair revenue from the village, and made
up from the common fund the short comings of individual members. . . . It
is obvious that the only difficulty was to see that the ryots did not imperil
the revenue [by] leaving cultivable land waste. This difficulty has continued
down to the present day. The founders of the system, however, had no hesitation as to the remedy to be applied. In such a case the waste escheated to
Government.

According to Crole, under Place and until the coming of the ryotwari system of individual assessment, the system worked well. However, Crole argued that this depended on "employing Padiyals" or day laborers. In fact, many of the paraiyars and pallis in the district were and had been debt-bonded laborers known either as Pannaiyals or Padiyals:

> Under the system of joint village rentals, the mirassi system was in its perfection. It amounted to a contract between the owners of full shares in the village as above, and the Government for the payment to the latter of the revenue of the village. The Mirasidars were to take their own way of getting this done, and as they performed their part of the contract and a fair revenue was paid to Government.

Crole contended that the system that developed under Place

> was one suited to a barbarous age, an unsettled country, and a Government needing money and little sedulous of the future. It was too rough and unequal, however, to stand long before our ideas of justice and policy, for it entailed a system of rack rent fatal to thrift and progress, under which the industrious had to make up for the short comings of his less energetic or careful co-sharer. It soon gave way to an individual [or ryotwari] settlement with each ryot on the Dittam system.

However, the ryotwari system struck the first blow at the integrity of that system. All the claims that the Mirasidars now made had therefore to be seen in terms of a system not only that Place had "exhumed" but to which the government had from time to time given sanction.[71]

If Place created the mirasi system out of chaos, he was also, according to Crole, responsible for offering a solution to any Mirasidar unwilling to allow any Payirkkari or tenant to come into the village to cultivate uncultivated arable land. To illustrate his point, Crole again quoted from Place's 1799 report to show that the government also had the right to replace any Mirasidar who was unwilling to allow a tenant to take up arable lands. Place had written that it was "not only justifiable, but a duty enjoined on Government on this principle, that it must not allow any individual to possess land for the purpose of keeping it waste, and further . . . that as the revenue of the State is derived immediately from the cultivators of lands, it ought not to suffer from the caprice or the inertion of an individual."[72]

In Crole's view, all the waste lands of the Jagir had become the property of the government many years earlier and therefore the Mirasidars no longer had any right to them. The fight concerning the rights of the Mirasidars over waste in part constituted a conflict over the rights of the state to increase cultivation to enhance its tax base and spread wealth among more people. However, the struggle with the Mirasidars also concerned the whole problem of the rise of a unitary state that was less and less dependent on other intermediate interests. Essentially, Crole felt that both the mirasi system and the Mirasidars were created by the British and Place. He believed that conflict would remain endemic so long as this antiquated system was strengthened to raise taxes without consideration of the problems posed for equality between the tenants and Mirasidars. Furthermore, he insisted that, during the nineteenth century, the government had stripped away more and more of the rights of the Mirasidars. Rights over the wastelands were in the gift of the government; if the state did not recognize the structure, the mirasi system would no longer exist. It could therefore be disposed of entirely for the benefit of the state.

Crole argued that far from the government making concessions to the Mirasidars, the reverse should be the case. "Almost every claim set up by the Mirassidars has been disallowed. They have lost their right over fisheries. The Government has declared it will not brook interference with mines and quarries. It levies seignorage on wood cut in jungles." Then in 1870, he said, the government finally decided that the Mirasidars had no right to any compensation for the same wastelands for which the levying of swatantrams was now proposed. "This rang the death knell of the whole system—Mirassi then became a mere name, a disembodied shade, which need frighten no officer, properly supported and prepared to do his duty."

Only one inference emerged from his entire analysis: the mirasi system no longer existed in the Chingleput district. All that was necessary to exorcise this "ghost" was to require that the word Mirasidar no longer be used in government documents and that in its place the word pattadar or title-deed holder be substituted. That act assured its elimination. The government, he said, should declare an end to the privileges of the Mirasidars over the hoarding of wasteland. Land consequently would become available to all and be granted to the first applicant. In the future, the state would not recognize any distinction between its tenants; all would simply be called pattadars or title holders.[73] Crole contended that if this were done, land would pass into the hands of those willing to cultivate it and to pay taxes regularly. "Half the trouble and all the frivolous objections, by which the Revenue Officer is now trammelled in granting land and receiving the assessment would disappear along with it." In other words, if the government followed his suggestions, the

Chingleput district would become emancipated and uncorrupted. There would be no conflict. Government would be simple. The state would collect its ample revenues and the entire country would prosper. Like Place, Ellis, and Smalley before him, Crole sought to make a case for a utopian transformation. But in Crole's case this utopia related not to the past, which was barbarous, but to the future. Unlike his administrative forebears, he wanted to get rid of the mirasi system altogether, but like them he aspired to the goal of creating a never-never land, a golden age of the future in which society would be harmonious and life would be peaceful and more cooperative. Like his forebears, he felt that this was possible through state intervention. This formulation of a golden age merely became another way to formulate the future as a more interdependent and cooperative society in which everyone's behavior would be self-restrained.

This helps to illustrate how vulnerable a single British officer, and perhaps the British administration generally, felt in situations in which decisions about proprietary usage were intimately connected with powerful feelings about cultural definition. Crole (with Place and Smalley) wanted to be free of all the trammels that prevented him from carrying out the kind of service that he felt he should render for the people of Chingleput and for the state. Here again, Crole blamed the uncooperative, corrupted Mirasidars for the fallen and decayed state of the Chingleput countryside. The Mirasidars created the conflict and contentiousness that prevailed in the courts. The Mirasidars were not only a political enemy but a moral enemy as well; they stood in the way of the district's golden age. It was they who prevented the emancipation of the land system.

Only a vestige of the former mirasi system remained—the right of the Mirasidars to "darkhast," to apply to cultivate wastelands. Why was there a huge amount of uncultivated wasteland in the Chingleput district and why was there so much tax arrearage? Crole said:

> I can discover for the former no sufficient reason but bad habit. From the time of the Dubashes up to the present there has always been a powerful body of officials in the Presidency town [Madras] in a position to procure at least a favorable hearing for any pretensions put forward. The Government, ever generously ready to protect and foster the vested rights of the cultivator [Mirasidar] has looked upon the Chingleput District with special interest. Owing to the above circumstances, and its nearness to Madras, disputes, claims, and complaints, which would never be heard of beyond the four walls of a mofussil Collector's cutcherry [office], have been ordered to be inquired into, investigated, weighed, and decided with a careful tenderness and too

often with expressions of hesitation, and doubt, and even admission of the exceptional nature of the tenure of land in this district. Out of this has grown up a custom of asserting pretensions regarding mirasi which really have no foundation in truth.[74]

In the middle of the century, a person who described himself as a "native revenue officer" had written that the peculiar nature of the mirasi system provoked an enormous unsureness in the application of rules; this allowed for much corruption:

> The jealousy and suspiciousness with which the ruling authorities looked upon this right as one opposed to their interests and the consequent disinclination which they evinced to face the matter directly, determine the rights distinctly and enforce them decisively, great vacillation has marked the proceedings of the Collectors in those cases which open a wide door to bribery.[75]

He also argued that this ambiguity had provided a wide variety of options, including certain cases in which Mirasidars were fully recognized and others in which Mirasidars could levy privileges but not interfere with the occupancy of the lands by others, or could levy privileges in some instances and not in others, or had no privileges at all. Additional options included the award of pattas (title deeds) that designated the holders by various denominations—Mirasidars, Payirkkaris, Coode-thanam (Kuditanam) purchasers, or individuals without any designation at all. Yet another option, issued in the name of the Mirasidars, particularized the names and extent of lands cultivated by their subtenants. Another option excluded subtenants from the pattas but entered their names into the adangal or cultivation accounts.[76]

Crole argued, however, that since the social groups from which the tenants were previously taken could now earn good wages in Madras, some had risen in status. The Mirasidars looked on these tenants as "insolent, [and] curse the present administration, and determine that if they cannot make anything of the waste themselves, neither shall any one else." The Mirasidars felt that even though they lacked tenants who bowed to their wishes, one or another member of their family would become wealthy through government service and the wasteland of the village could then be added to their family property: "A Payikari [tenant] therefore, though as good in other respects as themselves, has come to be hated and to be considered the enemy of the future advancement and the destroyer of the ancient dignity and position of the family of each mirassidar of the village." According to the Mirasidars, at any rate, the tenants stood as the cause of their straitened circumstances:

However, the main effect of all these processes was to make the mirasidars unwilling to change their position. By preventing competition, it has taken away the stimulus to honest labor and the desire for improving holdings. The mirasidars secure from intrusion, are utterly supine and indolent. [Moreover], many have sunk *pari passu* with their continued exclusiveness, until the Chingleput district which, from its superiority in having a fine market at its door, first rate communications, a very favorable climate and rainfall, and many other advantages should have been the best, has become the most wretched and the poorest in the Presidency.

"My remedy for this great evil," concluded Crole, is "to make land free." That is to say, he felt that the wasteland in the district should be made available to everybody. Though this was bound to produce a certain amount of derangement in the beginning, he felt that the land would find its way into the hands of individuals who wanted to improve it, and general prosperity and progress would result.

Considerable coercive activity in the district created significant problems

due to the reckless struggle for waste when a payikari [tenant] gives a Darkhast for it [applies for it]. If the Mirassidar secures it, he too often finds that he has not the means of cultivating it to advantage. It remains waste. He can't pay the assessment. Part of his holding (or maybe his household goods) is sold by Government in default. On the other hand, if the Payikari, often a pauper is successful, a similar result often teaches him too late the folly of his ambition to cultivate when he has no capital.[77]

The tenant then collapses and the land is sold and bought in by the government for a nominal sum.

In marginal years, much land was left uncultivated because, without cooperative work, the tanks and waterways were not repaired. Sufficient money was also not available to repair the tanks. The public works department, he felt, was quite hopeless. Even the straw collected from the paddy in the district was shipped off to Madras. That the district had poor soil Crole also mentioned in the *Chingleput Manual* to illustrate the fact that the district was "congenitally" unable to prosper.[78] In many ways, his arguments here, as in the manual, purport to show how a district invaded by Hyder and Tipu was destroyed first by war and later by rights inadvertently granted to the Mirasidars. This land had lost its capacity to produce good cattle or a sufficient amount of grain. First, by essentializing the environment of the district, Crole showed certain unchanging characteristics of the region while at the same time demonstrated what he conceived to be the decay of contemporary society and economy in the district. Second, he developed a certain xeno-phobia or anti-urbanism. He felt that the poverty of the district resulted from the extraction of ingredients indispensable for its prosperity (such as cow dung and straw) by "foreign" elements such as Madras and that selfish and uncooperative Mirasidars should have been numbered among the destructive agents. Structurally, the eighteenth-century Du-bashes were replaced by the nineteenth-century Mirasidars as the ex-tractors of the vital elements of the district.[79] He even decided in the face of such a poor record that the tax arrears in Chingleput could be elim-inated were he to collect them himself. He therefore dismissed the Ta-luqdar for the Chingleput taluk, eliminated all the arrears, and cleared up the accounts himself. "I have reduced them to order," he said.[80] He concluded that since the sloth and carelessness of the Mirasidars pre-vented any kind of economic growth, the government should make a declaration that it would not recognize mirasi rights on grounds that they did not exist.

Though Crole had argued against the reality of the mirasi system, the Board of Revenue concluded otherwise: "There can be no doubt as that it exists, not withstanding many years of persistent efforts to crush it, that it is of great antiquity, as is indeed implied by Mr. Crole's own expressions regarding it; and that it is dearly cherished." The Board decided therefore that it would support the compulsory payment of the swatantrams by the tenants to the Mirasidars and retain the Mirasidar's first option to access to the wastelands of Chingleput. It totally dis-counted Crole's ideas. Thus, the discussion resulted in rendering the now-modified mirasi idea even more powerful than it had been before.

During the 1880s and 1890s, however, other forces emanated from many different sources to help erode the Mirasidar position. Part of this transformation involved redefining the paraiyars as well as the position of those at the bottom of the social and land-holding hierarchy. Let us now turn to an examination of this new project emerging at the end of the century.

CHAPTER 4

From Slaves to the Original Dravidians

In the 1880s and 1890s, the utopian movement among Indian and British commentators became pervasive, forming another key epistemological moment in the dialogic process. Most critically, this utopian urge expressed itself in an effort to "understand" why the poor, whether in India or in Britain, were getting poorer. This movement, in many ways an extension of the Condition of England discussion or the Condition of India movement, was not a naïve activity designed simply to understand the effects of colonialism or industrialization. An increasing amount of evidence suggests that this discussion aimed to define modern society to confine all individuals, especially the poor, to a specific dwelling, to one place. Whether referring to the paraiyar bonded laborers in Chingleput district or the poverty-stricken people of the East End of London, analysts attempted to prevent the poor from moving around. As we will see, in the Tamil area as well, definite precolonial conceptions differentiated nomadic from sedentary populations. The dialogic construction of "the sedentary paraiyar" resulted from both local and British ideas and became a principal focus of discussions in the 1880s and 1890s.

The cultural interrelations presumed to exist between the virtues of a sedentary life and the state's interests in a prosperous society were so vigorous because a sedentary life represented a basic ingredient in the definition of citizenship. For the British, social commentator Henry Mayhew put this idea most stridently in 1861 in his famous investigation called *London Labour and the London Poor:*

There are the urban and suburban wanderers, or those who follow some itinerant occupation, in and around the large towns. Such are . . . the pickpockets—the beggars—the prostitutes—the street sellers—the street performers—the cabmen—the coach-men—the watermen—the sailors and such like. In each of these classes—according as they partake more or less of the purely vagabond, doing nothing whatsoever for their living, but moving from place to place preying upon the earnings of the more industrious portions of the community, so will the attributes of the nomade [sic] tribes be more or less marked in them. [These groups are marked by] their lax ideas of property— for their general improvidence—their repugnance of continuous labour— their love of cruelty—their pugnacity—and their utter want of religion.[1]

Catherine Gallagher has shown that Mayhew looked on these "itinerant" individuals as people who used up the nutriment that would ordinarily have gone into the bodies of productive workers: "The placement of the valuable, problematic body at the center of social discourse led, through the circular logic just outlined, to the division of the social organism into valuable (weak but productive) and problematic (strong but unproductive) bodies. Around this axis much nineteenth-century [British] social criticism revolves."[2] Furthermore, she has written, "Non-productivity has for its sign 'nomadic' movement, and movement has for its sign . . . a strong body."[3] Similarly, by the end of our period, the Madras government could take even the use of alcoholic drink as a sign of a settled, healthy (hence, productive) and economically stable agrarian work force. British assumptions thus joined with complementary local notions to produce the need for "proof" of a sedentarized and "emancipated" or "disciplined" pauper. Not surprisingly, such evidence was eagerly discovered and joyfully discussed.

Categories of Social Dependence and Loyalty

For many years, collectors in Chingleput had been preoccupied with perceived agricultural decay and the need for emancipating the land from the Mirasidars. As we have seen, Crole concluded that since the mirasi system no longer existed, land was free and available to any person who wished to buy it. Mirasidars no longer had a privileged prerogative over the lands they did not cultivate. He looked to the Madras government to state this authoritatively, to shift the monologic narrative to a new construction that aligned free land with fixed individual bodies to form a prosperous state. Crole interested himself in a wide variety of things but primarily in the soil, the productivity, and the tenure of the district. He was therefore part of what we can call an "old" school that could do its work without concerning itself with the social and economic positions of the underprivileged individuals around it. Rather, he considered that the land had been emancipated from the grip of outdated vestiges of an earlier age, and he sought the government's aid in that project.

In his claims for land that would be emancipated in the future, he did not address the question of social emancipation. Specifically, he did not address himself to the problem of the degraded position of the individuals who had been Pannaiyals or bonded laborers before 1861 and who were largely paraiyars. Thus, his comments about the manner in which proprietary relations operated in the district were in many ways a metaphor for the operation of social and economic relations between the Mirasidars and Padiyals and former Pannaiyals.

At the same time, Crole performed an important historical task by compiling the *Chingleput Manual*. In it, he referred to a large variety of perceived moral problems, seizing the opportunity to change the signification attached to elements of the society on whom the British depended. Among these groups were low-caste boatmen who operated along the coastal waters up and down the Chingleput district. They were theoretically important for the project to sedentarize agricultural groups because they occupied very different spatial areas than did those who spent their time on land.

The boatmen had long posed a problem. Some years before Crole, Cuniliffe, another collector of the district in 1855, had complained of the "unruly and insubordinate" behavior of the boatmen who carried the salt produced by government salt works. He argued that "when employed at Ennore [to the north of Madras], they strike work on the least provocation and last week on . . . my declaring that the two boats had put off short handed and had been stranded should not receive their hire they threatened to go off to Madras. . . . These men give much trouble—we are very much in their hands."[4] That is, although the British had become masters of the subcontinent, they remained unable to dominate the boatmen in the Madras area. Boatmen formed part of a large community of low-caste Tamils operating on the sea who performed essential services for the British and others in the region. Crole cited in his manual the historical example of an incident in the wars between the British and the French for the supremacy of the Carnatic. When the French commander Lally held Madras under siege in 1759, the boatmen (of what later became the territory called the Jagir) acted in a way that was considered to be "loyal." Crole deemed the incident worthy of record because it was a "pleasant exception to the greed and turncoat deception generally displayed by the natives with whom the Europeans had most to do."[5] This is the story.

On the night of 2 January 1759, the day when Lally opened fire on Madras, some European women were taken by "masula boats" during the siege of Sadras (slightly south of Madras), seeking the protection of the Dutch, whose settlement it was.[6] However, in the meantime, Sadras had itself been taken by the French, who also captured the boats and the passengers. In due course, on 8 January the French sent the three masula boats back to Lally and the French army in Blacktown (the "indigenous" or "black" part of Madras), with fifty barrels of gunpowder and other military stores accompanied by a French soldier in each boat. Crole quoted Robert Orme's description:

> At four in the morning when they were opposite the [English] fort [St. George], each of the soldiers had fallen fast asleep, on which the boatmen concerted in their own language [Tamil] with the certainty of not being understood, although overheard; and having first poured water into the firelocks, overpowered and bound the soldiers, and then landed the boats at the [English] sea gate. This uncommon instance of fidelity and spirit in men, who are deemed a mean and outcaste race, was rewarded and encouraged by paying them immediately the full value of the gunpowder and stores.[7]

Crole concluded his account of the incident by asking, "Does this spirit and fidelity continue as a monopoly of the mean and the outcaste?"[8] Crole thus used these accounts of the past to help him in the grand historical project of providing a new signification for "slave," "paraiyar," and "outcaste" that contained loyalty, trustworthiness, and productivity. At the same time, there appears to have been no real attempt to change the structural position of the boatmen or the paraiyars in the nineteenth century. Rather, Crole's statements formed part of a general attempt to put those low-caste persons within new categories being produced on a large scale by both Indians and British.

The Description of Poverty and Slavery as a Way to Sedentarize the Poor

Opposed to this set of ideas expressed by Crole, another group—of government servants, journalists, missionaries, and others—became concerned primarily with poverty. Specifically, they became preoccupied with the political and bodily effects of impoverishment. The members of this "new school" claimed that though the government had emancipated former Pannaiyals or debt-bonded men by a series of laws, they structurally still served as slaves. What this suggests is that the question of "emancipation" in the Chingleput district had two meanings to the officers of the government resident there in the 1880s. One sense alluded to the "liberation of the land" from the Mirasidars, providing "land" with a new signification. The other signification referred to the "emancipation of the slaves," providing "slavery" with a new signification.[9]

This development is important for our purposes because in Chingleput a direct connection existed between the emancipation of the land from the Mirasidars and the emancipation of the Pannaiyals from their vellala and brahman masters. Specifically, for the project of sedentarizing the peasantry of Chingleput to succeed, the construction of the Tondaimandalam village as immobile and antique had to be linked with an equally new production of "truth," in which the paraiyars, even though they were the poorest, became constructed as the most loyal and the most sedentary of anybody in the entire population. To effect this linkage, a general cultural project had to be undertaken in which all inhabitants, all voices would participate in creating the knowledge that ensured that all members of the population remained in identifiable places.

In Chapters 2 and 3, we examined the cultural thinking and practical working out of the first task of this historical project, the archaicizing of Tondaimandalam villages as a basis for a future state and society. In this chapter and the Conclusion, we will look at the strategies undertaken to accomplish a second historical task, that of creating a description of the situation of the poor. This attempt showed that the paraiyars of Tondaimandalam were the original settlers of the area in order to give them the right to individual dwellings so that they would not move. This naturally included the development of a separate ethnic identity for the paraiyars as the original Dravidians, who were in fact the original settlers of the area. The project of establishing a sedentary population became directly connected with ethnic singularity. The general movement toward an increasingly settled population in the nineteenth century incited all members of the community to discourse no matter what their location in the social hierarchy. As we know from many other contexts, this involved enormous excitement and pleasure for individuals at all levels of society. It also involved a vast elaboration of the description not only of the poor but of many other elements of the society as well. In a sense, the more social repression there was, the more knowledge was created.

The movement to sedentarize the population of Chingleput was mirrored by other similar developments in many other areas of India. As part of that general intellectual and economic activity, specific attempts were made to speak about what was conceived to be the growing poverty of India under British rule. In many ways, this discussion about the poverty of India became intertwined with and extended the earlier Condition of England debate in Britain. Both discussions had as their goal the continuing classification of the social community. Though much of the debate focused on the poor, the discussion aimed at defining the values of middle-class society and of citizenship generally.

As part of the extended Condition of England debate, a discussion about housing for the poor arose in the 1880s in Britain. This was particularly concerned with the destitute of East London. One of the most influential pamphlets on the subject, *The Bitter Cry of Outcaste London*, jointly authored by a nonconformist minister named Andrew Mearns and others, appeared in 1883.[10] As K. S. Inglis has noted, the pamphlet served as "a plea for parliamentary action, especially to provide decent cheap housing" for the poor.[11] It is also certain that *The Bitter Cry* was partly based on "a more vivid tract" by G. R. Sims entitled *How the Poor Live*.[12] These two publications joined a number of other pamphlets and articles, as well as reviews of the day by Joseph Chamberlain, Richard Cross, and others, and articles published in the *Pall Mall Gazette* in 1883 and later about the housing conditions of England's poor.

Some authors argue that this spate of publicity simply formed an attempt to disempower the dangerous classes. Anthony Wohl, for instance, has pointed out that Charles Kingsley had written a quarter of a century earlier that "better working-class housing would pay in many ways, especially by 'gradually absorbing the dangerous classes.' "[13] In the same way, Sims observed that "this mighty mob of famished, diseased, and filthy helots is getting dangerous, physically, morally, politically dangerous." He warned that "its lawless armies may sally forth and give us a taste of the lesson the mob has tried to teach in Paris, when long years of neglect have done their work."[14] Therefore, the concern of British middle-class reformers with the housing of the poor and their economic plight, according to Wohl's analysis, focused on making the poor powerless. What Wohl does not see is that this activity also helped to interactively create categories that defined both the poor and the middle classes in a society in which productivity and living to maturity became increasingly important.

Another work, printed toward the end of the period when the terms and vocabulary of the debate had already been largely set, was "General" William Booth's *In Darkest England and the Way Out*. This book appeared in late 1890 after the appearance of Stanley's *In Darkest Africa*.[15] Booth noted in his preface that the strategies traditionally employed by Christian philanthropy were totally inadequate for dealing with the "despairing miseries" of a group of people he called the "outcast classes."[16] Booth said, "As there is a darkest Africa is there not also a darkest England? Civilisation, which can breed its own barbarians, does it not also breed its own pygmies? May we not find a parallel at our own doors and discover within a stone's throw of our cathedrals and palaces similar horrors to those which Stanley has found existing in the great Equatorial forest?"[17] Whether it was prostitution in England or slavery in Africa, the problem was the same. "And when once," he wrote, "the poor girl has consented to buy the right to earn her living by the sacrifice of her virtue, then she is treated as a slave and an outcast by the very men who have ruined her."[18] Moreover, Booth asked whether any "African slave system, making allowances for the superior civilisation, and therefore sensitiveness, of the victims, reveals more misery," saying, "Just as in Darkest Africa it is only a part of the evil and misery that comes from the superior race who invade the forest to enslave and massacre its miserable inhabitants, so with us, much of the misery of those whose lot we are considering arises from their own habits. Drunkenness and all manner of uncleanness, moral and physical, abound."[19] Booth felt, as Stanley had indicated, that there was a way out, that change was possible.[20] In other words, with discipline, planning, and application of the appropriate methods, even poor people could make a social and economic contribution and live a better life.

Invoking the Scientific Method

What is important about the appeal of William Booth and the many social reformers like him is that the debate became bound by a particular vocabulary and an invocation of a particular method.[21] These ideas formed part of a new category of a normalized and productive society, with a vocabulary that included the words "slavery," "outcast," "uncleanness," "depravity," "drunkenness," and "misery." The method conjured up was the scientific method, with that use of abundant statistics considered to be the mark of many social reports.[22] Shaped by the desire to "describe the condition of the poor" through the use of collected detail, these reports eschewed sensationalism to make a point seem incontrovertible. As Charles Booth, William's namesake, said when he introduced his huge study called *Life and Labour of the People of London,* "The materials for sensational stories lie plentifully in every book of our notes; but, even if I had the skill to use my material in this way—I should not wish to use it here."[23] More important was the creation of an impression of great precision to communicate a perception of disinterestedness, completeness, and authority. By these devices, social reformers and their supporters sought to demonstrate the extent of the "problem" and the "solution" of the Condition of England. Even William Booth, who was both florid and sensational in his oral style, wrote that with the help of other writers he was appealing "neither to hysterical emotionalists nor headlong enthusiasts." Rather, he said, he sought to "understate" the problem in a spirit of "scientific investigation."[24] He also called himself "a practical man" who wanted to deal "with sternly prosaic facts."[25]

Conceptions of the scientific method helped to set the terms of the category of "normalized poor" in England. This is well illustrated by William Booth's focus on what he called the "submerged tenth," a total of three million poor, most of whom lived in London. He wanted to examine the living conditions of "the Lost, . . . the Outcast, . . . the Disinherited of the world." This group of people, "by their utmost exertions are unable to attain the regulation allowance of food which the law prescribes as indispensable even for the worst criminals in our gaols."[26] Booth also proposed that this group of people should be treated at least as well as a London cab horse. Naturally, it was presumed that like prisoners and domestic animals the poor should not only be given a decent diet but should also be trained, watched, and cared for—and enclosed. In this analysis, the condition of prisoners and household animals therefore became the standard for which aid was to be sought for this "outcast" population.

These arguments are important for our purposes because they applied not only to India in general but specifically to the Parakkudis or tenants-at-will and the Padiyals in the Chingleput district, many of whom were paraiyars or untouchable. Individuals, drawn from all levels of society, whether British or Indian, used these and other ideas to develop even further their utopian visions of progress and history.

Did the British Pauperize India?

The Condition of England debate also set the terms in which many Indians and British looked at the Condition of India. As in the case of the discussion about England, the debate in India was concerned with the impact of modern civilization, and particularly the administration of the British, on the poverty of India. Whether true or not, the sense among many Indians and British that the moral and economic condition of India had declined gave much urgency to the controversy. This debate extended for half a century from the 1870s onward. One individual influential in this dispute was Dadabhai Naoroji, "an older Parsi merchant who lived in London and acted as an informal ambassador for the nationalist cause for half a century."[27] Naoroji had argued that though the British made a solemn promise to bring wealth and contentment to India, they had gone back on their word. In an essay entitled "The Poverty of India," he demonstrated that the extent of poverty in India under the British had increased rather than decreased.[28]

Ideas about the decay of Indian economic and moral life were naturally reflected in the discussions on the Chingleput district. Both British officials and members of the local population in Chingleput had claimed that the area had been in a decayed condition since the end of the eighteenth century. However, not until 1871 did Dadabhai Naoroji, using statistics taken from government sources, concern himself with the problem, arguing that the problem involved the "continuous impoverishment and exhaustion of the country." During that time, then, local debates in Chingleput became specifically articulated with national and international controversies.[29] Indeed, the Chingleput discourse rested on Naoroji's demonstration in 1871 that the average annual per capita income of Indians was rupees 20 a year.[30]

Both in 1866 and in 1876–78, serious famines struck South India; the Bellary famine of 1866 and the famine of 1876–78 were both widely documented by photographers. William Digby, a journalist who had edited the *Madras Times,* also attempted to illustrate the growing pauperization of India through his book entitled *India for the Indians—and for England.*[31] Another author named Seymour Keay wrote a series of articles in *Nineteenth Century* entitled "The Spoliation of India."[32] Partly in reaction to the work of Digby and Keay, Samuel Smith, a liberal MP from Lancashire and friend of Naoroji, wrote a series of articles in the *Contemporary Review* following his second trip to India.[33]

Smith's ideas, like those of Keay and Naoroji, helped to focus awareness on the fact that some educated Indians felt that Britain had pillaged
India and continued to drain it of its resources. This thought contrasted
dramatically with the presumption in Britain that India was "immensely
indebted" to the British, who had converted a "land of anarchy and
misrule into one of peace and contentment, that poverty is giving place
to plenty, and a low, corrupt civilization to one immensely higher."
Smith went on to shock Englishmen with the discovery that "instead of
contentment one finds in many places great dissatisfaction, and a widespread belief that India is getting poorer and less happy."[34] Moreover,
he argued that the poverty in India "is extreme and more acute than
what we witness in Europe."[35] British culture and the government desire
for excise income were "rapidly spreading drunkenness among the people of Bengal in order to supply revenue to the Government."[36] Smith
also identified "not a little friction" between "native opinion" and official views. The Indians, said Smith, "think that the English officials
stand between them and their just rights and claims."[37] However, he
noted that "no such complaint" had been lodged against "the British
Nation" as such. There was, he stated, "a strong belief in their justice
and good faith, and the constant desire of the Indian people is to get
access to them, in order to lay their complaints before that august tribunal. They fully believe that if the British Parliament and people were
made acquainted with their grievances they would remedy them. It is
almost touching to see the simplicity of their faith."[38] In other words,
the British middle-class ideals of justice and good faith had also been
consensually supported and created in India by British and Indians from
all levels of society. At the same time, however, some British and Indians
blamed England for the impoverished state of India. The "loyalty" invoked by both Smith and Naoroji formed part of the same project, the
same invocation to which Crole referred in his account of the low-caste
boatmen in the fight against the French in the middle of the eighteenth
century. Fervent belief in these ideals by Indian writers and thinkers
made British policy in India seem particularly galling.

The tension between the two approaches was critical to the claims
made by both British commentators like Keay and many Indians and
led to great participation in the project to create a kind of "truth" regarding what had been pursued by the British rulers and others since
the last decade of the eighteenth century. As part of the same enterprise
to which Smith subscribed, Naoroji himself wrote in the *Contemporary
Review* a year later:

> Now, I have no complaint whatever against the British Nation or British rule. On the contrary, we have every reason to be thankful that of all the nations in the world it has been our good fortune to be placed under the British nation—a nation noble and great in its instincts; among the most advanced, if not the most advanced, in civilization; foremost in the advancement of humanity in all its varied wants and circumstances; the sources and fountainhead of true liberty and of political progress in the world; in short, a nation in which all that is just, generous and truly free is most happily combined.[39]

Gauri Viswanathan has recently argued that the introduction of literary study in place of religion by the British operated a veiled mechanism of social control to keep Indian society governable without the use of violence.[40] Viswanathan, however, describes this as a willed activity by a state that was fragile and therefore unusually vulnerable. By the end of the nineteenth century, she argues that this kind of literary study became used as a way to show Indians their subservient and appropriate social role in the colonial society established by the British. Viswanathan quotes essays written by two Bengali students in Calcutta in 1843 to show that British strategies of social control had effectively subdued and overpowered them and that therefore the policy of the government was effective. However, the process of creating a discourse involves both the rulers and the ruled. For example, in one of the passages quoted from an essay by Nobichunder Dass, a student at Hooghly College in Calcutta, a principal object of this education in India is identified as the creation of knowledge about future society, a project in which many Indians from all social levels also eagerly participated. Whether in the countryside or in urban environments, the general project to create a modern state incited people to discourse. As one of those participants, Nobichunder wrote

> The English are to us what the Romans were to the English; and as the English are the children of modern times, and command more resources and power than the Romans, we derive great advantage. The facility afforded to communication by the use of steam has enabled the English to govern our country with great prudence and vigilance, they do not appear to be at any time at risk of forbearing in the glorious work which they had commenced, of improving the native mind and condition, but prosecute it with honour to themselves and favour to their subjects, till they are styled the regenerators of India.

It may be argued that this one-way, top-down kind of social control and creation of knowledge through British education provoked Naoroji to say what he did. In reality, it formed another case of multiauthorship among many millions of Indians, Europeans, and others. There is much evidence to show other Indian writers acting and writing along the same lines at this time as part of this general dialogic project. Social values and policy reinforced one another in the last decade of the nineteenth century. In the late 1890s, when the two serious famines in South India "cast serious doubts on official estimates of increasing prosperity" in India, the value of British ideals—of justice, humanity, and fairness—suddenly became problematized, helping to fuel the debate over the impoverishment of India to an even greater extent.[41] W. S. Caine, an MP speaking on the Indian Famine Commission Report in 1902, referred to this fact when he spoke of the "evidence of the horrible poverty of the agricultural people of India, the evidence of recurring famine with ever-increasing intensity."[42] During that time, a substantial discussion in the press and in government circles questioned whether India was becoming poorer as a result of its connection with Britain (and by inference from its association with modern civilization generally). It is partly in this connection that Mohandas K. Gandhi wrote his utopianist booklet entitled *Hind Swaraj* in 1908.[43] William Digby, an editor of the *Madras Times* who had penned an account of the famine in 1876–78, also said that "Lord Macaulay, Mr. Grant Duff, and others believe that when the English tongue alone is spoken, and the Christian religion is generally professed, the difficult problems which are characteristic of European countries will be encountered in India."[44] Digby also noted that one unnamed individual had pointed out that "if India becomes Christianised, if all the people become converted to what the missionaries teach, a Poor Law will be a necessary consequence." This was true, he said, because in Europe all the poor were supported by the state while in India the poor were taken care of by the people themselves.[45] He thus pointed to the great disadvantages in bringing western modes of government and social organization to India, particularly the notion of the state's responsibility for the poor. However, in an address in 1900, in terms very similar to the debate between the anti-abolitionists and the factory reformers in early nineteenth-century England, Naoroji observed that "Indian Natives were mere helots. They were worse than American slaves, for the latter were at least taken care of by their masters, whose property they were."[46] Even W. W. Hunter, director general of statistics to the government of India, in his book *England's Work in India,* wrote that "forty millions of the people of India habitually go through life on insufficient food."[47]

The comparative nature of these assessments of Indian poverty helped to raise the stakes in the debate. Statements by intellectuals and writers of comparative wealth in India and elsewhere also produced much oversensitivity among government officers.[48] The debate involved a considerable number of individuals, ranging across a diverse spectrum including W. H. Moreland, whose *India at the Death of Akbar* did not appear until 1920, and S. Srinivasa Raghavaiyangar, whose *Memorandum on the Progress of the Madras Presidency during the Last Forty Years of British Administration,* commissioned by Lord Connemara, the governor of Madras, appeared in 1893.[49]

Many officials in the Indo-British administration sought to defend the government's policies in the face of attacks by individuals such as Naoroji. For instance, the former governor of Madras Mountstuart Elphinstone Grant-Duff wrote articles in 1886 to that effect, answering the views of Samuel Smith.[50] Grant-Duff's articles were answered in turn by Naoroji himself.[51]

Grant-Duff and others sought to discount the legitimacy of Indian complaints. Grant-Duff, for instance, argued that Smith had depended unnecessarily on the "pushing talkers of the big towns, full of the last new 'cleverisms,' just sharp enough to repeat the parrot cries of European mischief-makers, and to be ingeniously wrong on most subjects."[52] Grant-Duff admitted that "there is in many parts of India frightful poverty, but is there not the same and even worse, in our own country?"[53] For Grant-Duff, the question was not so much whether India was getting poorer but rather who was making those claims and what their unstated goals were. "What the pert scribblers in the native press, and the intriguers of the Presidency towns" wanted were "increased opportunities for themselves—Government employment and political changes, which may increase their personal importance."[54] "The only possible question," he said, related to the relative benefit obtained "between the rule of the Englishman and of the Brahmin, the Aryan of the West and the Aryan of the East." Grant-Duff wondered whether Samuel Smith would "do a good turn to the 254 millions of natives if he were to hand them over to a much greater extent to Brahmin domination?"[55] Much better to have rule by the British than rule by even the most educated Indians.

Could these Indians know anything about either India or Britain? Grant-Duff wondered how any Indians to whom Smith had spoken and who "made no complaint" about the "British nation" could even know what that "British Nation" represented:

A very few of them [Indians] have been able to cross the seas without ensuring their own damnation, have been received in England as strange and interesting creatures, petted, and made cub lions of. . . . Every English-speaking 'native' who finds his way to London is as interesting to the home-keeping Briton as is a mango in Pall Mall. In Bombay or Madras a mango is a mango.[56]

Grant-Duff argued that British rule had brought wealth and food to a needy India. He nevertheless admitted that "there is in many parts of India frightful poverty."[57] Grant-Duff also wrote, "The question worth answering is: Do the Indian masses obtain, one year after another, a larger or smaller amount of material well-being than the peasantry of Western Europe? Speaking of the huge province of Madras . . . and I have visited every district in it—I think they do."[58]

According to the critics of this opinion, the main problem related to British intentions. In the first of his rebuttals to Grant-Duff, Naoroji claimed that in 1833 and again in 1858 the British had pledged to make India prosperous.[59] He also claimed that they had not fulfilled those promises. Part of this controversy had occurred fifteen years earlier. In 1870, Grant-Duff as a member of the Commons had asked another member, Sir Wilfred Lawson, in the debate on opium, "Would it be tolerable to enforce a view of morality that was not theirs, which had never indeed been accepted by any large portion of the human race, we should grind an already poor population to the very dust with new taxation?"[60]

A year later in 1871, Grant-Duff, who had been the under secretary for India, focused on the contrast between the per capita annual income of a person in Britain (thirty pounds) with that of India (two pounds). Grant-Duff had concluded at that time that "even our comparative wealth will be looked back upon by future ages as a state of semi-barbarism. But what are we to say of the state of India? How many generations must pass away before that country has arrived at even the comparative wealth of this?"[61] Grant-Duff's estimates were also accepted by the viceroy Lord Mayo, who said, "We are perfectly cognizant of the relative poverty of this country as compared with European States."[62]

So long as they felt that they could set the terms of the debate on the Condition of India, British administrators were not defensive. However, when these critical statements were made by educated Indians, the accusations became intolerable. Naoroji had calculated that the average annual per capita income of Indians was rupees 20 and that in Madras it was a mere rupees 18.[63] Naoroji in his 1887 article on "Views about India" wrote that according to Sir George Campbell the bulk of the people of the Madras presidency were paupers. Naoroji also quoted the views of W. R. Robertson, agricultural reporter to the government of Madras, who called the condition of the agricultural laborer "a disgrace to any country [and that] the condition of the agricultural population of Ireland is vastly superior to the condition of the similar classes in this country."[64] These comments and ideas appear to have sensitized officers of the Madras government, particularly a subcollector named Mullaly in the Chingleput district.

What most offended the officials of the British government in India was Naoroji's comparisons of India with other parts of what we would now call the developed world: "The question at present is, Why, under the management of the most highly paid services in the world, India cannot produce as much even as the worst governed countries of Europe. I do not mean to blame the individuals of the Indian service. It is the policy, the perversion of the pledges, that is at the bottom of our misfortunes."[65] What is important in this debate is that Naoroji sought to invoke the value prized by administrators as the essential ingredient in the claims that the British had gone back on their word. Thus, the dialogue leveled two accusations against the British: they had impoverished India, and they had done so in direct contravention of their own pledges.

Had the British Impoverished Chingleput District?

Against this background, and specifically against this Naoroji's rebuttal, Subcollector Mullaly of the Chingleput district sought to show that in that area of India, the Mirasidars' agricultural Padiyals were being deprived of rights that the British had pledged to them. Moreover, Mullaly believed that the mandate of the government assured these Padiyals of a right to their houses. Let us look at the strategies that Mullaly and others followed to recreate the villages of Chingleput through the same sort of utopian urge that had characterized not only Place but also the Mirasidars, the tenants, and the Padiyals of the district.

Some time in 1888, the government of India sought to address what it defined as the problem of overpopulated tracts, apparently in response to a suggestion made by W. W. Hunter. As a result, the Indian government sent a resolution to all provincial governments asking them to review the measures taken for relief in these areas. This inquiry, said Hunter, encompassed some 250 districts in British India.[66] Then on 19

October 1888, the government of India sent a resolution to all provincial governments requesting a report on the condition of what it defined as the lower classes of the population and on relief operations in these overpopulated tracts. This formed part of the inquiry set in motion by Lord Dufferin, the viceroy of India, on "the condition of the lower classes of the population."

The inquiry resulted in a government of India resolution stating that the condition of "the lower classes of the agricultural population is not one which need cause any great anxiety at present."[67] This assertion could be maintained only with difficulty. For instance, one of the reports to the Madras government's inquiries had argued that the Chingleput district was in a bad state. To this report by Collector Lee Warner the Madras government took exception. They argued that "the condition of the people [of the Chingleput district] . . . had markedly improved within the past ten years" since the time of the decision to recognize the swatantrams of the Mirasidars and carry out the tax reassessment. Lee Warner had forwarded two documents, including one from Reverend Adam Andrew, a missionary of the United Free Church of Scotland Mission in Chingleput town, reporting the results of inquiries into living conditions and wages of the paraiyar Padiyals in Chingleput.[68] Lee Warner pointed out that the "wages ordinarily earned by the people are extremely low and that a large proportion of the population lives from hand to mouth, is badly housed, ill clothed, and compelled to be satisfied with a nutriment far below the sufficiency diet agreed upon by doctors as a necessity for life." Lee Warner's references to "scientific standards" for health and poverty emerged from the Condition of India discussion, which referred to the need for state intervention to protect the health of the poor. In rebuttal, the Board of Revenue in Madras agreed that the condition of the lower classes in the Chingleput district may not have been very satisfactory but said that " this is mainly due to the general poverty of the soil."[69] The Board did not feel that anything that Lee Warner had written or submitted had shown that "any large proportion of the population suffers from a daily insufficiency of food."[70]

According to the governments of both India and Madras, Britain had restored order to India and had "emancipated" the "slaves." Therefore "slavery" could no longer exist. Through the work of the emancipation laws and the working of British culture, the bad aspects of the master-slave relationship had been removed and the good qualities of a land-lord-laborer association had been retained. This individual and unilateral attempt aimed somehow to ban the "slave" category in favor of a category and terminology that used by turns "panchama," "depressed classes," "Harijan," "scheduled classes," and "Adi Dravida" or original Dravidian.

Indians and British during this period thus pursued a grand project to create knowledge about both "Indian" and "British" values. That project involved converting the Tamil paraiyars into ancient inhabitants of India by eliminating the "slave/paraiyar" signification and implanting a new signification of the paraiyars as the original Dravidians of India. As the "slavery category" was obliterated, the "Adi Dravida" or "Original Dravidian" category was summoned up in its stead.[71] This complex procedure of eradicating the "slave" sign and transforming it into "the original Dravidians" is a process still underway. The result of actions taken by both Europeans and Indians, this activity and documentation helped to create knowledge about those considered to be the ancient inhabitants of South India. It continued work initiated by a wide variety of forces already at work in the land before the westerners arrived. These ideas had been argued by Ellis even in the early part of the nineteenth century. Moreover, the sensitivity of Christian missionaries had in the nineteenth century recruited converts from a variety of subcastes such as paraiyars and other "panchamas." A sensitivity began developing among Hindu intellectuals, who wrote in the press about the difficulties of the paraiyars. Paraiyar leaders, largely Christian, used a journal called *The Paraiyan* to state how they perceived their present and past conditions. A significant number of British officers of the government also documented the positions of various populations of India in ancient times. British writers to the London press also contributed to this process.[72]

What appears to have united these disparate efforts at this historical point in time was the new susceptibility of the government of India and the provincial governments to assure both the world and themselves that India was not poor or disorderly and that no slaves remained there. Within this context, the discussions that had been proceeding in the Chingleput district over the previous century formed the basis of much new knowledge created about the way the past helped create future society.

Fixing the Paraiyars in Their Houses

Much of the activity attempting to eliminate the signification of "slave/ paraiyar" took place during the final two decades of the nineteenth century. To an unusual degree, this also became focused on the district of Chingleput. In August 1889, for example, Chingleput Collector Warner submitted an account of activities by his own subcollector, Mullaly, to his superiors, the Board of Revenue. This report concerned Mullaly's attempt to get free house sites for the paraiyar Padiyals or day laborers in the Chingleput district.[73] He noted that Mullaly had begun a process of trying to disprove the validity of the Mirasidars' claims to the house sites of the paraiyar Padiyals. Warner also said that Mullaly was very vexed by "my interfering with his well-meant schemes for the improvement of the condition of the labouring poor, [and had] brought these hundreds of applications for [paraiyar and palli] dwelling sites on himself." Significantly, though Warner and Mullaly occupied opposite sides of these reformistic impulses, both shared the goal of changing the "slave/paraiyar" signification.

Warner felt that it was best to let the people "settle such matters for themselves, merely watching the interest of Government that the total area allowed free of assessment is not excessive." Warner forced Mullaly to put the names of the Mirasidars back on the cultivation accounts as the owners of the house sites from which "they had been struck without an inquiry, and to advise Mr. Mullaly to be more careful about not disturbing the relations between the two classes, viz. the Mirasidars and their sub-tenants [tenants-at-will or Parakkudis, many of whom were paraiyars], in the future." Though many revenue officers looked on the entries in the old aḍangal or village cultivation accounts on cadjan or palm leaf forms as valueless, the courts referred to them as authoritative.

For his part, Mullaly had written in his report of 1889 that the problem of providing house sites for the paraiyar Padiyals had come to his attention four years previously, specifically in response to some allegations made by Dadabhai Naoroji.[74] Numerous cases occurred in which assignments of puṟambōkku or wasteland had to be made for Parakkudi house sites since the existing village site was claimed by others or was simply insufficient. He took his examples from the cheri (Tamil "cēri") or paraiyar settlement of Olalur, a village in the Chingleput taluk, using it as one of the many illustrations of "the determined opposition of the Mirasidars to any improvement in the condition of the laboring classes." On 21 March 1888, Mullaly reported that the condition of the poverty-stricken subtenants or Parakkudi Payirkkaris provided "an apt illustration of his [Dadabhai Naoroji's] statements and should be brought to the notice of the Government of India." Mullaly suggested that the present poor living conditions of the Parakkudis of the Chingleput district, who were partly paraiyars, should be communicated to the government of India as part of the general debate on the poverty of the poorer classes of India.

Mullaly said that the Padiyals received bare subsistence wages and could not get proper housing accommodations. He gave figures to show how little they were paid and how crowded were the cheris in which they lived. For example, the cheri or paraiyar settlement at Tirukkaluk-kunram in the present-day Chingleput taluk covered only 3.46 acres but had thirty-four houses in which sixty-five families lived. The total population living in that area was 333 individuals for an average of ten persons per house: "To form a proper conception, it must be remembered that each house consists of only one room 12 feet by 8 feet. It reminds one of the penny low East End lodging houses in London where several families—men, women and children—are huddled together in one room. There it is due to dense population and dire poverty, here it is due to a particular tenure and system of registry." This comparison illustrates his participation in a general discussion about the condition of India and the problems of what William Booth came to call the "submerged tenth." The way the poor lived in London's East End provided one of the bases for a discussion of the paraiyars of the Chingleput district, using all the definitions and categories employed by those who wrote in the London press of the period.

Paraiyar living conditions were too disorderly, too slavelike, and too threatening to be acceptable to Mullaly's definition of British-Indian culture. Mullaly responded much as William Booth would have, declaring that "I determined to improve the miserable and overcrowded condition of their houses." The fact that the paraiyars could not get land "renders these unfortunates nothing more than the slaves of the mirasidars who exact from them labor for nothing or at a much lower rate than the market rates."[75]

Perceived Disorder of Paraiyar Settlements

From Mullaly's perspective, the claim by Mirasidars to housing they did not inhabit reflected perhaps the most disorderly aspect of these paraiyar settlements. In some villages, the paraiyars would do nothing to alter the situation because the Mirasidars threatened to throw them out. He described in his diary entry for 7 July 1888 the situation in Paler village, in what is today the Madurantakam taluk:

The village [of Paler] is in a disgracefully dirty state when I visited it on the 13th. I was nearly sick three times by the stench. The Revenue Inspector was ordered to go to the village to allot sites for the Pariahs this morning. I find that most of the Paracheri [paraiyar cheri or paraiyar living area] lands are entered in the names of the Mudaliars [vellala Mirasidars] and that they threaten to evict them [the paraiyar] if they don't work gratis or very cheaply for them. . . . This is a regular instance of slavery. . . . Of the Local Fund allotment of Rs. 200/, Rs. 41 have been sanctioned for removal of prickly pear and a further allotment will be made for it if it is very badly required.

One important element in this sense of chaos was the existence of prickly pear, one of the common cactuses in the South Indian environment. During the period of Tamil cultural and political history shortly after the time of Christ, certain cactus plants were considered to be typical of the pālai tinai or wasteland territorial category.[76] Eaten in the New World and Europe, prickly pear originally came to India from America but became naturalized all over the South Asian subcontinent and many parts of Europe. Since it had thorns, it was used for hedges and boundaries in India; Tipu Sultan used prickly pear around his fortifications, for example. However, for Europeans it came to have an entirely different signification in the South Asian environment. Yule and Burnell, the authors of *Hobson-Jobson,* point out that prickly pear was "objectionable, from harbouring dirt and reptiles."[77] They also cited the author Hugh Cleghorn, a nineteenth-century conservator of forests in Madras, who wrote that the use of prickly pear for hedges was "unsightly"; he commented that "the use of prickly pear [for hedges] I strongly deprecate; although impenetrable and inexpensive, it conveys an idea of sterility, and is rapidly becoming a nuisance in this country."[78] In the *Madras Manual of Administration,* the compiler C. D. Macleane noted that Tamils called the plant nāgatāli and valued it as a cure for whooping cough and asthma. Macleane also noted that many attempts had been made either to get rid of it or use it for "industrial purposes." He said that "it has a distinct preference for waste arid soils that will grow nothing else, and it does not flourish freely on rich well-cultivated land. . . . As hedge plant prickly-pear is both impenetrable and uninflammable; the unrestrained growth of the plant around villages which generally arises from its employment is however very inimical to sanitation."[79]

British officers of the government therefore looked on prickly pear as outside cultivation and outside habitation. Considered as a threat to order, it appeared chaotic from this British perspective. An account from the *Madras Times* suggests the extent of this characterization. Editor William Digby compared prickly pear to the criticisms of the Madras government by a visiting MP named W. S. Caine, who criticized government antitemperance policies:

> Prickly pear is the enemy which the Board of Revenue in Madras has to contend with, next to Mr. Caine. If Mr. Caine does not succeed in planting himself as a thorn in the side of the Board [of Revenue], the other enemy succeeds, but too well, and establishes itself as a veritable thorn in highways and byways and, unlike Mr. Caine, is present here, there and everywhere throughout the country. The Collector of Trichinopoly waged a particular war, successful as far as it went against this omnipresent enemy last year.[80]

The prickly pear compounded the dirt and overcrowding found by Mullaly; together they epitomized disorder in the Chingleput environment.[81]

Redefining "Slavery" to Sedentarize the Paraiyar

Beyond physical conditions, the mention of "slavery" suggested moral disorder. To eliminate the appearance of the anomaly of "slavery" meant recording the paraiyars' houses as their own property and removing the prickly pear as well. Both strategies aimed at one goal. Wrote Mullaly of Paler village in Madurantakam taluk: "A new street of comparatively large and new houses [was] built. The village was considerably improved when I visited it again this year on 25 June 1889 and more houses are going to be built. On my first visit in 1888, the Pariahs were loud in their complaints, but on my last visit they seemed well contented." Mullaly sought to satisfy his own hopes for order based on a dialogically constructed conception of the function of the "prickly pear" and a desire to house the poor "properly." He also tried to list all the houses in the cultivation accounts in the names of the paraiyar Padiyals and other subtenants or Parakkudis themselves, since he believed that entries in the names of the Mirasidars indicated the existence of what he considered to be slavery.

As a result of Mullaly's actions, many paraiyars petitioned him to undertake similar changes in other parts of the district. Mullaly wrote that he "was determined that they should be disposed of in spite of the strenuous opposition raised" by the Mirasidars. "All I wanted," he wrote, "was an account showing occupied and vacant sites in order to dispose of the 222 Chingleput applications" from subtenants or Parakkudis. However, the karnams or village accountants rebelled against his orders and themselves complained directly to Mullaly's superior,

Collector Warner, who in turn ordered that only present occupation
should be recorded and that "old occupation must not be interfered with
arbitrarily." Mullaly then had an account made only of present occupation and vacant housing sites. "I was not going to let all the petitions
slide simply on account of the difficulty raised," he wrote.

Mullaly realized that he could easily reject the applications for house-
sites of the subtenants by telling the petitioners to settle the matter themselves.[82] He felt that "to adopt this course would be to deny justice and
to aggravate the wretched condition of a numerous class." Mullaly and
some others in the British bureaucracy here decided to confront what
they called "the opposition." All these cases cast the Mirasidars as en-
emies of the welfare of the people represented by "the poor," the tenants,
and particularly the paraiyar Padiyals. These were the "submerged
tenth" of William Booth. For Mullaly, identifying the paraiyar Padiyals
and subtenants accomplished both a personal and ultimately a larger
historical task, as well as a transformative one. In lodging an appeal to
a former time and former place, Mullaly's ambitions sought to overcome
all obstacles and to ameliorate the living conditions of the paraiyar Padiyals. He appears also to have used all the legal and administrative
options available to him to create what he felt was a new world. Probably unaware that in "fixing" the houses of the paraiyar tenants he
helped to contain them, Mullaly not only prevented them from moving
about but also helped the state and the population to cast their gaze
over them, define them, and ultimately reform them. He probably also
did not realize that his activities and thinking would in many cases be
taken up excitedly by the paraiyars themselves. They became part of this
dialogic, creative process, for the very act of being "fixed" in their dwellings helped them to become embedded and enmeshed in the society.

In the end, Mullaly decided to assign what he considered vacant land
for paraiyar Padiyal and Parakkudi houses. He employed one or another
of these alternatives according to the nature of each particular case. By
far the largest measure of Mullaly's attention focused on the registration
of village sites. He believed that a proper system of registration of house
sites in the village should show the existing recognized rights of each
palli or paraiyar Padiyal or subtenant occupying it rather than the presumed rights claimed by the Mirasidars. This constituted a "distinct
assertion of the proprietary right of Government over village sites."

Already in 1886 the Board of Revenue had decided that the mirasi
claim over the absolute right of the village site was "anachronistic and
inconsistent with the welfare of government and its subjects and have

refused to recognise it."[83] The problem was that registration of these
house sites in the names of the Mirasidars threatened the assertion that
slavery did not exist in the area. For instance, the Tamil expression
"innar manai" in the cultivation accounts meant "the plot of such and
such a person." This corresponded to mirasi pretensions of ownership
of the paraiyar settlement itself:

> A widespread belief prevails that the mirassidars are absolute owners of
> the village site, and although wrong, the entries in the account perpetuate
> and strengthen this belief, and on the strength of them the grossest acts of
> oppression are perpetuated. The abuses are not rare but of almost daily oc-
> currence, and it was impossible for me to remain inactive with such a stain
> on the administration. It seemed as if there was a direct official recognition
> of villainage [sic].

What is important here is that Mullaly understood the symbolic and
pragmatic function of categories of oppression as categories perpetuated
through state collusion. Second, Mullaly looked on certain categories
and activities as a "stain on the administration," suggesting that the
government had a mandate to eliminate these. Of necessity then, Mullaly
felt obliged to eradicate all marks of what he believed was slavery wherever they existed. He understood this as a task partly to "free the slaves"
but partly to save the prestige of the state and Britain, in whose name
these actions were ultimately undertaken. The discussion over the tenants and over the paraiyar Padiyals and Parakkudis therefore may have
been started mainly as a way to explicate British ideals of justice and
fairness rather than any attempt to change the structural position of the
poor and the weak per se. According to Mullaly, the social system in
the Chingleput district had been unjust, but what needed to be confronted was that it continued to be unjust. That is, the kinds of information and movement within the bureaucracy and elsewhere had as
much to do with what the individuals felt about definition of their own
values as with the unjust social system that they were describing. Thus,
the kind of social description that emerged from this discussion was as
oriented to British requirements as to the system of social hierarchy and
degradation operating in the Chingleput area.

The dialogic interaction often substantiated Mullaly's interpretation.
As the result of what Mullaly did in a village named Oragadem in the
present-day Sriperumbadur taluk, a Mirasidar told a paraiyar Parakkudi
to leave his house or pay the costs of a civil suit against him. The house
site had been entered as Kandadu Rangachari "Innar Manai" (property
owner) and Parasuraman as "Kudiyiruppu" (resident). Following the

general instructions issued by Mullaly, the first entry was omitted by the village accountant. After the Mirasidar appealed to the collector, Warner ordered the restoration of the old double entry. Immediately, Rangachari, the Mirasidar, served a lawyer's notice on Sivanda Natan, a relative of Parasuraman, to "remove the house in 8 days and to pay up to Rs. 10, the value of the chilies grown in the backyard, on pain of having to incur the cost of a civil suit. . . . Thus on the strength of an entry 'innar manai' in some old accounts, a threat is made to evict one whose family has been occupying a site for years."[84]

Mullaly also found in these old accounts Tamil entries in the form puṟamaṉai iṉṉar āl, or "the person who was the possession of the man who owned the land." These entries were "relics of the time when the Pariahs were ascripti glebae or villains [villeins] attached to and transferred with mirasi shares." If title deeds were given to all paraiyars or tenants for the houses they occupied, "this would cause a great improvement in most villages; in place of ruined walls and sites overgrown with prickly pear, brushwood, etc., we would have neat houses and properly kept backyards."[85] In other words, his actions introduced a process of renewal aimed at bringing to light his own idea of middle-class British order out of local chaos and misery.

Mullaly requested that, if Warner were unable to change his mind and support him, his account be sent to the Board of Revenue for a decision. The Board indicated that the Mirasidars should be resisted over the question of house sites in Chingleput. However, the fluid heteroglot nature of the discourse around Chingleput emerged in this decision as well. Mullaly, according to the Board, "should not have used the term slavery, a term which does not describe their condition accurately."[86] At the same time, the note went on, Mullaly had shown that "the wages earned by the labouring class [Padiyals] barely amount to subsistence wages, that they are compelled to live in overcrowded miserable huts, that they often have to pay rent when the Government intend them to live rent free, and that they are compelled to give their labour for little or nothing at the order of the mirasidars." However, it said that Mullaly had not exhibited sufficient caution in dealing with "what he ought to have known was the great difficulty of the Chingleput district." Yet another Board member wrote that Mullaly had shown "the condition of the non-Mirasidars in some villages at all events . . . [to be] almost that of slavery, and worse than slavery in some respects because in this case there is none of the feeling of responsibility which at all events in many cases attaches to the master in countries where real slavery exists."

The fourth member of the Board, W. S. White, said that Mullaly used "exaggerated expressions that ought not to appear in official correspondence unless supported by the strongest evidence. One of these is the application of the word 'slavery' to the condition of the low caste cultivators of Chingleput."[87]

The Decay of the District and the Paraiyar Position

During the rainy season of 1890–91, the rains failed almost entirely in the area around Madras. As a result, during the year 1891 considerable scarcity emerged in the Chingleput region. In December 1890, the editor of the *Madras Times* announced that in both the Chingleput and Tinnevelly districts a new movement of resistance by groups below the caste system had begun. These people were the "multitude of people who are practically slaves in British India."[88] He continued, "To all intents and purposes he [the paraiyar Padiyal in Chingleput] is as much in the hands of the caste people of this country as the villeins and serfs of the west were in the hands of the Barons 800 or 900 years ago, under the old Feudal system of the Anglo-Norman kings." Under the "power and protection of English law . . . within fifty miles of the seat of government," wrote the editor, there were people in Chingleput who were

> practically the property of others. How is it to be expected that India can be other than poor so far as the masses of her people are concerned, when idle land-holders live luxuriously on the spoils they take by means of a cowardly sweating system, and forced labour, for which they give in return perhaps two meagre meals a day; when the old inspiration of the labourers, is the fear for his oppressors. Let the Pariahs be emancipated![89]

In the middle of 1891, the editor again noted that under the old Pannaiyal system the paraiyars received kindnesses, but when they were granted their "freedom" they experienced much greater vulnerability. The Mirasidars could be pitiless, but the government was to blame. The government had loosened the bond and had relieved the Mirasidars. It had "separated the Pariah and left him helpless, only it has told him that he is free."[90] Many of the paraiyar Padiyals in the Chingleput district existed in a state "little removed from actual slavery; bound to their caste masters by a species of serfdom similar to that which formerly obtained in Russia." Yet Tiruvaḷḷuvar, the Tamil author of the *Tirukuṟaḷ*, the great Tamil poetess Auvaiyār, and the architect of the classical city of Hastinapur had all been paraiyars. This, he believed, showed that in former times the paraiyars occupied a much higher position than they did later. "What a striking contrast there is between these men [the paraiyars] and the lazy but important Brahman who will condescend to anything to get a salary so long as it does not include hard work." The English should therefore be much more sympathetic to the paraiyars even though they were illiterate.[91]

The vulnerable situation of the paraiyars formed the focus of formal government concern in the district as well. In March 1891, the collector of Chingleput J. H. A. Tremenheere described the sixty or seventy paraiyars in Senneri village in the present-day Chingleput taluk. Their condition, he wrote, would have moved a "heart of stone."[92] Their state was

> not appreciably lower than usual; a large proportion of them are always badly nourished, clad if at all in the vilest of rags, eaten up with leprosy or other horrible diseases, hutted like pigs, untaught, uncared for and unpitied. I must apologise to the Board [of Revenue] and Government for picturing the position, which is indeed already known, but the day cannot be far distant when the public conscience of England, if not of India, will wake up to the condition of these unhappy wretches and to the easy way of ameliorating it. [Someone has written in pencil, "What is the easy means?"][93]

He also noted that "The black word slavery, which is so much objected to, can hardly be avoided when for any disobedience the Pariah is turned out of his house on pretext of long occupation by a family which for generations, or perhaps, for centuries, has not, and from caste prejudice, could not come within 50 yards of it."[94] The scarcity in the district underscored Tremenheere's comments and sharpened the epistemological moment for signifying the paraiyar. However, such comments also provoked government officers and others to contribute to a new definition of the paraiyar. As a result of this movement within the bureaucracy, in October 1891 Tremenheere submitted a long report on the paraiyars of Chingleput district. In that report, he noted that it was "easy to picture Chingleput. We have a district with a fair rainfall; with a soil excellently adapted to wells; traversed by a canal and two railways, tapped by a harbour; with an enormous market at its centre; and with a land tax so moderate that an acre of irrigable land is taxed only 3.5 rupees against a presidency average of 4.5 rupees. This should be an Indian paradise."[95] However, the district was not a paradise. Rather, as the under secretary of state for India had described it, Chingleput district was, "owing to its infertile soil and to certain accidents of tenure, . . . among the most backward parts of Madras Presidency."[96] In another context, Tremenheere wrote,

From Chingleput take the train further south, or leave the railway at Chingleput or Vandalur and strike eastwards to the coast. On either hand you can shoot partridges over miles of useless bush which in an ordinary district would be waving with grain, feeding and employing thousands of people. . . . There is at present in the mirasi villages 73,912 acres of unoccupied arable land, crying out for tillage like the fields in the fairy tale. The annual loss of revenue to Government is Rs. 99,887. The mirasidars will not take this up, and will not let it be taken up by the non-mirasi residents of the village; while neither class would for a moment think of waving [sic] its privileges in favour of a despised and rejected Pariah.[97]

The wasteland of the district had become an epistemic site of moral decay.

But why was Chingleput district so underdeveloped? To understand how this situation arose during the nineteenth century, we should summarize the way in which the Mirasidars and the state operated in that period. Under the rules instituted by the ryotwari proprietary system after 1818—a system of taxation that abandoned settlement with the entire village and instead made agreements with each individual Mirasidar or landowner—the Indo-British administration claimed that it had the right to take any unoccupied wasteland away from Mirasidars and give it to other persons who could improve and cultivate it. However, the Mirasidars again resisted what they considered an attempt to invade their traditional rights. Ellis supported the Mirasidars in this position, but it was hotly disputed by Thomas Munro in 1824. By 1841, Ellis's ideas had become accepted as authoritative and momentarily monologic. In the years after mid-century, the Mirasidars of the district sought again to resist state attempts to bring in tenants to unoccupied land. They did this by assuming more land than they could cultivate or pay taxes on. As a result, they impoverished themselves as well as the state. Some irrigable land went out of cultivation.

Creating a New Pannaiyal System Out of the Old One

Naturally, this system produced enormous disparities of wealth. Tremenheere said:

> The divorce of the Pariahs from the land and the insecurity of their homes . . . place the agricultural labourer under the heel of the large landholder. In the result the district shows worse farming, has fewer resident landlords, is fuller of sub-tenants and bond-labourers, and altogether produces more striking contrasts of wealth and poverty than any of which I have had experience.[98]

Specifically, the system allowed effective debt bondage and much of the relationship implicit in the Pannaiyal system to remain. He showed that "in the Southern States of America, before the Civil War, it would have been accounted madness to suggest that the Negroes should be enabled to take up land on their own account. Prejudice and fear of a free labour market would have stood in the way. In Chingleput, though legal slavery has been abolished there is a similar prejudice and a similar fear."[99]

The "laws of emancipation" in Madras (3 and 4 William IV, 5 George IV of 1843, and Act XLV of 1860) prohibited the Mirasidars from using violence against the Pannaiyals. But, he said, "the serfs [Pannaiyals] continued to work for their old masters and their descendants continue so today under the name Padiyals [laborers who worked for padis ('measures' of about 100 cubic inches each) of rice or payment in kind]." This was due, in part, to the operation of the Breach of Contract Act of 1859, which made it hard for a Padiyal to escape the control of a master. To prove his point, Tremenheere quoted a series of fourteen deeds of men who gave their brothers, themselves, or their sons as security for loans of rupees 10 to 15 after the "emancipation laws." "Adimai," the Tamil word for slave, was still used in the deed texts. According to these deeds, the debt-bonded individual said that he would work gratis instead of paying the interest on a loan undertaken to pay off an old debt or for a marriage. . . . "Such bondage [notes were simply] . . . specimens of the thousands that exist. One single man having been known to produce 150. They are more common in this district than elsewhere, but have been brought to the notice of Govt . . . from other districts."[100] He also pointed to the fact that though these deeds of debt bondage could not be legally enforced the bonded individuals were not aware of this. Instead, the Mirasidars constantly threatened the laborers with lawsuits. Tremenheere believed that as long as the terminology and ideology existed alongside the mechanisms that prevented any true emancipation, "slavery" was bound to continue in the Chingleput district.

He buttressed this agreement with his own historical construction. When the British took over the Chingleput district, he said, "the mirasi system was discovered in a more or less disintegrated form." Three causes had contributed to arrest the progress of decay, including "the conservative effects of the decisions in the Mayor's Court" during the latter half of the eighteenth century, "the researches of Collector Mr. Place," and the fact that the ryotwari system had been introduced into the district by "Mr. F. W. Ellis, a distinguished and fond student of ancient tenures, and author of a treatise upon mirasi."[101] Moreover, although the courts had depended on Ellis and his assistant Shankarayya for interpretations of mirasi, "perhaps enough weight has not been given to the consideration that for different reasons the antiquarian Ellis and the Brahman [Sankarayya] were both extremists."[102] In other words, both Ellis and Shankarayya had strong investments in making claims about the antiquity of mirasi, but their great cultural and personal interests in these claims were quite different from one another's and even possibly contradictory. This illustrated in a clear way that the historical requirements of the times had led both Ellis and Shankarayya to enter the dialogue, to create knowledge, and to find answers to their questions from different epochs and different cultural realms.

In building his case, Tremenheere rejected the argument proffered by some of his contemporaries that the mirasi system would die of its own weight. He felt that this idea

> does not harmonize with the view expressed at the same time, that the [mirasi] privilege is still highly prized by its owners and that a non-recognition would undoubtedly meet with strong opposition. It is neither probable that a privilege should be falling into disuse, when the growing wealth of the country makes it everyday more valuable; nor does history support this view. We have seen that it was not thoroughly established till 1842, and I know of little that has since occurred to weaken it.

Tremenheere argued that the state had degraded the position of the lower castes in the past and had made their niche in society more vulnerable. He urged that "the state must retrieve its mistakes. We have permitted privileges to survive until they have become anachronisms, we have created new privileges."[103] He argued that, in the complex mechanisms surrounding the rise of an increasingly nonmobile society, the Padiyals and debt-bonded laborers and Parakkudis or tenants-at-will had been left without state support.[104] The recognition of what he considered "new privileges" such as the swatantrams, which had been made part of the tax reassessment provisions in 1877–78, had further exaggerated the social and economic distance between groups. He believed that since the state was responsible for creating these inequities it should rectify them. Finally, he argued the anachronism of the entire construction of the mirasi system because it perpetuated serious social and economic disabilities. Finally, Tremenheere invoked the Africa-England resonances of Stanley and William Booth. "Indeed," he wrote, "when one inspects the residents of a Chingleput or Madurantakam paracheri— poor objects, some of them look as if they had been brought from Cen-

tral Africa to exhibit the depths of human debasement—one of the sad-
dest thoughts is that there is no one to care for them."[105]

The New Definition of the Paraiyars as the "Disinherited Children of the Soil"

In his long statement, Tremenheere also argued, seeking to recreate a
former age, that "the Pariahs were not always in their present condition
of degradation. The most popular poem," he wrote, "ever produced in
the Tamil country, the Kural, was written by a Pariah named Tiruvalluvar 'the divine Pariah' as he has been called." In undertaking these
tasks, Tremenheere was simply one of thousands of individuals who
wanted to eliminate the previous "dishonest" and "inappropriate" signification of the paraiyars:

> Nor is the Pariah of the present day by any means destitute of sense and
> good qualities. He shakes of his folly with his degradation and exhibits re-
> markable acuteness in a European household, and in the Colonies. As for
> devotion to his master in danger or in sickness, no part of our Eastern pos-
> sessions, however wild or deadly, but can bear witness; While his courage
> has made the reputation of our finest regiment.[106]

In another context, a Wesleyan missionary named William Goudie
working in Ikkadu near Tiruvallur just west of Madras wrote in 1894
that the paraiyars were "the disinherited children of the soil, and to give
them again some small possession in it is only to restore them to a
position which their fathers held with honour long ago when their race
saw better days."[107] "There are people," he wrote, "who have a kindly
feeling for decayed aristocracies: to such I would suggest that the Pariahs
are amongst the most ancient of that class in this country and for that
reason alone should find a place in their generous sentiments."[108] Ellis
also pointed to the fact that the paraiyars were fiercely proud of their
own mirasis or hereditary rights to land. He had written that the paraiyars of Tondaimandalam

> affect to consider themselves as the real proprietors of the soil; the vellalar,
> they say, sells his birth right to the Śānar, the latter is cajoled out of it by the
> Brahmans, and he is swept away before the fury of a Mahommedan invasion;
> but no one removes or molests the Pareiyar, whoever may be the nominal
> owner or whatever the circumstances of the times, they are safe in this insig-
> nificance, and continue and will forever continue, to till the ground their
> ancestors tilled before them. The villeins [paraiyar Pannaiyals] possess estab-
> lished rights and privileges of which they cannot be deprived, which consti-

tute their mirasi and which are prized by them as much and maintained ostentatiously as the more valuable privileges of the higher orders.[109]

These constituted part of the large-scale dialogic project to construct the paraiyars as the autochthons of South India, the "original Dravidians."

Up until his time, Tremenheere noted, the battle had been between the Mirasidars and the "caste non-Mirasidars" or Payirkkaris (tenants-at-will). Only very recently had the British collectors and the paraiyars themselves realized that it might be possible for the paraiyar Parakkudis to obtain land, thus shifting the stakes that would incite participation by new contributors to the dialogic process. Tremenheere wrote that "the one question that can bring a smile to their care-worn faces is why they [paraiyars] did not apply for land." He reported that the paraiyars of Kaniver village in the Tiruvallur taluk replied, "But what is the good . . . of applying for this [land]? The Mirasidars will take it up merely to keep us out." "Well," replied Tremenheere, "at least you will have the satisfaction of forcing them to pay the assessment. Make an attempt and see." Tremenheere and other individuals like him, on the other hand, sought to get rid of an oppressive and artificially produced structure. Nevertheless, by opposing the Mirasidars they assisted in creating a new mirasi system. These paraiyar Padiyals and Payirkkaris thus became as involved as the British or the Mirasidars in helping to construct "truth" about the mirasi system and hierarchy in general. Their immediate goals, however, appear to have been very different. By placing pressure on the Mirasidars to take on more land than they could possibly cultivate and pay taxes on, the paraiyars helped to oppose the Mirasidars but support the mirasi system.[110] In the process, paraiyars aided in the grand historical task of sedentarizing the Tamil population. This process included the enhancement of agriculture as a superior expression of economy and culture. It kept people from moving around as had been the case in the eighteenth century and before. As a result of these activities, the paraiyar voice, however low in status, played an important heteroglot function in creating meaning and participating in important historical tasks. Margaret Trawick has used the ideas of Bakhtin to understand heteroglot expressions in paraiyar songs of the Chingleput district in the twentieth century concerning authority, love relationships, and agency. Her data shows how "the distinction between voices is sometimes very vague" and that the voices in these songs are "united by strategies of ambiguity." In one song, Trawick notes, "between the two voices, there is no strict turn-taking, so that we can only know who is saying what on the basis of the content of what is said." In another context, she notes that "one experiences the very powerful illusion that not one person is speaking, but two, because the single voice one hears is so responsive to the silent other." Her point is that there is always a merging of the "author's voice" and the "other's voice." She concludes that in her work the paraiyars "see themselves as comprised of multiple and independent voices, which may speak to each other in dreams or in trance or in songs."[111]

According to Tremenheere, there were of course many reasons for the paraiyar being excluded from the land.[112] Tremenheere's appeals to a former time shared similarities with the appeals of Place, Ellis, White, Hastings, Shankarayya, Place's Telugu and Tamil informants, and many other individuals of both low and high status. They simply constituted additional ways by which the interactive construction of knowledge continued.

The New Paraiyar Body

Tremenheere had said too much in his report on the paraiyars. His contentions had to be addressed by the government in a direct way. As a result, his superiors on the Board of Revenue tried not only to discount everything that Tremenheere had said but also to identify the redeeming aspects of the current paraiyar social situation. However, to do this, they had to prove above all that the village system in the district was not as oppressive as Tremenheere had pictured it. They had to establish the fact that over the previous century British cultural mechanisms and the state had usefully translated the situation from slavery to benevolence, from oppression to kindness. In sum, the alternative position had to demonstrate the inaccuracy of the analysis put forward by Tremenheere and others.

In its counteranalysis of Chingleput rural social relations, the Board pointed to the fact that even when Pannaiyals and debt bondage had existed, many beneficent aspects to those relations could be identified. For instance, they quoted Place's century-old account of ritual reversal between the Mirasidars and their paraiyar Padiyals and Pannaiyals. Place had written:

> There is a peculiarity in the mutual conduct of cultivators [Mirasidars] and their servants [Padiyals] partaking with regard to the latter both of bondage and freedom . . . the servant [Padiyal] engages in the service of a cultivator [Mirasidar] at the beginning of the year, on the customary terms of the village to which he is conciliated, and binds himself by the acceptance of

betel, unless in those cases which I before noticed as inducing one party to demand and the other to grant exorbitant terms, and his servitude expires with the year, during which it seldom happens that he is guilty of desertion if those terms are faithfully observed towards him. Many from good treatment acquire an attachment to their masters whom none almost could prevail with them to desert; yet the ceremony of withdrawing themselves at the end of the year and recontracting for their labour is invariably renewed; for the disposition of each party towards the other is so well understood, that this retirement is never further than the adjoining village, and if, under such disposition, one should not allow a reasonable time or the other refrain to offer a renewal of the contract within that time, the complaint would be equally heavy; the long residence creates attachment and a kind of inherent right, which it is for the interest of both not to violate and in fact perpetuates a servitude which is reconciled to the bare forms of freedom with but few of its privileges. There are some servants [Pannaiyals] who are considered altogether slaves attached to the soil and are transferred with it from one purchaser to another, entitled however to all the privileges of the former class.[113]

It then quoted a description of this same ritual written by Ellis in 1814. At the close of the Tamil month of Ani (mid-June to mid-July) when the revenue year ended and just before cultivation began,

> The whole of the slaves [paraiyar Padiyals] strike work, collect in bodies outside of the villages and so remain until their masters [Mirasidars] by promising to continue their privileges, by solicitation, presents of betel [a nut offered to show honor] and other gentle means, induce them to return. The slaves [Padiyals] on these occasions, however well treated they may have been, complain of various grievances, real and imaginary and threaten a general desertion. The threat, however, they never carry into execution, but after the usual time everything having been conducted according to mamul [custom], return quietly to their labour.[114]

Then the Board proceeded to quote from the *Chingleput Manual* in which Crole commented on the passage by Ellis just quoted:

> The above is a description of slavery under its mildest and most benignant aspect. An institution from which the mind revolts, owing to the horrors and degradation incident to it in other modern countries is here presented so as to contrast favourably with the state of conquered peoples, even when normally free, elsewhere. It is not astonishing therefore that without any formal act of emancipation, the British administration has been able to work a silent revolution, which, while it has left the proper relations between the cultivating class and their farm servants undisturbed, has made the latter as free as any of Her Majesty's subjects.[115]

Crole thus sought to show how much better was the situation of bonded men and farm laborers in Chingleput than in other places where slavery existed in the modern world. Crole also wanted to demonstrate that even though hierarchic Mirasidar-Pannaiyal relations in effect still existed in Chingleput, these relations remained the basis for a later peaceful and benevolent transformation that had been effected by the British. This evolution had made it possible to retain the benign aspects of these relations, to leave them "undisturbed," while at the same time emancipating the debt-bonded Pannaiyals by a "silent revolution" so that they were as free as anybody in the British Empire. In essence, Crole argued that the relations between Pannaiyals and Mirasidars differed from the relations ordinarily at work between individuals in that kind of situation "elsewhere, even when normally free." In other words, such unusual relations could form the basis of a transformation that did not require any government measures to ameliorate them.

However, the Board also suggested another way to look at the paraiyars in their economic position. They could also be seen as consumers of liquor. Tremenheere had noted that the paraiyars, "whether from the proximity of salt factories or from other causes," sometimes got paid well. But, he said, the state allowed an "excess of public-houses" to exist. This policy encouraged paraiyars to spend this new money on drink.[116] The Madras Board of Revenue used the excise statistics to prove that each paraiyar man drank rupees 5 worth of liquor a year. This consumption enabled the Board to measure "a substantial surplus of income over expenditure and [thus] disprove . . . the existence of any widespread destitution." Tremenheere had looked on drink as an indication not of wealth but of paraiyar poverty and dissipation; the Board, by contrast, believed that in the Chingleput district no relationship between drink and crime could be established as had been done for Great Britain:

> Drunkenness does not obtrude itself. On the contrary, drink is to a great extent consumed as part of or as a supplement to, food, by certain classes to which it is not forbidden by custom, dating long before British rule. It is, for instance, a matter of common observation that during the palmyra toddy season, the physical condition of the lower orders all over the country undergoes unmistakable improvement. It is mere toying with a serious subject to suggest that, if a Pariah drinks in moderation, it is a cause of moral degradation, and is evidence of general poverty, and not of a measure of prosperity. Even the Reverend Mr. Andrew [missionary of the Free Church of Scotland in Chingleput town] describes the pariah community in Chingleput as "hard-working and muscular." This is totally incompatible with besotted excess in strong drink, or with a condition of chronic starvation.[117]

Here the Board had decided that the paraiyars were more productive because they drank liquor, that they had the money to indulge their fancy, that they were certainly not paupers, that liquor enabled them to remain strong, healthy, and active, and that they drank only in moderation and along with food. The only conclusion to be drawn was that the paraiyars were not poverty-stricken but well off and healthy. Paraiyar drinking thus proved to be good for society. The main goal was to focus on the productive bodies of the paraiyars. Ironically, both those who thought that the paraiyars were healthy and had enough to eat and those who did not helped to formulate conceptions regarding the nature of the useful paraiyar body.

In another context, the Board argued that since the Padiyals who had previously been Pannaiyals had access to British legal institutions and a labor market in Madras, they enjoyed important protection:

> Long before the Negroes of America were emancipated the Pariah was freed from his bondage [through the "emancipation laws"], and he could carry his labour wherever he chose. With a free and good labour market (at the Presidency town) almost at his very door, and with numerous courts to redress his wrongs, there is no reason whatever for him to submit to "iniquitous contracts" or to work "for a rack rent or for starvation wages."[118]

"Emancipated" Pannaiyals of the Tondai country could not therefore be considered disadvantaged.

To strengthen their position still further, the Board of Revenue invoked Place's reasons from another cultural realm for not trying to change the position of the paraiyars. To do this, they quoted his "evidence" that the paraiyar Pannaiyals and Padiyals benefited from various contributions in grain throughout the year, and particularly at harvest time:

> But there are other advantages, which the families of these labourers [Pannaiyals and Padiyals] derive from extra services, which they contribute to the village, and for which they receive, although a regulated hire, yet a requital which satisfies them; and it is often their only support, from the dissipation of their head. . . . For this reason, I have doubted whether it would be politic to attempt, because not clearly possible to effect, an improvement in the situation of the cultivator's servants [the paraiyar Padiyals and Pannaiyals] since it would only tend to weaken the government of themselves; and leave their families, who now excite, and benefit by, the compassion of the inhabitants, utterly destitute.[119]

In other words, social forces united and made the paraiyar groups cohere and formed the basis of their survival. If they received government assistance to better their position, this social solidarity would vanish. They could no longer attract the sympathy of other people. Therefore, it was inappropriate to change the social position of the paraiyars. The Board had quoted Place's report, they said, because he had "devoted his special attention to this subject." The Board considered that the situation of the paraiyar family and the conditions under which it worked had not altered in a century. The Board sought to create an essentialist world in which the relations between state and society had not changed in a hundred years, or perhaps a millennium. Data on the contemporary situation of the paraiyars was as good for the 1790s as for the 1890s. The Board quoted Place because he said what they themselves wanted to say. In the operation of heteroglossia, they chose a meaning out of the past to perform a task both for the present and the future, a task whose meaning and requirements had altogether changed. Therefore, Place's authorship of these ideas was itself put at risk because the historical construction had grappled with totally different kinds of historical imperatives. Now, not only did the past have to be transfigured but past transfigurations had to be used to see future social usefulness. By invoking dialogically produced ideas from Place and Ellis, the Board sought to bring the paraiyars into a larger productive community whose requirements for full competence could exclude no one. Similarly, although Tremenheere and the missionary Goudie approached the paraiyars not by citing Ellis and Place but by invoking local ideas about their present decayed condition and their former greatness, they attempted to promote the same general project. Their initiative concerned the need to make all elements of the society reach physical maturity and be productive.

In this dialogic interaction, then, the Board discounted statistically Tremenheere's contentions about paraiyar debasement. It also claimed that this social project should not be the state's responsibility but should rely primarily on private philanthropy. For this purpose, it employed not only the contemporary accounts and data provided by its own staff members but also those of Place from the previous century. The Board said that "very strong assertions are made, but every statistical fact and all the information at the Board's disposal tell the other way." However, the Board had still other more basic objections to Tremenheere's suggestions:

> It is quite beside the question of Government action that, in the opinion of certain persons, the caste system of the Hindus is an abomination, or that certain classes of the population have been relegated, under the custom of the country, for ages, to certain professions or employments and that the result is social degradation. The British Government is pledged to abstain

from direct interference with caste and custom just as it is bound to respect the rights of private property in land. Yet the proposals presented for acceptance of Government would revolutionize the one and confiscate the other. There is no question here of sympathy with poverty, or of the propriety of raising the fallen or degraded into positions of respectability. In India, as in all countries, efforts to ameliorate such unavoidable evils form the proper field of private philanthropy. The State can certainly not intervene with effect, at least not in the way of creating a social revolution and confiscating private property; yet, these are the measures proposed; for Government is asked to make landholders out of farm servants [the word "slaves" is not used], who are already too few, partly at least by making over to the Pariahs land over which their masters have undoubted legal rights. In regard to Sub-Tenants [Parakkudis], in the same way, it is proposed to deprive the mirasidars of the ownership of the soil in every case in which a Pariah has paid rent for twelve years. It is, likewise, proposed to repudiate the undoubted rights of the mirasidar in the waste. Mr. Tremenheere correctly anticipates that his proposals will be spoken of as revolutionary. It is hard to imagine how they can be otherwise characterised.[120]

In this expression, the Board invoked a strategy of noninterference that had evolved over several decades after the Great Rebellion of 1857. However, this conservatism did not just result from the desire to preserve political stability; it also shows that the Board thought that the responsibility for a person's bodily condition was no longer the responsibility of the state but of missionary and other charitable organizations. It admitted that the state no longer exercised control over a person's body. Rather, it asserted that this responsibility had been placed in the hands of nongovernmental agencies.

Structurally, this admission indicated an important step in the withdrawal of the state not only from violence and control of the body but over immediate control of the individual in general in modern society. That is, we may trace significant movement over a century's time: the dialogic construction of religious culture and the temple in the nineteenth century had also increasingly involved the dissipation of the sacred into the bodies of each individual. The comments of the Board of Revenue about its "noninterference" in the lives of the poor formed another phase in this structural dissipation of the sacred, leading to the increasing responsibility of individuals themselves and agencies outside of the state for people's bodies. In a sense, the state was withdrawing from local interference.

Thus, according to the government of Madras (the governor, his council, and the superiors of the Board of Revenue), Tremenheere's report had "greatly exaggerated" the conditions in Chingleput, and it was "questionable whether there is anything like as much misery among the poorest classes in India as there is in any large European city." On the contrary, they felt that though the poorest could make a living in India, this was not true in Europe. Moreover, Tremenheere's "highly colored description of the Pariah of Senneri [the subject of a question in Parliament about the village in the Chingleput taluk] would apply with equal truth . . . to the lowest classes in European countries."[121] Other individuals used some of these same materials to claim the benign nature of the Mirasidar-Padiyal relationship. Baden-Powell, in his *Land Systems of British India,* published in 1892, argued that these "villeins" "worked for the mirasidars in rotation. . . . They got a house and yard free, also certain dues in grain (kalavasam, etc.), and presents in clothes, grain, and money, at stated festivals. The 'slavery' was therefore not a very hard bondage."[122]

Ultimately, whether the paraiyars were considered besotted and poverty-stricken or not proved unimportant in the emerging discursive production. Instead, the main historical task focused on eliminating the unproductive signification of slavery and creating another that bore an entirely different meaning, whether it was one of honesty, loyalty, productivity, or legitimacy as the original Dravidians of the Tondaimandalam area. The newly created paraiyars formed part of a general discussion of what the poor ate and drank and where they lived, both in India and in Europe—whether that was the British urban "submerged tenth" or the Chingleput rural paraiyars who made up one quarter of the population. In effect, therefore, the elimination of the "slavery" signification helped to create another, more useful identity, which gradually claimed the paraiyars as the most fixed inhabitants of the entire population. The idea of being riveted to Tondaimandalam was not new. According to Place and his local Tamil informants, the story about the vellalas indicated that the Chola king had fixed their affections on the soil of the Tondai country "so strongly" that they could not even harbor a wish to leave.[123] The process of eliminating the "slave" signification for the paraiyar therefore became an attempt to transfigure the past in order to deal with contemporary "peasantizing" historical requirements. In this case, the future offered the possibility of a society in which individuals would be more and more able to transfer their labor and be individually responsible for their own bodies.

Conclusion

Sedentarization, the State, and Its Citizens

One of the most important aspects of Indo-British civilization was the rise in esteem of sedentary agriculture as a form of culture. This judgment separated those who practiced agriculture from groups who wandered and traveled across the land in search of a livelihood, to pursue commerce, to beg, or to become saints. It also, ultimately, separated those seen to be "authentic Dravidians" from cultural interlopers—an immensely significant distinction to which we will return. The privileging of sedentarization resulted from an attempt on the part of both British and Indians to define citizenship strictly in terms of a society whose members possessed given places of residence, who were embedded, and who did not move about. The focus on sedentary society emerged as part of a general development in which the British and local agricultural groups interacted to create a high place for agriculture as the basis of the state. This meaning formed a bedrock of agreement to which many British, Indians, and others came very early in the relationship; it cannot be explained by the imposition of European values on a weaker India.

In essence, European and local groups shared a conception about the quintessential mark of citizenship in a modern unitary state. Agriculture and the transferability of land, then, became the basic form of economic life in India and elsewhere. It became sharply differentiated from all those forms of social and economic activity marked by peripatetic movement. The preceding chapters have examined key epistemological moments in the dialogic process surrounding this sedentarization to create a modern state.

An integral part of a British and Indian definition of a normative village included the notion that people who were citizens of the same nation did not move. They had a residence. Moreover, this construction, this "truth" also presumed that when agriculturalists were forced by circumstances to temporarily move away from their villages, they nonetheless always returned to the same villages, the same houses, the same lands, and once there engaged in the same exchanges and other ritual activities to maintain the status quo. These rituals, perceived retrospectively by both Europeans and local individuals in the Jagir and elsewhere, aided the process of preventing people from moving about and helped to bind people together into sedentary, embedded structures. It gave them an address.

We have seen in the previous chapter how the Board of Revenue in the 1890s invoked the existence of ritual exchanges between Mirasidars and the paraiyars in the late eighteenth and the early nineteenth centuries. The Board conjured up the benign aspect of master-slave relations to shape future figurations for the society. In the nineteenth century and before, the golden age and utopian ideas of Indian commentators expressed themselves in similar ways. We have seen in the Introduction how a "native revenue officer" from Madras presidency in 1858 wrote of a time "not far back when universal content, concord and mutual sympathy reigned amongst the landholders and their labourers."[1] This was repeated in many other contexts and shows that the golden-age ideas relating to the Indian village simply formed another part of the dialogic creation of a normative, utopian face-to-face settlement. Nor was this activity a naive and artless one; it was an attempt to shape the "truth" for the future.

This intellectual and discursive interaction proved particularly vigorous whenever British and Indian agrarian groups sought to describe why and how these groups had migrated to the locations where British and Indian participants in the debate said they found them. Although we can say that the interaction resulted from the British attempt to gain juridical power and to control the Indian population, it is also true that the British sought to identify who they themselves were by using the Indian environment to work out ideas about citizenship and the precise nature of the European nation-state. Therefore, the kinds of information that they developed in the Jagir in the eighteenth and nineteenth centuries formed part of a general cultural production that related as much to British self-definition and self-ascription as to the specific description of a colonized India or even to the Jagir or, later, to the Chingleput district. Hence, we can no longer accept Said's contention that the cultural categories of the colonized operated in a willed, unidirectional, top-down way on an unthinking and unresisting colonized group, an inert object. Despite the juridically dominant position of the British, who theoretically had a monopoly on the use of violence, these kinds of knowledge were not imposed. Rather, categories emerged from interactive, heteroglot cultural formations that had no author. To put it in another way, these formations were so multiauthored that the ideas and interactions that went to make up these cultural productions made it impossible to locate any real provenance for them.

The development of an embedded society and a nonsegmentary state in India, as we saw in Chapter 2, led to the diminution of the ritual reversals among Indians themselves and between the Europeans and the local population. Once the state ceased to be segmentary, peasants could no longer engage in rituals of flight to reduce the state to impotence. Moreover, as this sedentarization process proceeded, the kind of emotional swings between caution and restraint followed in many specific situations also diminished or took on new meaning. These extremes of emotional behavior became less and less structurally possible and less and less tolerable in the bureaucratic state toward which British India headed.

A principal historical project—focused on the nature of sedentary life, of work, and of agriculture as a productive activity—therefore became associated with how proprietary forms developed in India. Though this project appeared under the rubric of an attempt to understand the antique and "original" forms of proprietary usage, above all it represented an attempt to legitimize sedentary agriculture, which had higher status and more social and economic validity than the activities of urban or wandering elements of the population.[2] The legislative and juridical apparatus developed to deal with land simply reflected discursive mediation required to create a sedentary, productive population. These requirements constituted the imperative to define who worked, who had a residence, and who did not.

Discussion about the critical nature of agricultural activity concerned the fact that "agricultural" settlers (whether they were the vellalas or the paraiyars) were defined both as being different from and superior to those who preceded them. Predecessors included both the so-called kurumbar or "forest people" prior to the rise of Tondaimandalam as a cultural region and those people who wandered about the country—styled by the Indo-British administration as "criminal tribes." Similarly, people who practiced agriculture stood as very different from the brahmans of the Tamil country, who did not cultivate.

The discussion regarding the nature of the Tamil mirasi or coparcenary system set in motion by many British and local individuals in the late eighteenth and early nineteenth centuries, then, simply attempted to define what a sedentary, productive life should be. This project, often unwittingly pursued, claimed to foster various proprietary forms conceived to be the "indigenous" elements of local Tamil life. State support of these forms of proprietary behavior promoted sedentariness and raised the status of agriculture and productive labor among all of the Indian population while at the same time incorporating them into British law. It attempted to retain a coparcenary form of social, economic, and political behavior on the one hand while relating it to the British and European practice of individual ownership on the other. These activities were not a form of oppression or subjection. They were a way by which knowledge was created so that people would represent themselves in more interdependent ways.

They also promoted the definition of citizenship characteristic of a modern society based entirely on people who worked for their living and did not move. However, this interaction also encouraged the creation by Indian Mirasidars of a series of cultural productions designed to protect mirasi prerogatives, not only after the "insurrection of the Mirasidars" in the Jagir in 1795–96, but throughout the nineteenth century in Chingleput. One aspect of that "protection" took the form of providing oral histories in the Mackenzie manuscripts' accounts of the vellalas coming into Tondaimandalam to displace the kurumbar. Indeed, part of the definition of the vellalas as an important sedentary group in the Tondai area emerged from the production of texts by Tamil writers such as Rāmaliṅgaswāmi, Maraimalaiyatikal, and hundreds of other people. These texts had as their basis the ideas in a Tamil text called the *Toṇḍa Maṇḍala Satakam* (Hundred Verses on Tondaimandalam) and sought to demonstrate that the vellalas of the Tondai cultural areas possessed all the essential ingredients of successful, productive agriculturalists.

Another way the Mirasidars helped to "protect" the definition of mirasi was by resisting the assumption of arable land by people who were not Mirasidars, people who were considered "outsiders," such as sukavasis, and tenants or Payirkkaris. This general historical process intensified when Lionel Place in 1795–96 introduced cooperative tenants who paid taxes regularly. He could eliminate Mirasidars who did not support his attempts to raise taxes at the moment when the East India Company desperately needed money. Historically speaking, the cultural discussions arising out of and around the power struggle between the Mirasidars and the Payirkkaris or tenants became the single defining characteristic of Madras—specifically the Jagir, and later Chingleput—agriculture in the nineteenth and twentieth centuries. Throughout the nineteenth century, this historical process had its main effect in gradually pulling the Mirasidars away from highly taxed lands in favor of lands that were less so. The Mirasidars pursued this policy to reduce the yearly income from land as a way to set long-term taxation rates at a low level. This occurred at the same time as the proposed "invasion" by tenants, some of whom had been paraiyar Pannaiyals.

Part of this "protection" also involved tracing elements of the society who did not move at all. Not the vellalas but the paraiyars themselves proved to be by far the most persistent and most sedentary element of the population from this perspective. This project was carried out by the paraiyars in the thousands of Tondaimandalam villages and also by British writers such as F. W. Ellis, Mullaly in the 1880s, and J. H. A. Tremenheere shortly afterward. Ellis's attempt clearly explicated the nature of the project when he argued that the paraiyars had lasted over the years in the Tondai country long after other elements of the population had been destroyed by invasions because nobody paid attention to them.

Henry Baden-Powell also demonstrated the nature of this project when, in his *Land Systems of British India,* he claimed that the authors of the passage by Ellis quoted above were the Mirasidars themselves.[3] Behind this argument lay a system of heteroglossia in which Ellis argued views that had been constructed collaboratively with local individuals to produce "truth." These statements were then taken over by C. S. Crole in his *Chingleput Manual,* who quoted them in a changed form. Baden-Powell next quoted these remarks from Crole as being authored by the "new Mirasidars," who had wheedled mirasi rights away from the vellalas, who were said to be their "original owners."[4]

The Voices that Help to Create "Authentic Tamils"

When the Madras Native Association formed in 1855, it asserted that a village tax settlement, rather than the individual settlement that had been newly brought in by the ryotwari system, was "consonant to native usage."[5] The project in which many individuals and groups—Ellis and his brahman assistant Shankarayya, Place and his Tamil and Telugu informants, and hundreds of other people from Mirasidars to paraiyar Pannaiyals and Padiyals—had been engaged now had a formal Indian political voice.

One of the main goals of the ryotwari system had been to give each cultivator a title deed or patta and to assess each cultivator for taxes he owed the government in cash. In 1796, Mirasidars in the Jagir numbered 8,387 out of a total population of 271, 371.[6] By 1850, however, out of a population of 583, 462, the number of individual assessed holdings in the district had risen to 28,396, held by 33,124 persons.[7] As opposed to this, the idealized system of mirasi that had been "exhumed by Place" from the rubble of the war of 1780, and which the ryotwari system of tax assessment was seeking in part to alter, always presumed the necessity for a "productive, sedentary village community" where the Mirasidars acted in common to deal collectively with the state's tax demands.[8] We can therefore say that the combined effect of the interaction of "ryotwari" with the "common village system of mirasi" generally provoked reasons for retaining the Mirasidars as the land controllers even though their existence complicated the tax collection process immensely and greatly impoverished the state. Retention, in its turn, both presumed and fostered a sense of collectivity that could be translated into political action. Even in 1891, Tremenheere felt that the combined effects of British legislation and mirasi manipulation of that legislation had perpetuated a sense of Mirasidar commonality that excluded outsiders. He wrote that "the mirasidars form a close body accustomed to act together, and consolidated by tradition, prejudice and self interest. Surrounded for a century by ryots hungry for an extension of holdings, they have succeeded marvelously in keeping these at bay."[9] One of the main effects of British and Indian practice, legislation, and thinking about the "sedentary village community" in the Tondai area, then, was to help to perpetuate the boundary between the Mirasidars and the rest of the agrarian community.

Mirasidars did not speak alone on the Indian side of this dialogue. An early attempt by an Indian to relate the vellalas to agriculture was made by a religious leader named Ramalingaswami (d. 1875). More famous for his formulations of a new kind of civil religion (marking the transition toward a new civil society) that he articulated in his *Tiruvaruṭ Pā* (Song of grace), Ramalingaswami also wrote in 1855 a commentary on the *Tonda Mandala Satakam*. The first line of introduction to that poem says that the *Satakam* is about "vellalas who are like a cloud" that brings prosperity.[10] Besides the contents of the poem itself, Ramalingaswami's commentary provided a sustained attempt to describe the vellalas of the Tondai country in terms of their peculiar abilities both as agriculturists and as persons of great generosity. In addition to their ability to overcome all opponents, Ramalingaswami wrote that the vellalas "through agriculture produced wealth both for this mandalam [or sociocultural region] and for the other groups who live there."[11] According to him, the vellalas were "benefactors who give without limit . . . without dreaming of a reward." Because of their agricultural equipment and what they produced in agriculture, not even the most powerful could do without them. They supported all forms of life wherever they were. They were persons of deep learning and high morality and were also successful warriors. They had aided kings who had ancient lineages. They were people of honesty and compassion:

> The vellala group through their good behavior, that is their competence [as agriculturists], leads the cloud to make it rain here and there, and of all the five tinais [Tamil emotive-cultural areas differentiated by land use, ecology, and behavior], they make the marutam tinai [paddy land] prosperous that gives life and protects it. They become the kings of the agricultural sacrifice and are those who possess the instruments for agriculture that give results and never fail.[12]

Like Indra who led the fertility-bringing cloud, Vishnu who protected, and Lakshmi who shone brilliantly as the goddess of wealth, the vellalas were endeared to everybody. "They give sweet tasting nectar to those who ask for it, they always stand [possessing the earth], and have a right to the earth goddess, they behave with the good quality of sattuvam [goodness, purity] and they are those who possess straightforwardness and courage."[13]

During the 1880s, discussions arose about the position of the vellalas in the Hindu varna system that formed part of the Indo-British definition of Hindu society (as perpetuated through the new census). Vellala groups in Madras asserted to the census commissioner that they formed part of the vaisiya varna group and were not sudras.[14] They sought support for these claims through a wide variety of literary sources in Tamil, Telugu, and English. However, by far the most persistent attempt to define the ritual and cultural status of the vellalas came through a series of books and articles written by another Tamil writer named Maraimalaiyatikal (d. 1950). His thesis, explored in a book called *Vēḷāḷar Nākarikam* (Vellala civilization) published originally in 1923, asserted that it was "the vellalas themselves who had been responsible for correcting and 'civilizing' the Aryas [or Aryan Brahmans], [for] originating Śaivite worship and the Tamil language, and through the civilization of our Sentamil̲ [pure Tamil] people, were living in a civilized way, [a style] which had existed from the earliest times."[15] After he had described how vellalas had given food, clothing, and shelter to what he says were uncivilized Aryans, he concluded that the meaning of the word "vellala" was "benefactor" and that the meaning of the Tamil word "vēlān̲mai," which is usually taken to mean simply "agriculture" (on which the word "vellala" was based), meant, rather, "help and charity."[16]

He sought to eliminate the signification "agriculture" and replace it with "charity" or "generosity." This replacement is important, given that the essential characteristic of contemporary Tamil society was considered to be generosity and charity. Later in the twentieth century, as Arjun Appadurai and Carole Breckenridge have noted, the Indian preoccupation with the connection between prosperity and generosity has given way to a preoccupation with prosperity and acquisition.[17] In the 1920s, however, Maraimalaiyatikal said that the Āryas, unlike the Tamil vellalas, showed little pity for the sick and the poor since they could not empathize with the difficult life that these poverty-stricken people led. The vellalas also helped to protect all forms of life instead of killing them. They developed the tradition of reciting the books that had been written by their forefathers. He concluded that the word "velanmai," which he felt was a synonym for charity, in turn became a synonym for the instruments of productive cultivation.

Ultimately, then, these two qualities, charity and the instruments of agriculture, became the synonyms for the ruling vellalas.[18] "During ancient times when the vellalas enhanced civilization and carried on agriculture, the Aryans were shepherds who herded cattle and sheep and lived by hunting."[19] The Aryas, that is, were mere wanderers and nomads and were not agriculturalists. They were, so to speak, the opposite of being productive according to his definition. By quoting selections of the *Mānava Dharmaśāstra*, a Sanskrit text that argued that good Aryans should deliberately not engage in cultivation, Maraimalaiyatikal sought to show that the Aryans had condemned the practice. By contrast, he wrote, all books in both Tamil and Sanskrit said that agriculture was peculiar to the vellalas. Maraimalaiyatikal also quoted a number of Tamil texts to prove the centrality of agriculture to the development of civilization in the Tamil area. He specifically referred to the *Tirukural* or sacred *Kural,* one of the most ancient texts in Tamil, to illustrate this point. It said that "those who practice agriculture are the most excellent in the world" and also that "those who have the character of eating (subsisting) by doing things with their hands / Do not beg and do not hide even a single thing from those who do beg."[20]

An extension of this privileging of the vellalas came in Maraimalaiyatikal's contention that, as opposed to those who performed other sorts of tasks, the vellalas as agriculturalists did not work for other people. They were dependent on nobody. Maraimalaiyatikal had previously called himself Swami Vēdāchalam and was preoccupied with discovering what were the origins of what he believed was Tamil culture. As part of his general project to characterize this civilization, he wrote that "the English authors of books concerning both the origins of people and the development of civilization have demonstrated clearly that from the very beginning it was from the people who had discovered agriculture that civilization originated and developed."[21]

One such British author was Baden-Powell, who remarked in his *Land Systems of British India,* in connection with the discussion concerning Mirasidars in the Tondai country, that

> we have an instance of the formation of joint-villages over a considerable area: the strength of the claim to the allotted areas and the principle of sharing it, being due not to the growth of particular chiefs grantees of the State, or scions of noble houses, but to the co-operative work of colonists, of a good agricultural caste, who in virtue of their conquest over natural difficulties, and of their equal rights, formed bodies which exhibited marks of coherence.[22]

Further on, Baden-Powell says that the "colonists were of the Vellalar caste, or tribe, who are good agriculturists." In a footnote, he says that the word "vellalar" is from "vēlan," which he says means "white." Nevertheless, contrary to Maraimalaiyatikal, Baden-Powell also says they have some "Aryan blood: Their tradition derives from the North. It is possible that there may be some connection between them and the Kunbis or Kurmis, who are such excellent cultivators."[23]

As we have seen, in the project to create a sedentarized peasantry, participants used techniques and ideas from a variety of times and places. The images and tactics of "General" William Booth and other reformers of urban life in nineteenth-century Britain were employed to "fix" the rural paraiyar and palli tenants in their houses. At the same time, the poverty of the tenants and Padiyals was used in Britain as a way to identify bourgeois values and requirements for citizenship in Britain. Simultaneously, this process resulted, in the period starting in the eighteenth century in South India, in banditry and nomadic behavior becoming totally unacceptable. Therefore, ancient values about agriculture were transformed by modern requirements into "essentialist" values. They were presented as though there had been no societal or structural change in two thousand years. In fact, the project to sedentarize the agricultural community in the modern period had a very different set of requirements, responding as it did to the demands of a unitary state with bureaucratic needs in an increasingly embedded society. Embeddedness altered fundamentally the nature of South Indian society: violence became more and more a prerogative of the center and could be used less and less openly; sacrality became less concentrated in the king or the deity and was dissipated into the bodies of the many individuals of the countryside (in a sense, anybody could be a king); people became more interdependent in society and were more restrained by these ties.

Implications of Heteroglossia and Historical Dialogue

Recognizing the epistemological moments important in the dialogic process by which South Indian history has been produced leads me to different conclusions than those reached by other scholars. The fact that Tamil Sangam literature exulted in the material culture of the time (c. A.D. 300), for instance, has been used by scholars such as Christopher Baker to argue a linear development between the fourth century and the nineteenth, when the project of sedentarization preoccupied those in South India. He rightly notes that three things stood out in this fourth-century enthusiasm. One he calls a celebration of the agricultural economy on which the civilization was founded; another, the classification of the ecological regions or tinais, firmly stressed the superiority of arable land; and the third, the combination of fertile agriculture and martial prowess, laid the basis for a proudly aristocratic culture.[24] Baker is correct in emphasizing the importance placed on agriculture by Sangam society. However, the linear connection he seeks is more problematic. We must keep firmly in mind that the moral values that came to be associated with the immobile peasant in "ancient" villages were dialogically constructed evaluations produced in the eighteenth and the nineteenth centuries, using the models of another time and place to deal with modern needs. In other words, because the society, economy, and polity had changed, the intellectual and moral requirements for those new structures necessarily differed as well. Therefore, we cannot equate the agricultural emphases of the Sangam period and those of the nineteenth century.

Similarly, Nicholas Dirks has shown that where vellalas settled in the Pudukottai region south of Madras they became known as good agriculturalists.[25] He also notes that, unlike many of the maravars and the kallars who were declared to be criminal tribes by the Indo-British administration, the vellalas stood as the caste that met British expectations as loyal and productive supporters of the administration.[26] Here, Dirks has usefully pinpointed the importance of the vellalas for the eighteenth-, nineteenth-, and twentieth-century project of constructing agriculture's premier position in the Tamil area. However, he does not stress the fact that these ideas about the vellalas as good agriculturists were historical creations out of the past dialogically produced for contemporary requirements. Their characterization did not emerge as a product of the British alone but formed a project resulting from many voices, high and low, past and present. Nor was vellala loyalty and agricultural productivity important merely because it was supported and recognized by the British. Rather, the recognition granted to these concepts could not have the authority it gained without participation from all levels of society.

Projects to populate the Chingleput district had been undertaken by Europeans and Indians since the Company acquired the Jagir from the Nawab of Arcot in 1783. The intellectual work group included a wide variety of individuals. It involved the committee of assigned revenue, who supported the settling of a Telugu Christian population by the Jesuit Padre Manente from Guntur in the vicinity of the Jagir village of Mappedu; Place, who had bamboo and fruit groves planted near Karanguli; the local assistants of Colonel Colin Mackenzie and their active and interested informants, who were delighted or felt incited to speak about the arrival of the vellalas in the Tondai area; and the local informants of Ellis, who evoked the kurumbar souls in and about the mounds of mud at Nerumbur and other areas.[27] Throughout the middle of the century, district officials interacting with the Mirasidars, Payirkkaris, and Padiyals became deeply involved in this activity. Mullaly in the latter part of the century wanted to destroy the perceived chaos of prickly pear and unruly paraiyar cheris to sedentarize and make the paraiyars more useful. Reverend Adam Andrew, a missionary of the United Church of Scotland in Chingleput town, established a village called Melrosapuram in 1894 as one of three pristine sites for Christians from the area created from the "chaos" of the scrub jungle.[28] Henry Sumner Maine used the materials from the official publication *Papers* on *Mirasi Right* to create an imaginary Tondaimandalam from the verses of the Tamil paraiyar poetess Auvaiyar.[29] The author or authors of the *Tonda Mandala Satakam,* Ramalingaswami's commentary on that text, and Maraimalaiyatikal all sought to populate and make sedentary the population of the Jagir or the Tondai country. This list employs socially accepted ideas of authorship, but we must include in this group the many nameless individuals in the thousands of villages and towns of the area and elsewhere who participated in this cultural production. Maraimalaiyatikal later incorporated many of these heteroglot interactions in works published up to the present. Most significantly, these ideas have become an important part of the religious and political culture of contemporary Tamil Nadu during the nineteenth and twentieth centuries.

Indeed, what later came to be called the Non-Brahman movement is an outgrowth of this general world project that linked ethnicity with sedentariness and culture. The Non-Brahman movement, in seeking to displace brahmans from positions in the administration and politics, hastened a general demographic project already in operation to move brahmans out of the villages to the cities of the region, to other cities in India, and elsewhere. Though it began as an elitist movement, during the 1930s and after World War II it became a mass movement that sought to make society more equal not only between men and men but also between men and women. By the years after World War II, the "land of the Tamils" had become firmly wedded to "the culture of the Tamils." The Non-Brahman movement was therefore based in part on constructions interacting with two ideas of spatiality that operated in the area before the coming of the Europeans. One of those was represented by the right subcastes such as the vellalas, who had a strong sense of local connection whether they lived there customarily or not. Their institutions and temples placed them in a local regime. In a sense, the castes that belonged to this right hand were local agrarian communities that did not consider themselves to be a part of a wider psychic and intellectual community. Their perspectives were typically those that situated the local regime in a place of prime importance. Unlike these right subcastes, those in the left division had a special outlook that denied the prime validity of local division and local loyalty. The spatial orientation of these left-caste groups such as the sengunthars was to a much wider region. This involved their senses of both politics and religious practices. Not only did the subcastes of the left move much more, this mobility gave them a totally different idea of what constituted the total social and the political community, for the making of a modern nation. As noted in Chapter 2, one of these left groups, the kailolars or sengunthars, looked on themselves as having a particular responsibility to Tamil as a language and used it as a cultural tool to spread Tamil beyond the traditional boundaries of that language. In the case study to which we referred, these sengunthars still see themselves as performing a kind of sacred cultural role in reciting the Tamil Ramayanam.

This is important for a study of the way in which cultural nationalism developed in the Tamil area before the availability of modern means of communication. The most publicized elements in the Non-Brahman movement were undertaken by individuals of the left division, many of whom later played dual roles in film and politics. Many of their forebears had relations to temples and to the performing arts. Their skills as orators and as showmen were directly related to these performance functions in society. These individuals took it upon themselves to propagate Tamil as the basis of a cultural movement, whether in the specifically nativist Self Respect movement or in the Indian National Congress. Significantly, these left subcastes—who were made a part of the sedentarizing process by a series of dialogic activities and felt themselves responsible for the propagation of Tamil—still had broad spatial orientations that predated the sedentarization process described in these pages. It is primarily these people who were effective in using spoken or written Tamil.

We can say that by the end of the nineteenth century the sedentarization of the Tamil population meant that the local constitutive cultural elements of the region were in place. At the same time, one of the main effects of the cultural discussions occurring during the nineteenth century over the cultural role of Tondamandalam was to create a center for Tamil culture. In other words, the dialogic process helped to formulate what was seen to be quintessentially Tamil in spatial terms. This provided the idea of the original Dravidians as having been in the territory from the time of the beginning of the Christian era. The identification of Tamil culture with agriculture helped to sacralize all villages as thousands of points of light on what came to be considered the broad and sacred map of the Tamil country. The creation of this sacred map and sacred community enabled C. N. Annadurai, born in Kanchipuram and a member of the sengunthar left-caste group, to proclaim that "everybody is a king of the country."[30] It was almost two centuries from the time when Place and his Tamil and Telugu informants undertook to make a new kind of more useful religion that related religiosity to pleasure and productivity. From that time until the time of Annadurai, both the villages as points of light and the broad canvas of the Tamil country were constituted into one continuous sociopsychic structure.

Therefore, though Tamil was given a new kind of sacrality in the course of the cultural discussions in the century between 1890 and the present, the place of "Dravidian culture" on which these discussions built referred back to an old set of relationships that combined spatial with sacral ideas over the use of Tamil. Thus, the rather facile connections scholars make between the creation of nationalism and the hegemonic discourse of the imperial state tell but a small part of the picture. If we are to understand the processes that created a sense of place connected to powerful cultural identities, we must look to a much broader and more inclusive dialogue. The example of South India shows us how a dialogue in history has prepared the way for a modern nation.

Abbreviations

ARL	Assigned Revenue Letterbooks
BC	Board's Collections
BARP	Board of Assigned Revenue Proceedings
BOR	Board of Revenue
BORP	Board of Revenue Proceedings, Madras and London
CCR	Chingleput Collectorate Records
GO	Government Order
HMS	Home Miscellaneous Series
IOL	India Office Library and Records, London
JB	Jaghire Books
JR	Jagir Records
LR	Land Revenue
MB	Miscellany Book
MCR	Madras Collectorate Records
MOML	Madras Oriental Manuscripts Library, Madras
NLS	National Library of Scotland, Edinburgh
PCP	Police Committee Proceedings

PL   Private Letterbooks

PP   Public Proceedings

RSLRA   Revenue Settlement, Local Records, and Agriculture

SCPSP   Special Commission on the Permanent Settlement
          Proceedings

TNSA   Tamil Nad State Archives, Madras

UFCSM   United Free Church of Scotland Mission Archives

Notes

1. Lionel Place, Report on the Jagir, 1799 (hereafter Place, 1799 Report), para. 164, BOR, Misc., vol. 45, TNSA.

2. Mark Wilks, *Historical Sketches of the South of India in an Attempt to Trace the History of Mysoor,* ed. Murray Hammick (1810; reprint, Mysore: Government Branch Press, 1930), 1:2.

3. Place, 1799 Report, para. 95.

4. We know that Englishmen performed a version of dharna (a hunger strike to force a person to pay a sum of money) on the Nawab of Arcot either to get back money that the Nawab owed them or to get him to do things that he did not want to do. It has been shown that Lord Pigot, governor of Madras, in early 1776, shortly before the "revolution" that removed him from power, sought to place a close surveillance on the relations of the Nawab of Arcot with the Muslim prince Hyder Ali and to assure the return of certain important areas (Arni, Sivaganga, Ramnad, Ariyalur, and Variyarpalayam). Lord Pigot accomplished this by a hunger strike directed against the Nawab. Paul Benfield, an English merchant and moneylender, also used this tactic on many occasions against the Nawab of Arcot to get his tankhwahs—assignments on the taxes of certain tracts of land—paid. John Gurney, "The Debts of the Nawab of Arcot," (Ph.D. diss., Oxford University, 1964), 303. Benfield was by training an engineer and civil architect. It was his demands for restitution for claims on the Nawab relating to some of the revenues of Tanjore that were the basis of the "revolution" that overthrew Lord Pigot. H. Davidson Love, *Vestiges of Old Madras, 1640–1800* (London: John Murray, 1913), 3:104.

In 1760, Eyre Coote was leaving Kanchipuram on his way to Vandavasi (in the contemporary South Arcot district) to fight the French under the command of Lally. Coote was at Uttiramerur, southwest of Madras town, where his progress was impeded by the lack of grain for his troops. Coote found that "the renter [tax farmer], though he depended on Madras [i.e., the British], had sold his store [of rice] to some agents, probably employed by the French at Sadras [on the coast forty miles south of Madras]; on which he was seized, and confined without eating, until the army was supplied; and his people in a few hours brought enough for the immediate want, and promised more." Robert Orme, *Transactions of the British Nation in Indostan,* 2d ed. (London: John Nourse, 1775), 3:576.

5. Eric Hobsbawm and Terence Ranger, eds., *The Invention of Tradition* (Cambridge: Cambridge University Press, 1983).

6. A Native Revenue Officer, *On Bribery as Practiced in the Revenue administration of the Madras Presidency* (Madras: Hindu Press, 1858), 15.

7. In the pages that follow, I use the word "power" in two different senses. When I speak about "juridical" power, I refer to the capacity to coerce an individual or a group by violence or the sanctions of law. When I use the word "power" without any modifier, I refer to the function that discourse has on the creation of values that constrains individuals.

8. Edward Said, *Orientalism* (New York: Vintage Books, 1978), 204.

9. Place to BOR, 10 September 1798, BC, no. 2109, IOL.

10. See the account in Bernard S. Cohn, "Representing Authority in Victorian India," in *An Anthropologist Among the Historians and Other Essays* (Delhi: Oxford University Press, 1990), 658, in which the dominant British rulers sought desperately to freeze and "make manifest and compelling the sociology of India." This darbar of 1877, says Cohn, sought to invite participants "in relation to ideas which the British rulers had about the proper social order in India."

11. For a view of the state as "limited," see Anand Yang, *The Limited Raj: Agrarian Relations in Colonial India, Saran District, 1793–1920* (Berkeley: University of California Press, 1990), Judith M. Brown, *Gandhi: Prisoner of Hope* (New Haven: Yale University Press, 1989), 390. Brown writes, "The British raj was a light-handed, amateur affair compared to the state of the later twentieth century, with its greatly increased numbers of employees and functionaries, its bigger revenues, higher expenditure on the army and the police, its economic planning and control of the economy through directives and a pervasive system of licenses."

For a view of the state as "repressive," Gyanendra Pandey, " 'Encounters and Calamities': The History of a North Indian Qasba in the Nineteenth Century," in Ranajit Guha and Gayatri Spivak, eds., *Selected Subaltern Studies* (New York: Oxford University Press, 1988), 122–23. Pandey writes, "What the advent of colonialism meant for the people of Mubarakpur is perhaps not unfairly summed up in the following terms: more rigorous administrative demands and control following the establishment of a centralized colonial powers; improved communications, increased traffic and a significant change in the direction of the cloth trade; and higher prices of food and of the raw materials needed for the local cloth industry, at least for important stretches of time."

12. Ashis Nandy, *The Intimate Enemy: Loss and Recovery of Self Under Colonialism* (Delhi: Oxford University Press, 1983).
13. Nandy, *Intimate,* xiv–xv, 32.
14. See the account of the "meaning" attached to Gandhi in Shahid Amin, "Gandhi as Mahatma," in Ranajit Guha and Gayatri Spivak, eds., *Selected Subaltern Studies* (New York: Oxford University Press, 1988), 288–350.
15. M. M. Bakhtin, *The Dialogic Imagination: Four Essays,* trans. Caryl Emerson and Michael Holquist, ed. Michael Holquist (Austin: University of Texas Press, 1981); Bakhtin, *Rabelais and His World,* trans. Helene Iswolsky (Cambridge, Mass.: M. I. T. Press, 1968).
16. Alvin Gouldner, *The Two Marxisms* (New York: The Seabury Press, 1980), quoted in Richard Fox, *Gandhian Utopia: Experiments with Culture* (Boston: Beacon Press, 1989), 72; H. M. Collins, "The Core-Set in Modern Science," *History of Science,* 19:6–19, quoted in Fox, *Utopia,* 82.

CHAPTER 1

1. During the war of 1780, the inhabitants of the village of Paruttipattu, in the present-day Saidapettai taluk, stayed in the fort at Poonamallee about twelve miles from Fort St. George. Others who remained there were betel growers from Uttiramerur (in the Jagir southwest of Madras), Vandavasi (in what was later called the North Arcot district), Narinaveram, and Kalahasti. Some of the villagers from Paruttipattu made an agreement to grow betel leaves there. As a result Paruttipattu became an important source for the betel leaf chewed in Madras. Dighton to Charles Oakley and Members of the Committee for Managing the Jaghire, 25 June 1785, JB, vol. 8, TNSA. Another important center was the village of Numbal. Charles Baker to BOR, 6 January 1798, MB, BORP, R. 286/3, IOL.
2. Wilks, *Historical Sketches,* 2:2.
3. This is what has been characterized as "military fiscalism" by David Washbrook in "Progress and Problems: South Asian Economic and Social History c. 1720–1860," *Modern Asian Studies* 22, no. 1 (February 1988): 89.
4. Comm. of Assigned Revenue to Governor in Council, 31 January 1785, BARP, vol. 8, TNSA.
5. Comm. of Assigned Revenue to Governor Lord Macartney, 7 August 1783, BARP, vol. 4, TNSA.
6. W. J. Wilson, *History of the Madras Army* (Madras: E. Keys at the Government Press, 1882), 1:100.
7. Wilks, *Historical Sketches,* 2:22.
8. Quoted in Love, *Vestiges,* 3:210.
9. Mattison Mines and Vijayalakshmi Gourishankar, "Leadership and Individuality in South Asia: The Case of the South Indian Big Man," *Journal of Asian Studies* 49, no. 4 (November 1990), 776. The Kamatci idol was carried off to the Udayarpalayam jungles in what was then the domain of the Raja of Tanjore many miles to the south. The image of Kamatci was made of gold,

called the Bangaru Kamatci, and it is said that the Raja of Tanjore took possession of it. This image was then installed in the Bangaru Kamatci temple in
Tanjore.

10. Letter of John Baillie, a cadet in the Madras Army, to his father, 14 June
1784, HMS, vol. 223, IOL. An account of the battle was also published in
Hickey's Bengal Gazette, 23–30 September 1780. Quoted in Love, *Vestiges*,
3:200.

11. C. S. Crole, *The Chingleput, late Madras, District* (Madras: Lawrence
Asylum Press, 1879), 126.

12. Cloth version shown in "Tigers Round the Throne" Exhibition in London, Zamana Gallery, August 1990. In 1991, in a video presentation by Granada Television called *Empire!* commentator John Keay transformed the British
commander Sir Hector Munro into Thomas Munro, a later governor of Madras
and a well-known figure in Britain. *Empire!* was concerned with showing that
the Great Trigonometrical Survey of India helped not only to define its exact
boundaries but also to "control" the subcontinent with a series of triangles that
would imprison India. In *Empire!* scenes from Tipu's mural of the battle of
Pullalur were shown and John Keay argued that the battle of Pullalur (in which,
he said, eight thousand men were either killed or lost) was a classic example of
a battle in which there were no good maps.

13. Proclamation of John Chamier, secretary to the government, 7 August
1790, BARP, vol. 1, TNSA. This had been done several times in the past without
any effect, many times because the Company employees had presumed that their
moneylending activities would not be abridged. Furthermore, in the 1770s, the
money that Company servants lent to Indian tax farmers was essential to allow
the Company to later extract its taxes from the Jagir.

14. Wilson, *Madras Army*, 2:142.

15. In 1749, the Company acquired St. Thome, which produced pagodas
6,346 a year in taxes; Poonamallee produced pagodas 35,000 a year; Triven-
dipuram (in the present-day South Arcot district) produced pagodas 26,250 a
year; and a remission on the tribute or peshkash for Madras amounted to pagodas 1,200 a year. Gurney, "Debts," 31.

16. The grant appears to have been coerced from the Nawab. According to
him, he had several encounters with Pigot, who was governor in 1763. "At
first," wrote the Nawab, "he asked me in very civil terms for a few villages,
afterwards he wanted four parganahs [territorial subdivisions] and when I required the conditions under his hand he answered me in severe terms and demanded twice as much as he first asked for. I am not so weak a person as to
grant the Jaghire which is the choicest part of my country to the Company
without any conditions in my favour, while my debt to the Company and to
individuals and a long arrears of pay to my sepoys etc. remains undischarged."
Nawab Muhammad Ali to Governor Du Pré, 26 November 1770, HMS, vol.
113, IOL.
Dimensions of the Jagir are taken from "British Acquisitions in the Presidency of Fort St. George," *Madras Journal of Literature and Science*, 1879, 121.

17. Phillimore, author of the account of the survey of India, refers to a series
of maps that were produced of the Baramahal. These maps of the area, which

later became the Salem district, came into the possession of the British in 1792 as a part of the treaty with Tipu Sultan. They were made by John Mather, a man engaged by Captain Alexander Read. Philmore notes that the survey of the Baramahal "was the most thorough and complete survey of any district in India made since Barnard's survey of the Madras jagir." *Historical Records of the Survey of India,* collected by R. H. Phillimore (Dehra Dun: 1945) 1:114.

18. Place to BOR, 27 March 1796, BORP, vol. 161, TNSA.

19. Gurney, in his study of the Nawab of Arcot's debts, said that Barnard put the income of the Jagir in 1762–66 at pagodas 275,372 a year, in addition to which the Nawab also issued a large number of individual land grants. Gurney, "Debts," 52.

20. President and Council and the Jaghire Committee to Collector, November 1784, CCR, vol. 441, 1784, TNSA.

21. "The Committee have besides sufficient reason to be assured that this attack of the Kallans was occasioned by Col. Herron's carrying away a large number of the religious images from *Kovilkudi* Pagoda [temple]." S. C. Hill, *Yusuf Khan: The Rebel Commandant* (London: Longmans, Green and Co., 1914), 42n.

22. Crole, *Chingleput,* 117.

23. Governor to Lt. Joachim Lundt, Commanding at Chandragiri, 31 January 1785, ARL, vol. 13, TNSA.

24. Jaghire Committee to Superintendent, 23 May 1785, CCR, vol. 441, 1784, TNSA.

25. The word "tom" is an Indian word that seems to be an onomatopoeia, "not belonging to any language in particular." Henry Yule and A. C. Burnell, *Hobson-Jobson* (1903; reprint, New Delhi: Munshiram Manoharlal, 1968), 929.

26. The tamukku was used in Madras by municipal officials to communicate decisions and policy in the scavengers' and street cleaners' settlements until the 1940s. In this particular case, it was remarked that troops would be sent if necessary. Jaghire Committee to Resident in the Jaghire, 12 May 1786, CCR, vol. 441, 1784–86, TNSA.

27. Richard Dighton to BOR, 16 February 1787, BORP, vol. 6, TNSA.

28. Richard Dighton to the President and Committee for Managing the Jaghire Farms, 20 January 1785, Extract from the Madras Revenue Proceedings, HMS, vol. 259, IOL.

29. Nattars were heads of the right subcastes such as the Tamil-speaking Tondaimandala vellalas. Right and left castes are terms applied to a series of caste groups in South India, and particularly in the Tamil area. In South Indian society, as in many other cultures, the left hand has many associations with impurity, while the right hand has many positive ideas associated with it. However, according to Arjun Appadurai, the use of "right" and "left" expresses not only a particular contrast or even opposition but also is a manifestation of "the unity of conflicting units." This is the formal function of the idea of right and left castes. Arjun Appadurai, "Right and Left Hand Castes in South India," *Indian Economic and Social History Review* 11, nos. 2, 3 (June–September 1974): 221–22. At the risk of oversimplifying, we can say that though there are

exceptions, right subcastes were mostly agrarian and left subcastes were artisan and other groups. As noted in the Introduction, moreover, right and left subcastes had different spatial orientations. Right subcastes were more rooted in a given locality and worshipped at local temples. Left subcastes worshipped at more distant and even regional temples. Right subcastes looked on the left subcastes as being ritually inferior.

30. Richard Dighton to the President and Committee for Managing the Jaghire Farms, 20 January 1785, Extract from the Madras Revenue Proceedings, HMS, vol. 259, IOL.

31. See Bernard Cohn, "Political Systems of Eighteenth Century India," *Anthropologist Among the Historians*, 484. See also the comments in André Wink, *Land and Sovereignty in India* (Cambridge: Cambridge University Press, 1986), 190, 199, 206.

32. Alexander Read to Board of Revenue, 31 March 1793, BORP, vol. 9, TNSA.

33. Board of Revenue to Government of Madras, 13 April 1793, BORP, vol. 70, TNSA.

34. Minute of C. N. White, 21 October 1793, BORP, vol. 81, TNSA. The benefits that were to be granted to the lower classes were only one way by which this great increase in tax revenues could be rationalized.

35. According to an account presented in Love's *Vestiges of Old Madras*, the British in 1779 expected to derive about pagodas 2,969,109 from all sources. Of that amount, the Nawab was responsible for pagodas 700,000 and the Raja of Tanjore for pagodas 400,000, while the taxes from the circars (which came into the hands of the British in 1767) provided pagodas 776,800. The combined revenues of the Jagir and Poonamallee (both rented out to the Nawab of Arcot himself) were pagodas 368,350. However, none of this was a product of a European officer dealing directly with the Company tax employees. Love, *Vestiges,* 3:142.

36. G. R. Gleig, *The Life of Major General Sir Thomas Munro, Bart.* (London: Henry Colburn and Richard Bently, 1831), 1:161–62; minute by Lionel Place on his resignation from the Special Commission, 7 October 1802, BC, F/4/150, IOL, complaining about the appointments of Thomas Munro, Alexander Read, and John Ravenshaw; and letter from Benjamin Roebuck to Paul Benfield, 3 March 1795, PL, vol. 41, TNSA.

37. C. N. White, Minute 23 December 1793, BORP, vol. 88, TNSA.

38. Minute of C. N. White, member of the Board of Revenue, 21 October 1793, BORP, vol. 81, TNSA. These reports were from John Clerk, the collector of the northern division on 31 August 1793, and from Walter Balfour, the collector of the southern division on 10 October 1793.

39. C. N. White Minute, 23 December 1793, BORP, vol. 88, TNSA. The annual tax income from the Jagir in this period (1786–93), in round numbers, was (in pagodas):

1786–87	115,180
1787–88	176,534
1788–89	111,806

1789–90	162,617
1790–91	53,941
1791–92	141,182
1792–93	193,107
Average	136,332

40. F. G. Bailey, *Stratagems and Spoils* (Oxford: Basil Blackwell, 1969), 1.

41. Bailey, *Stratagems,* 172.

42. BOR Minute on Badarnavisi, 30 June 1796, BORP, vol. 168, TNSA. In 1828–29, the total cultivated area was only 88,769 kanis (about 264,087 acres), whereas by 1850–51 it was 162,828 kanis (484,413 acres). A. Sarada Raju, *Economic Conditions in the Madras Presidency, 1800–1850* (Madras: University of Madras Press, 1941), 64. In 1940, the proportion of wet cultivation to dry cultivation was 605,500 acres sown in wet and 332,600 sown in dry. "Statistical Atlas for the Decennium ending Fasli 1350 (1940–41): Chingleput," in *A Statistical Atlas of the Madras Province* (Madras: Superintendent, Government Press, 1949), 453.

43. Benedicte Hjejle, "Slavery and agricultural bondage in south India in the nineteenth century," *The Scandinavian Economic History Review* 15, nos. 1–2 (1967), 80.

44. The early German Lutheran missionaries in Tranquebar in 1727 reported the baptism of a slave who had been beaten so badly by his master that he was about to die and had to be baptized right away. They said that he knew the Lord's prayer in Portuguese and something more about Christianity. *Der Königl. Dänischen Missionarien aus Ost-Indieneingesandter ausführlichen Berichten, Erster Theil, Vom ersten ausführlichen Bericht an bis zu dessen zwölfter Continuation mitgetheilet* (Halle: Verlegung des Weysenhauses, 1735); Continuation 25 (26 October 1727).

45. Dharma Kumar, *Land and Caste in South India: Agricultural Labour in the Madras Presidency During the Nineteenth Century* (Cambridge: Cambridge University Press, 1965), 41.

46. William Adam, *The Law and Custom of Slavery in British India* (Boston: Weeks, Jordan, and Company, 1840), 177.

47. Edgar Thurston, *The Tribes and Castes of South India* (Madras: Government Press, 1909), 7:380.

48. Lionel Place called this period "years of mutual robbery" when all parties "preyed on each other." Place, 1799 Report, para. 185.

49. See the discussion in Susan Neild-Basu, "The Dubashes of Madras," *Modern Asian Studies* 18, no. 1 (February 1984): 1–31.

50. Neild-Basu, "Dubashes," 11.

51. Place, 1799 Report, para. 218. Place's bête noire was a man named Kesava Mudaliar who "conducted frequent lavish festivities at the family-managed temple in his native Tottikkalai village." Neild-Basu, "Dubashes," 12. Walter Balfour, collector of the southern division of the Jagir in November 1791, wrote, "I only say 'formed an opinion' because no man (let his conceit be what it may) can possibly unravel or get to the bottom of the whole truth in any dispute between Black Men, more especially amongst those in the Jagheire,

who from their vicinity to Madras are daily engaged in intrigues and litigations, which are fermented, and kept up to such a degree that a collector has a most difficult part to act." Walter Balfour to BOR, 8 November 1791, BORP, vol. 51, TNSA.

52. Richard Dighton to Charles Oakley, 6 December 1785, JR, TNSA.

53. Lionel Place, 1795 Report, para. 20, in BORP, 25 January 1796, vol. 142.

54. Bailey, *Stratagems*, 172.

55. In 1791, John Clerk had pointed to the same set of strategies. He said that under a system of what was called amani tax collection (as opposed to a village settlement), in which the state had to collect the tax from each individual cultivator rather than (as in a village tax collection system) through a few head people, "it is impossible for one person to be guarded against the artifices, which all descriptions of the inhabitants find it in their interest to adopt in order to defraud the circar [the state]." John Clerk to BOR, 14 May 1791, BORP, vol. 46, TNSA.

56. Place, 1799 Report, para. 179. The previous section was based on paragraphs 174–79.

57. Committee of Revenue to the President and Council, July 1775, Appendix to a letter of John Turin to the Committee of Assigned Revenue, 31 March 1784, JR, vol. 3, TNSA.

58. Charles Oakley to Governor and President of Council, 17 December 1785, and John Chamier, Secretary to the President and Council, to Oakley, 24 December 1785, JR, vol. 5, TNSA.

59. John Clerk to William C. Jackson, Secretary to Military Department, 26 December 1791, BORP, vol. 40, TNSA. The matter of the "desertion" of the cultivators or their Pannaiyals (bonded laborers) was, naturally, of central importance. In May of that same year, when the horsemen of Tipu Sultan entered the Jagir, Clerk reported that "the crops have suffered very materially in several of the districts, by the enemy's horse, and by our own army, and the whole of the northern division of the Jaghire sustained a heavy loss in consequence of the entire desertion of the inhabitants, at a period when their presence was particularly necessary to cut and gather in the crop." John Clerk to BOR, 14 May 1791, BORP, vol. 46, TNSA. Walter Balfour, the collector of what was then referred to as the southern division of the Jagir reported that in early 1791, "The paddy fields presented every appearance of a rich and fruitful harvest and had the reapers not fled from the fields on account of the alarms it was generally supposed the crop would have been equal to the produce of [the revenue year] 1199 [1790–91]. The Board must be well aware the very reverse of this took place and before the reapers returned to the fields more than three fourths of the paddy was totally dried up and otherwise destroyed by the grazing and marauding of horses, cattle etc." Balfour also asked for authorization to recruit a group of armed retainers "as the only mode of preventing a total desertion of the ryots from the paddy fields." He said that if he were to attempt to leave Kovalam—on the coast south of Madras—"every inhabitant in this town and Tripalore would instantly desert their homes."

Seeking to illustrate how villagers would take advantage of any kind of armed invasion into the area to settle old scores or to deprive the tax collector of what he wanted, Balfour continued, "Those very memorialists who petitioned the Board absolutely stole from the Renter [of Salivakkam] between three and four thousand Calams of paddy which after a good deal of trouble on my part they openly confessed they had taken a part of but that they believed the looties had plundered the rest. Nay they absolutely paid back to the renter the amount or value of what they confessed to have taken and to show with what a vindictive spirit of revenge they were activated, and as if they only hated the man to injure him more deeply. They instantly repaired to Madras with a ready pen'd petition of which every third line is a falsehood. The other circumstance, which I alluded to, is the extreme modesty of the petitioners, who insist in their settlement with the renter that he shall pay their shares in money valuing the grain at the market price of the day. But the Board must be perfectly aware the Renter has nothing to do with this, but has only to pay them a certain quantity of grain agreeably to Mamool. . . . When the weather is a little settled I shall send for the meerassydars and other village servants together with the renter, and petitioners, and endeavour if possible to find out the real state of the cultivation for Phasely [Fasli] 1200." Walter Balfour to BOR, 8 November 1791, BORP, vol. 51, TNSA.

60. Ibid.

61. BOR to Governor in Council, 15 May 1796, BORP, vol. 156, TNSA.

62. One marakkal (or "marakkalam") was twenty-seven or twenty-eight pounds. Therefore, three marakkāls would be between about eighty-one and eighty-four pounds. One kalam was equal to twelve marakkals or approximately 336 pounds.

63. Hjejle, "Slavery," 81.

64. Place, 1799 Report, para. 136.

65. BOR Minute on Place's 1795 Report, 24 March 1796, BORP, vol. 151, TNSA.

66. John Turin to Committee on Assigned Revenues, 31 March 1784, JR, vol. 3, TNSA.

67. "Petition of Head Tenants," 25 July 1783, JR, vol. 2, TNSA. Even later, in 1807, after the zamindari settlement was introduced into the area the Company officers were confronted by requests that the Chembrambakkam tank near Poonamallee be repaired. One collector named Cazalet wrote that "the zamindaris watered by the tank have been assessed in proportion to the benefits calculated to be derived from the same and government receiving the marahs [merais] have engaged to keep this valuable reservoir in due repair the Zamindar of Colatore [southwest of the tank] one of the principal landholders under this tank has frequently stated the necessity of more being done than the repair now submitted." Cazelet to BOR, 22 April 1807, BC, no. 7177, IOL.

68. The Mayor's Court was originally established by the charter of 1687 and could try all civil or criminal cases and punish offenders by imposing fines, imprisonment, or even corporal punishment. Love, *Vestiges*, 1:499.

69. Charles Oakley to the Governor in Council, 6 January 1786, JR, vol. 6, TNSA.

70. A pagoda was worth about rupees 3.5. Dighton to Oakley, 21 January 1786, JR, vol. 2, TNSA.

71. "Amani" meant "the collection of the revenue direct from the cultivators by the officers of Government on the removal or suspension of an intermediate claimant." H. H. Wilson, *Glossary of Judicial and Revenue Terms* (1855; reprint Delhi: Munshiram Manoharlal, 1968), 21.

72. Oakley to Dighton, 14 December 1785, JR, vol. 5, TNSA. Evalappa Mudali was also deprived of 40 kanis (52.8 acres) of maniyam land or land on which there was no tax.

73. Dighton to Oakley, 15 November 1785, JR, vol. 5, TNSA.

74. Dighton to Oakley, 26 November 1785, JR, vol. 5, TNSA.

75. Dighton to Oakley, 15 November 1785, JR, vol. 5, TNSA.

76. Ibid.

77. Oakley to Dighton, 8 November 1785, JR, vol. 5, TNSA.

78. Neild-Basu has shown that these strategies continued to be followed in the nineteenth century. In 1818, the superintendent of police in Madras said, "[The principal leaders of the right subcastes] seldom actually commit riots themselves, but are always those who incite the Pariars [paraiyar Pannaiyals or bonded laborers], over whom their influence is very great." Superintendent of Police to Head Assistant Magistrate, Chingleput, 21 June 1818, Public Consultations, 30 June 1818, TNSA, quoted in Susan Neild-Basu, "Madras: The Growth of a Colonial City, 1780–1840" (Ph.D. diss., University of Chicago, 1977), 211–12. The paraiyar Pannaiyals also "resisted with vehemence" any attempts by the British or by their own caste rivals to diminish the prestige of their traditional right subcaste leader. Neild-Basu, "Madras," 217.

79. Oakley to Governor and President in Council, 20 December 1785, JR, vol. 5, TNSA.

80. BOR Minute on Place's 1795 Report, 24 March 1796, BORP, vol. 151, TNSA.

81. Charles Princep, *Record of Services of the Honourable East India Company's Civil Servants in the Madras Presidency from 1741 to 1858* (London: Trubners Co., 1885), 115.

82. BOR Minute on Place's 1795 Report, 24 March 1796, BORP, vol. 151, TNSA.

83. Ibid.

84. Place to BOR, 26 November 1795, BORP, vol. 140, TNSA.

85. Ibid.

86. Ibid.

87. In Wilson's *Glossary*, "badar-nawīsi" (a Persian term) was defined as a "writing off of items of an account which are objectionable or excessive," 43. One of the main objections of the Poonamallee Petition had been that Place was seeking to tax the Mirasidars on a part of their areas (called kollais) adjoining the more immediate enclosures (called pulakkadai) next to their houses. A pulakkadai is defined by Wilson as "a small portion of ground or a yard adjoining a dwelling held rent free by a mirasidar, used as a kitchen garden, or one for vegetables requiring a richer soil, as tobacco, sugar, turmerick—it is not transferable except with the entire Mirasi property and rights," 422. The kollai was

defined in the same source as "dry soil, high ground not capable of artificial irrigation; a backyard, or, rather, an inclosed piece of ground belonging to one of the proprietors of a village, whether or not contiguous to his dwelling," 293. Place proposed to tax the kollais and said that the mirasidars were claiming them as badarnavisi or charges to be written off.

88. All the details of the Poonamallee Petition are from Translation of a Petition from Poonamallee inhabitants to the Board of Revenue, 23 November 1795, BORP, vol. 139A, TNSA.

89. Place was specifically reprimanded by his superiors for having been too severe in having Aiyakutti, the Amil of Shamier Sultan, and Venkatarayan flogged at Numbal near Madras. Venkatarayan was given forty stripes of the cane and Aiyakutti thirty stripes. This was shortly before he decided to resign. BOR to Place, 13 September 1798, BC, no. 2110, IOL. See chap. 2.

90. The way that Place employed pieces of carved granite that were obviously parts of temples can be well seen in the stone work of the Madurantakam tank, the earth portion of which burst most recently in December 1985.

91. See Chapter 2 for a discussion of Place's dispute with the sons of a well-known Armenian merchant who called himself Shamier Sultan over the shelter of some robbers in a village named Numbal. Numbal had originally been made an inam or gift to Kheir ul Nejsa Begam by the Nawab in 1763. Petition of Chateput Ponniappah, 13 February 1784, JB, vol. 3, TNSA. Numbal was an important village in the present-day Saidapet taluk. After the war of 1780, it became an important center for the production of betel leaves for export to Madras. Charles Baker to BOR, 6 January 1798, MB, BORP, R. 286/3, IOL.

92. Place to BOR, 2 December 1795, BORP, vol. 140, TNSA; BOR Minute, 2 December 1795, BORP, vol. 140A, TNSA.

93. In its Minute, the Board referred to its letter to Place indicating its desire for extending individual property in the villages "and consequently of securing the improvement and prosperity of the country—but they [the Board] never entertained the most distant idea that this could be effected by coercion or by rendering property less secure." The Board also had no authority to threaten Mirasidars with the "forfeiture of their meerassees if they did not agree to the rent [tax]." Board's Minute, 7 December 1795, BORP, vol. 140A, TNSA.

94. Ibid.

95. Place to BOR, 5 December 1795, BORP, vol. 140, TNSA.

96. Place to BOR, 27 March 1796, BORP, vol. 161, TNSA.

97. Ibid.

98. Place to BOR, 25 July 1797, BORP, vol. 168, TNSA.

99. Governor in Council, 8 January 1796, BORP, vol. 142, TNSA.

100. Ibid.

101. Ibid.

102. Place to BOR, 26 February 1794, BORP, vol. 147, TNSA.

103. Place to BOR, 1 March 1796, BORP, vol. 149, TNSA.

104. Michael Moffatt, *An Untouchable Community in South India: Structure and Consensus* (Princeton: Princeton University Press, 1979), 213–14.

105. Dirks, in his account of Pudukkottai, says that "in most cases [paraiyar] marriages take place between karais [lineages] inside single villages. This

suggests the limited nature of the natu as a territorial unit except in so far as it creates an identity between the untouchables and the natu of the dominant caste lineage or village under which they serve." Paraiyar natus are the same as the natus of the dominant castes. Nicholas Dirks, *The Hollow Crown: Ethnohistory of an Indian Kingdom* (Cambridge: Cambridge University Press, 1987), 273–74.

106. Place to BOR, 29 March 1796, BORP, vol. 151, TNSA. If we were to transcribe these names into more modern spelling, they would be called Pettiya Totti, Puntamalli Kutti, Mangadu Kamban, and Pammal Kanniyan.

107. Ibid.

108. Place to BOR, 13 December 1795, BORP, vol. 153, TNSA.

109. Moore to Darvall, 28 February 1794, BORP, vol. 143, TNSA.

110. Hodgson to Place, 12 January 1795, BORP, vol. 143, TNSA. One of the gramani men was severely wounded in the head; another had his leg broken.

111. This dispute continued on until 1808 when it was decided that Place's decision had been illegal and that the vellalas were the legitimate Mirasidars. However, by that time the Gramanis had sold all the land in Tondiarpet. "Even the residential site of the mirasidars and village artisans, which had been situated on a central spot on the main road to Tiruvuttriyur, no longer existed, for the Shanars [or Gramanis] had destroyed all its former buildings." Though the Kondaikatti vellalas, who had now regained the title of Mirasidar, tried to get the courts to challenge the deeds of sale granted to the Gramanis, they would not do so. Neild-Basu, "Madras" 102.

112. Stephen Allen Barnett, "The structural position of a south Indian caste: the kondaikatti vellala-s in Tamil Nadu," (Ph.D. diss., University of Chicago, 1970), 92.

113. Place to BOR, 29 March 1796, BORP, vol. 151, TNSA.

114. This was the western part of Blacktown originally inhabited both by local people and Europeans; it lost its fashionability as a place for European dwellings in the early part of the eighteenth century. With the exception of a few streets in its southeast portion, it was designated the living area of the right subcastes by Thomas Pitt in 1707. The other part of late eighteenth-century Blacktown was Muthialpet, which after 1799 came to have an important European presence along the beach as well as on that street which was called the Esplanade. Neild-Basu, "Madras," 179; Love, *Vestiges*, 2:472 and 3:162.

This Periya Tambi, of course, is not to be confused with an important Tamil-speaking Labbai Muslim merchant named Pareya Tambi Mastry, who owned an "elegant, large, upper-roomed house on Meera Labbai Street in Muthialpet, but also a house and ground on Krishnaswamy Pagoda Street, a Hindu Street, and three other grounds near Hindu temples." *Madras Courier*, 2 March 1808, quoted in Neild-Basu, "Madras," 182n.

115. Although these particular paraiyar Pannaiyals were not imprisoned by the British, eight others, who could not have been involved without the assent and encouragement of their Kondaikatti vellala masters, were put into irons to work on "public works" in the Jagir. These eight paraiyar Pannaiyals were to be employed until the arrival of the threshing season. They were Padavatan of Kovur, Sooren of Kovur, Padavatan of Kunnatur, Coraven of Kunnatur, Au-

niyam of Mangadu, Ninan of Mangadu, Ninan of Palantandalam, and Sadien of Pakkam. Palantandalam, Kunnatur, and Mangadu are villages near the Chembrambakkam tank. I cannot identify Pakkam. BOR to Place, 14 July 1796, BORP, vol. 168, TNSA.

116. I am grateful to Stuart Blackburn for this and many other suggestions.

117. Declaration of Periya Tambi, Mastry of the Great Paracheri and by Ranjan (an employee of the Company) to the Board of Revenue, 22 April 1796, BORP, vol. 153, TNSA.

118. Declaration of Uttakartan Maistry of Periyamedu in Madras on 21 April 1796, to the Board of Revenue, BORP, vol. 153, TNSA. In an apparent reply to the letter of these three untouchable subcaste leaders in Madras, the Karanguli untouchables are supposed to have written, "Agreeable to your orders that we should repair to Madras for protection we are assembling together. If you will intercede with the Gentleman [Place] on our behalf when we arrive, and defray our expenses, send your answer by the bearer and we will accordingly come."

119. Place, 1799 Report, para. 280.

120. Ibid., para. 244.

121. Ibid., para. 280. In 1799, at the time he submitted his report on his activities, he prided himself on the fact that he had demonstrated that the Jagir would yield a tax revenue of pagodas 400,000 and that it had been established on a "footing of increasing and durable prosperity." Place to Governor, 11 June 1799, BC, no. 2111, IOL. Moreover, he conceded that when he came to the Jagir to carry out the village settlement—an assessment with the head inhabitants of more than two thousand villages—it "produced violent commotions, which required every exertion to quell." Nevertheless, he believed that his successor, John Hodgson, by contrast, was able to carry out the tax assessment "without a struggle and this too, under the prevalence of a drought unexampled in the memory of Man"; the implication was that only Place's actions enabled Hodgson's success. Place to Governor, 12 June 1799, BC, no. 2111, IOL. Now, he felt, a collector would no "longer [be] distracted by overawing the cabals of intrigue, or quelling the disturbances of contending factions, but have full leisure to prosecute the suggestions on [their] own terms, for the improvement and happiness of his charge." Place to Governor, 11 June 1799, BC, no. 2111, IOL. This, of course, was a period of gradual institutionalization or reaggregation involving the process of setting both the terms of the relationship between the Mirasidars and the collector and the exact words that the collector and his seniors would use about this relationship. See also Lionel Place's Minute, 7 October 1802, BC, F/4/150, IOL.

122. BOR to Governor in Council, 15 May 1796, BORP, vol. 156, TNSA.

123. Place to BOR, 16 July 1796, BORP, vol. 161, TNSA.

124. Ibid.

125. Ibid.

126. Place was particularly incensed with Appa Mudali because he was "exciting opposition" against Place's efforts to make tax assessments with the villages that were watered by the Chembirambakkam tank, close to the village of Poonamallee. Ibid.

127. Ibid.
128. Ibid.
129. Ibid.
130. Ibid.
131. Ibid.
132. Governor in Council to BOR, 4 June 1796, BORP, vol. 157, TNSA.
133. Place, 1799 Report, paras. 281, 286, 299. The final count on the number of individuals who left their villages (presumably all men, not counting Pannaiyals) was 293 Mirasidars from these subdivisions of the district. They were divided up as follows:

93 men from 83 villages in Karanguli pargana.
38 men from 14 villages in Kanchi pargana.
73 men from 24 villages in Uttiramerur.
88 men from 25 villages from Kavantandalam.

The Board of Revenue noted that, of those who had deserted from Karanguli, eighty-five had come from five villages close to the Madurantakam tank and that the remaining seventy-eight villages had on average "not lost one each." Place to BOR, 2 July 1796, BORP, vol. 168, TNSA; BOR Minute of 14 July 1796, BORP, vol. 168, TNSA.

134. Although, according to Place, everybody on his list had actually deserted, some of these were replaced by others for a wide variety of reasons not ultimately having anything to do with the "insurrection." For instance, an appraisal of the list indicates that only forty-four of the Mirasidars were actually removed by Place for having deserted. These included the five "ringleaders"—Mudu Venkatapati Reddi, Agastiyappa Mudali, Kollapa Nayak, Muttu Mudali, and Ramaswami Mudali—as well as Venkatachari, Vadaman, Muttuman, Sastri Narayana Mudali, Chakrapa Mudali, Muttu Mudali, Rangappa Mudali, Tirumala Srinivasa Iyengar, Appa Srinivasa Iyengar, Venkatachala Giramani, Varadapa Giramani, Marumuttu Nayak, Pudunakadu Mudali, Arumuttu Mudali, and Swami Mudali. None of the Mirasidars listed above came from Poonamallee pargana. There were, in addition, twenty-four Mirasidars who "gave up their mirasi when I began to rent the Purganah, and the conduct of the inhabitants at large having never yet been decided on, no other meeraseedars have been appointed." These Mirasidars (all from Poonamallee pargana but not among the "ringleaders") were Subbaiyya and Venkataiyya from Kilmanampetu; Vida Mudali from Cokkanallur; Viraswami and Aiya Mudali, Chengalroy Mudali, and Anna Mudali from Ariyanallur; Venkatachalam, Muttiyappan, Vira Perumal, and Ramaswami from Koranjeri; Venkatanarayan Pillai, Venkatachala Pillai, Ranga Pillai, Muttu Pillai, Lakshminarayan Pillai, Mallaya Pillai, and Kanaka Pillai from Pidikalakuppam and Varadarajapuram; Bankar Rao, Narayan Raj, and Kumara Pillai from Putadlum(?) and Puttakaram(?), Saidapettai Taluk; and Muttu, Nainappa, and Chinna Muttu from Netunjeri. Though these persons were deprived of their mirasi rights, no persons had been given them by Place at this time. Place to BOR, 4 November 1796, BORP, vol. 168, TNSA.

135. BOR to Governor in Council, 21 November 1796, BORP, vol. 168, TNSA.

136. The "volunteers" included Suburayudu, Ramanujachari, Venkachala Mudali, Viraswami, Venkata Nayak, and Rayaliya. The two earlier ones were Hari Pantulu and Venkata Rao.

137. The missing Mirasidar was Ramachandra Pantulu; the other five were Karta Mudali, Surya Narayan Mudali, another Karta Mudali, Muttu Mudali, Vira Pillai, and Lakshmana Mudali.

138. His name was Mritunjay Sastri. All of these materials are drawn from Place to BOR, 4 November 1796, BORP, vol. 168, TNSA.

139. The one group of brahmans who had originally protested against Place's behavior was from the village of Tirumalisai.

140. The numbers of Mirasidars who deserted are drawn from Place to BOR, 2 July 1796, BORP, vol. 168, TNSA; BOR Minute of 14 July 1796, BORP, vol. 168, TNSA.

CHAPTER 2

1. Special Commission on Zamindari in the Jagire, 9 April 1802, BC, no. 2117, IOL.

2. Public violence is illustrated in what are obviously somewhat hostile accounts of behavior among the group called the kallar in the southern part of the Tamil country. In these accounts, the kallars are called "colleries." An account of 1817 says, "The women are inflexibly vindictive and furious on the least injury, even on suspicion, which prompts them to the most violent revenge without any regard to consequences. A horrible custom exists among the females of the Colleries when a quarrel or a discussion arises between them. The insulted woman brings her child to the house of the aggressor, and kills it at her door to avenge herself. Although her vengeance is attended with the most cruel barbarity, she immediately thereafter proceeds to a neighbouring village with all her goods etc. In this attempt she is opposed by her neighbours, which gives rise to clamour and outrage. The complaint is then carried to the head Amblacarar, who lays it before the elders of the village, and solicits their interference to terminate the quarrel. In the course of this investigation, if the husband finds that sufficient evidence has been brought against his wife, that she had given cause for provocation and aggression, then he proceeds unobserved by the assembly to his house, and brings one of his children, and in the presence of witness, kills his child at the door of the woman who had first killed her child at his. By this mode of proceeding he considers that he has saved himself much trouble and expense, which would have otherwise have devolved on him. This circumstance is soon brought to the notice of the tribunal, who proclaim that the offense committed is sufficiently avenged. But should this voluntary retribution of revenge not be executed by the convicted person, the tribunal is prorogued to a limited time, fifteen days generally. Before the expiration of that period one of the children of that convicted person must be killed. At the same

time he is to bear all expenses for providing food, etc., for the assembly during those days." Account of T. Turnbull (1817), quoted in Thurston, *Tribes and Castes*, 3:54–55. In the first Tamil novel *Piratāpa Mutaliyār* by Mayūram Vetanāyaka Piḷḷai (1879; reprint, Madras: Sakti Kariyālayam, 1957), the hero's grandmother orders that when Piratapa, the hero, made a mistake in his lesson, the teacher should not beat Piratapa, his student, but should beat his own son, Kanakasabai. Should Kanakasabai not be not there when Piratapa made mistakes, the teacher should instead beat himself on the back (p. 6).

Bhats were used by local Indian kings and others to force into submission people considered to be "turbulent." A Bhat was able to control the behavior of individuals by the use of his own body and the bodies of his family through the performance of traga. According to a member of that subcaste, a Bhat who performs traga "generally exposes himself before the house (of the person against whom it is aimed), or in some public part of the village in which the person whose misconduct causes the resort may reside, fasting during such observance, and if unsuccessful in this mode he will next inflict wounds on himself in different parts of his body, such as I now exhibit ('shewing a deep cut above his wrist') to the court, till he obtain his end. In extreme cases, all the members of his family are collected; all of whom sit down at the entrance of the village in which the offender may have his abode, and if by such means he fail as he seldom does, he then severely wounds himself or sacrifices one of his relations. A Bhaut never commits violence on the person of his opponent." Letter from the Commissioners [Board of Control] for the affairs of India to the Directors of the East India Company, Whitehall, 6 October 1815, BC, IOL. All the information about traga is taken from this document. I am indebted to Dharmpal for its use.

3. An ūḷikārru is the "destructive wind that prevails at the end of the world." *Tamil Lexicon* (Madras: University of Madras, 1982) 1:502; A. L. Basham, *The Wonder that was India* (London: Sidgwick and Jackson, 1954), 320–21. I would like to express my thanks to George Hart for useful discussions on this matter.

4. Place, 1799 Report, para. 49.

5. Place, 1799 Report, para. 66.

6. Bundla Ramaswami Naidoo, *Memoir of the Internal Revenue system of the Madras Presidency, Selections from the Records of the South Arcot District* (Madras: Superintendent, Government Press, 1908), no. 11:5. The preface is dated 1 January 1820. The document is filled with many such observations. Bundla Ramaswami Naidoo was "the most prominent nineteenth-century member" of the Madras Bandla family. Beri Timmana, one of the seventeenth-century members of that family, served as a chief merchant of the Company. The family belonged to the Perike or Perikaver weaving caste. Neild-Basu, "Dubashes," 5.

7. Letter from "Observer," *Madras Observer*, 26 April 1792, quoted in Neild-Basu, "Madras," 175. She also notes that the use of carriages by Indians was a significant change. In the 1770s and the 1780s, with the exception of the family of the Nawab of Arcot, only one carriage was kept by an Indian in all of Madras. Ibid., 176n.

8. Place, 1799 Report, para. 53.

9. Place, 1799 Report, para. 280. Place resigned from the Board of Revenue three years later because he felt that the collectors such as Alexander Read and Thomas Munro, both military appointees, received treatment not accorded to that of the civilian appointees in the revenue line. At that time, he also reported a "crisis" to be overcome. Part of his irritation concerned the fact that the special commission, competing with the Board of Revenue in setting the terms of what came to be called the Permanent Settlement, left the Mirasidars of the Jagir unprotected. Place's Minute, 7 October 1802, BC, vol. 150, IOL.

10. S. Arasaratnam, "Trade and Political Dominion in South India, 1750–90: Changing British-Indian Relationships," *Modern Asian Studies* 13, no. 1 (February 1979): 24.

11. Love, *Vestiges*, 3:402.

12. Arasaratnam, "Trade and Political Dominion," 25.

13. Minutes of Council, 7 December 1781, July–December 1781, PP, 240/53, quoted in Arasaratnam, "Trade and Political Dominion," 24–25.

14. Minute of C. N. White, 28 March 1793, BORP, vol. 27, TNSA.

15. Minute of C. N. White, 15 March 1793, BORP, vol. 27, TNSA.

16. Minute of C. N. White, 23 December 1793, BORP, vol. 88, TNSA.

17. Place, 1795 Report, para. 25.

18. Quoted in Love, *Vestiges*, 3:485.

19. Committee of Police to Governor in Council 8 July 1786, PP, TNSA, quoted in Neild-Basu, "Madras," 146.

20. GOM to BOR, 24 February 1798, BC, no. 2109, IOL.

21. See Crole, *Chingleput*, 66. "The presidency town close by [Madras] is at the bottom of the backwards nature of the district which is called the 'most backward in the whole Presidency.' The chief land owners, some holding government appointments, live in Madras, either wholly, or in great part, and the district is thus deprived of a capital of its own. Living there is costly, and expensive tastes are formed, for the gratification of which the farm or estate is rack rented, and the expenditure for its improvement, or even for its maintenance, curtailed. Little interest in good farming is shown by the rich and well to do, and the cultivation . . . is not advancing because it is left in the hands of the ignorant." Later Crole argued, "The effect of [neglect] is disastrous for the land is generally too inferior to stand bad farming without resenting the neglect." Crole also remarked against the carrying off of what were called by the British "brattis" (Tamil "viraṭṭikaḷ")—dried cakes of cow dung used for fuel. Ibid.

22. Hastings to Lord Mansfield, 25 August 1774, G. R. Gleig, *Life of Warren Hastings* 1:401, quoted in Eric Stokes, *The English Utilitarians and India* (Oxford: Clarendon Press, 1959), 3.

23. Peter Marshall, *The British Discovery of Hinduism in the Eighteenth Century* (Cambridge: Cambridge University Press, 1970), 42.

24. George M. Foster, "Colonial Administration in Northern Rhodesia in 1962," *Human Organization* 46, no. 4 (Winter 1987): 367. I am grateful to Elizabeth Colson for bringing this article to my attention.

25. F. W. Ellis, "Lectures on Hindu Law," Mss Eur. D. 31, Erskine Collection, IOL. I am indebted to Dharampal for leading me to this source.

26. Norbert Elias, *The Civilizing Process,* vol. 1 of *The History of Manners,* trans. Edmund Jephcott (New York: Pantheon Books, 1978), 104.

27. Fox, *Gandhian Utopia,* 93–95.

28. See the account in Mattison Mines, *The Merchant-Warriors: Textiles, Trade and Territory in South India* (Cambridge: Cambridge University Press, 1984), 70.

29. See the account of the dispute over mirasi rights and the right to build in the village between the reddis and agamudaiyars in Viravorum, near Manimangalam, about sixteen miles southwest of Madras, in 1785. Eugene F. Irschick, "Peasant Survival Strategies and Rehearsals for Rebellion in Eighteenth-Century South India," *Peasant Studies* 9, no. 4 (Summer 1982), 218–19. Many other instances emerged in the 1780s.

30. Irschick, "Peasant Survival Strategies," 237–38.

31. Place to BOR, 28 January 1796, BC, no. 940, IOL; Place to BOR, 28 June 1796, BC, vol. 36, IOL.

32. Place to BOR, 28 June 1796, BC, vol. 36, IOL.

33. In the Jagir, the site of the village itself and that of the village temple was called the nattam. The Mirasidars believed that they could only build their houses in the nattam and nowhere else. Minute of the Board of Revenue, 5 January 1818, BOR, Misc., vol. 257A, TNSA.

34. Place, 1799 Report, quoted in *Select Committee on the East India Company: The Fifth Report on the Affairs of the East India Company* (reprint, Madras: J. Higgenbotham, 1866), 2:43 (hereafter Fifth Report).

35. President and Council and the Jaghire Committee to Collector, November 1784, CCR, vol. 441, 1784, TNSA.

36. This discussion of Place's policies toward the temples in the Jagir is based on Place, 1799 Report, paras. 450–61.

37. Place, 1799 Report, para. 452.

38. Visitors to the large Madurantakam tank in the southern part of what is today the Chengalpattu MGR district can attest to the strategies that Place employed in constructing the dam for that tank. See also the complaints of the Mirasidars who composed the Poonamallee Petition that Place forced villagers to use bricks and stones taken from temples to repair the Chembirambakkam tank just west of Poonamallee, in "Translation of a Petition from Poonamallee inhabitants to the Board of Revenue," 23 November 1795, BORP, vol. 139A, TNSA. There is much evidence to show that the Company employees often used stones and bricks from temples to make fortifications during the defense of Madras against the French in the late 1740s.

39. Place to BOR, 27 March 1796, BORP, vol. 168, TNSA.

40. See the account of the estimation of the population of Varanasi as a dialogic activity to create the notion of size. Bernard S. Cohn, "The Census and Objectification in South Asia," in *Anthropologist Among the Historians,* 234.

41. These religious beliefs and practices were not referred to as Hinduism at this time. The expression "Hinduism" is a product of a wide-ranging con-

struction about religious behaviors in South Asia during the nineteenth and twentieth centuries.

42. Place, 1799 Report, para. 458.

43. Place, 1799 Report, para. 460.

44. Place to BOR, 15 May 1795, BORP, vol. 128, TNSA. It was typical at that time to have an office that was simply a thatched house. This was still true for the municipal office in Madurai in the 1970s.

45. Place, 1799 Report.

46. The context of the agreement itself was significant: "We will never enter our cultivation under false names, in order to take more than our proper Warum [share of the crop]—also we will not enter in the account Mauniams [tax-free lands], for which there are no Heirs, nor for Pagodas [temples] where there are no Ceremonies going on. But we will exert ourselves to the utmost in order to restore such ceremonies as have been stopped, so that we may pray to God to make us happy and prosperous in our village." Place to BOR, 10 November 1796, BORP, vol. 168, TNSA.

47. Place to Colonel David Baird, Officer commanding at Walajabad, 8 May 1797, MB, BORP, R. 285, vol. 63, IOL.

48. Greenway to BOR, 17 July 1801, BC, no. 2113, IOL. In 1801, the festival began on 24 May. Of this figure, the preparation of the prasadam—the sweetmeat that is ceremonially offered to the deity and then redistributed to the devotees after it has been ceremonially eaten by the god or goddess—was only one of the costs (it used nineteen kalams of rice and almost thirty-five pollams of gingelly or sesame oil). Other important costs included fireworks costing pagodas 34, gold ornaments for the deity costing pagodas 14, and flowers costing pagodas 10. By far the most expensive items were the presents to the dancing girls, which cost pagodas 111, one third of the total third-day's ceremony costs.

49. Quoted in John William Kaye, *Christianity in India: An historical narrative* (London: Smith, Elder and Co., 1859), 380.

50. Ibid.

51. "India and its Evangelization: a lecture delivered by Dr. Duff to the Young Men's Christian Association" (Exeter Hall, December 1850), quoted in ibid., 380.

52. Love, *Vestiges*, 1:72.

53. During the wars between the French and the British from 1744 to 1760, these forts (Chingleput, Tiruppaccur, and Karanguli, among others) became some of the important reckoning points in placing the military actions of the English, the French, and their allies. Even afterward, in 1783, when the French were aiding Hyder Ali and later Tipu Sultan, the same ideas applied. For instance, Bussy, the French commander, and one of the few French military men who had had formal military training, said that he had certain news that the march of the British army on Cuddalore placed it between Chingleput and Karanguli, awaiting the appearance of Admiral Hughes at Madras. Bussy to Suffren, 2 May 1783, Feuilles Volantes no. 595, Fond Inde, Archives d'outre mer, Aix-en-Provence.

54. "Historical account of the government of Chingleput Rajah," translated from the Marathi into English in the early nineteenth century, in Mackenzie (General), vol. 9, IOL.

55. Place, 1799 Report, para. 473; Place to BOR, 28 January 1796, BC, no. 940, IOL.

56. Place to BOR, 11 January 1798, BC, no. 2109, IOL. In fact, Place focused his activity on relatively few of the total number of Palayakkars. He apparently also took away the "watching rights" in some of the villages belonging to Palayakkars with whom he was friendly, such as Rayalu Nayak. The Palayakkars from whom he took away privileges were Maddikayala Teppalraj, Kuppum Venkatachala Nayak, Damerla Venkatapati Nayak, Strirama Singama Nayak, Rayalu Nayak, Vadamaraja Tanappa Nayak, Rangappa Nayak, Anapambattu Harikrishna Raj, Nakka Venaktarama Nayak, Adavi, Venaktapati Raj, Kulur Venkata Raj, Itambi Subburoya Pillai (the only Tamil of the group), Mul Raj, and Madupakam Ramachandra Nayak. The total monetary amount that Place took away was pagodas 16,324-9-70 out of a total of pagodas 47,774-6-22. In terms of numbers of villages, Place took away privileges or benefits for "watching rights" in seventy-seven villages out of a total of 1,286. Greenway to Special Commission, 30 October 1801, SCPSP, vol. 3, IOL.

57. Place to BOR, 6 April 1795, BORP, vol. 128, TNSA.

58. Thomas Munro, writing as principal collector in the Ceded Districts, 10 April 1810, quoted in the Report of the Committee on Police, PCP, vol. 4, IOL.

59. Richard Dighton to BOR, 16 February 1787, BORP, vol. 6, TNSA.

60. Place to BOR, 29 July 1798, BC, no. 2110, IOL.

61. John and Nuzur Jacob Shamier to Governor Harris, 7 April 1798, BC, no. 2110, IOL. The letter cadjan or a strip of palmyra palm leaf (Tamil "olai") was placed in a holder made for the purpose, the style at the time.

62. See Douglas Hay, "Property, Authority and the Criminal Law," in Douglas Hay, Peter Linebaugh, John G. Rule, E. Thompson, Cal Winslow, eds., *Albion's Fatal Tree: Crime and Society in Eighteenth Century England* (Harmondsworth: Penguin Books, 1975), 45–47. Place was castigated by the Board of Revenue for being unnecessarily severe in imposing these floggings. BOR to Place, 13 September 1798, BC, no. 2110, IOL.

63. BOR to Place, 13 September 1798, BC, no. 2110, IOL.

64. Woolf and Sewell to BOR, 16 December 1795, BC, no. 855, IOL.

65. Place to BOR, 10 September 1798, BC, no. 2109, IOL.

66. Greenway to Special Commission, 30 October 1801, SCPSP, vol. 3, IOL.

67. Crole, *Chingleput*, 171–72.

68. Place, 1795 Report, para. 86.

69. Crole, *Chingleput*, 178–79.

70. Place to Committee of Police, 4 May 1798, BC, no. 2109, IOL.

71. Place to Committee of Police, 4 May 1798, BC, no. 2109, IOL.

72. This formulation of society, the individual, and the sacred is derived from Durkheim and Goffman's definition of the "individual's personality . . . as one apportionment of the collective mana." Erving Goffman, "The Nature of Deference and Demeanor," in *Interaction Ritual* (New York: Pantheon Books, 1967), 47. Durkheim had also written that "the human personality is a

sacred thing; one dare not violate it nor infringe its bounds, while at the same time the greatest good is in communion with others." Emile Durkheim, "The Determination of Moral Facts," 37, quoted in Goffman, "Deference and Demeanor," 73.

73. Dirks is directing his points to Arjun Appadurai, *Worship and Conflict under Colonial Rule: A South Indian Case* (Cambridge: Cambridge University Press, 1981), 71, and Carol Breckenridge, "From protector to litigant—changing relations between Hindu temples and the Raja of Ramnad," in Burton Stein, ed., *South Indian Temples* (New Delhi: Vikas Publishing House, 1978); Dirks, *Hollow Crown,* 287–89.

74. Ibid., 290.

75. Mines and Gourishankar, "Leadership and Individuality," 765.

76. Mines and Gourishankar, "Leadership and Individuality," 765. See also Stanley Tambiah, *World Conqueror and World Renouncer: A Study of Buddhism and Polity in Thailand Against a Historical Background* (Cambridge: Cambridge University Press, 1976).

77. Ibid., 766. In addition to the work of Dirks, they refer to that of C. J. Fuller, *Servants of the Goddess: The Priests of a South Indian Temple* (Cambridge: Cambridge University Press, 1984), 46, in which he says that temple honors "are presented to particular persons, precisely to single them out."

78. Ibid. The citation is to Dirks, *Hollow Crown,* 261.

79. Stephen Mennell, *Norbert Elias: Civilization and the Human Self-Image* (London: Basil Blackwell, 1989), 79. See also Norbert Elias, *Power and Civility,* vol. 2 of *The Civilizing Process,* trans. Edmund Jephcott (New York: Pantheon Books, 1978), 107. I want to acknowledge many helpful discussions on these issues with Cecilia Van Hollen and particularly the insights that I have derived from her unpublished paper, "The Role of the Civil Society in Orientalist and Anti-Colonial Discourses: Women as Model Citizens" (Berkeley, 1991).

80. In the struggle that developed between Place and the Board of Revenue on the one hand and the Mirasidars and Place on the other, the entire definition of the mirasi system came into question because (as was explained by the Board of Revenue twenty years later in 1818) Place "removed the Meerasidars from some of the finest villages, and conferred the meerassy of them . . . on the Pycarries [Payirkkaris or tenants], or even on strangers." Minute of the Board of Revenue, 5 January 1818, BOR Misc., vol. 257A, TNSA.

81. Place to BOR, 27 March 1796, included with the minute of the BOR on Badarnavisi, 30 June 1796, BORP, vol. 160, TNSA.

82. Place to Board of Revenue, 25 July 1797, BORP, vol. 161, TNSA. The Board of Revenue wrote, "The consideration of the very great labour which is discoverable in the whole of the Collector's proceedings, and of the successful reform which he has introduced by the realization of a very large revenue, convinces us that a donation of this kind granted to his principal confidential servants will be a judicial reward of positive merit." Govt. to BOR, 3 June 1797, BORP, vol. 179, TNSA; see also BOR Minute, 31 July 1797, BORP, vol. 182, TNSA.

83. Place to BOR, 3 May 1797, BORP, vol. 177, TNSA.

84. Mines and Gourishankar, "Leadership and Individuality," 770.

85. Quoted in Mines and Gourishankar, "Leadership and Individuality," 764n.

86. Place to BOR, 10 November 1796, BORP, vol. 168, TNSA.

87. Place, 1795 Report, para. 180. The following discussion of Madurantakam and Uttiramerur is based on this account in Place's report.

88. Place to the Board of Revenue, 27 March 1796, included with the Board's note on Badarnavisi, 30 June 1796, BORP, vol. 160, TNSA.

89. The Nawab also reported other encounters with Pigot in 1763. Nawab Muhammad Ali to Governor Du Pré, 26 November 1770, HMS, vol. 113, IOL.

90. Place, 1795 Report, para. 180.

91. Crole, *Chingleput,* 32.

92. Toṇṭaimāṉ cakkiravartti carittiram [History of Tondaiman Cakkiravartti], Mackenzie MSS R 8350, MOML; Nerumpūr kurumpar kōṭṭai kaipīṭu [Narrative account of the Kurumbar fort at Nerumbur], Mackenzie MSS R. 7754, MOML; Kurumpar carittiram [History of the Kurumbar], Mackenzie MSS R. 8189, MOML, translated into English in the early nineteenth century in another version in Mackenzie MSS Class 2, no. 21, IOL.

93. Extract of letter from the secretary to government in the Revenue Department to the president and members of the Board of Revenue, 2 August 1814. F. W. Ellis, *Replies to seventeen questions proposed by the Government of Fort St. George relative to Mirasi Right with two appendices elucidatory of the subject* (Madras: Government Gazette Office, 1818), v.

94. Ibid.

95. F. W. Ellis, Appendix [to the] replies to the questions respecting meerasi Right (hereafter Appendix), 1814, BOR, Misc., vol. 233, TNSA. The following discussion of Ellis's work is based primarily on this document.

96. Letter of 17 April 1814 from the Government of Madras to the Board of Revenue in Ellis, Appendix, v.

97. Ellis even computed what he believed to be "vellala villages," "brahman villages," and "other caste villages." That is, he said that, of the area described by Place (the Jagir, the center of the Tondai country), there were 680 villages in which vellalas were Mirasidars, 256 in which the brahmans were Mirasidars, and 346 in which other castes were Mirasidars.

98. The Chingleput district came later to be called the Chengelpattu district. At one time it was called the Chengai Anna district because "Chengai" is a shortened form for Chengelpattu. A former chief minister of Tamil Nadu, C. N. Annadurai (d. 1969) whose nickname was "Aṇṇa" or "elder brother," was born in Kanchipuram, the headquarters of the district.

99. Stuart Blackburn, *Inside the Drama-House: The Rama Story as Shadow Puppet Play in Kerala,* ch. 1 (forthcoming). It is not without interest that the performers of the Kambaramayanam call themselves simply Mudaliyars, not Sengunthars, a strategy that hides their ethnic origins.

100. In Tamil, two kinds of Payirkkaris or tenants could be identified. The Ulkkudis had lived in a village for a considerable time; they could not be dispossessed and had the right of hereditary succession but did not have the right to mortgage or sell the land so long as they paid the stipulated rent to the Mirasidar. The second type, the Parakkudis, were migratory or nonresident

tenants who had no proprietary rights. They could simply cultivate lands in the village for a stipulated term at will. Wilson, *Glossary*, 401, 531.

101. Francis Ellis, "Account of a Discovery of a Modern Imitation of the Vedas, With Remarks on the Genuine Works," *Asiatic Researches or Transactions of the Society Instituted in Bengal for Enquiring into the History and Antiquities, the Arts, Sciences, and Literature, of Asia*, 14 (1822): 1–59. Ellis says on p. 57 that Nobili, "who was looked upon by the Jesuits as the chief apostle of the Indians after Francois Xavier took incredible pains to acquire a knowledge of the religion, customs, and language of Madura, sufficient for the purposes of his ministry. But this was not all: for to stop the mouths of his opposers and particularly of those who treated his character of brachman as an imposture, he produced an old dirty parchment in which he had forged, in the ancient Indian characters a deed, shewing that the Brachmans of Rome were of much older date than those of India and that the Jesuits of Rome descended, in a direct line from the God BRAHMA. Nay, Father Jouvence a learned Jesuit, tells us, in the history of his order, something yet more remarkable; even that ROBERT DE NOBILI, when the authenticity of his smoky parchment was called in question by some Indian unbelievers, declared, upon oath, before the assembly of the Brachmans of Madura, that he (NOBILI) derived really and truly his origin from the god BRAH'MA. Is it not astonishing that this Reverend Father would acknowledge, is it not monstrous that he should applaud as a piece of pious ingenuity this detestable instance of perjury and fraud?"

102. *Dictionary of National Biography* (Oxford: Clarendon University Press, 1917), 6:694.

103. See "Mayilapūr kantapparācan caritam," [History of Kandapparajan of Mylapur], Mackenzie MSS R. 8141, MOML.

104. Place, 1799 Report, para. 59. "Mudali" is the shortened form of "Mudaliyar," the surname of all Tondaimandala vellalas.

105. In 1786, the Board of Revenue was presented with a petition by some "Kondakutty Vellarahs" from Kuvam and Mappedu in what is today the Tiruvallur taluk, saying that "in very old times this country being a wilderness, Tondamon the famous monarch, after whose name this part of the world still goes viz. Tondamandalam, sending for the inhabitants from the kingdom of Sera [Chola] promised them that if they would cut down the woods, turn them into fields and cultivate the country each at his disposal, and give him one sixth part of the product, he would let them have the remaining 5 parts and the rights of settling and mortgaging their property of lands and thus they having brought about the business, such rights were accordingly conferred upon them. Many centuries after the days of the said monarch, the different rulers of the country being of cruel disposition curtailed the inhabitants' shares and put in practice many injustice[s] over them yet none of them ever think of so encroaching upon the usurping the inhabitants with their inheritance. . . . [The petitioners continued that the Nawab,] tho' capable of doing any injustice over the inhabitants at his disposal, yet he being bound by the cord of justice, was obliged to take grounds he lately wanted from the inheritors of Chennappa Naicker's Coopam not by violence but by their general consents and by paying them money for it." The petition was an attempt to head off the takeover of property by the Com-

pany after the war of 1780 in the villages of Kottur, Mappedu, and Kuvum in order to regrant the land to a group of Christians under a Jesuit missionary named Padre Manente, who was part of the Mission du Carnate.

106. Place, 1799 Report, paras. 62–63, 65.

107. BOR minute, 25 January 1796, BORP, vol. 149, TNSA.

108. Regarding population movements inspired by trade concerns, see D. H. A. Kolff, "Sannyasi Trader-Soldiers," *Indian Economic and Social History Review* 8, no. 2 (June 1971): 211–18; C. A. Bayly, *Rulers, Townsmen and Bazaars* (Cambridge: Cambridge University Press, 1983), 142–43.

For an account of flight in the face of war, see the description of the coming of the Maratha Bargirs into Bengal by Ganga Ram, *The Maharashta Purana: An Eighteenth-Century Bengali Historical Text*, trans. and ed. Edward Dimock and P. C. Gupta (Honolulu: East-West Center Press, 1965), 26–28.

For an account of flight during the Bengal famine of 1769–70, see W. W. Hunter, *The Annals of Rural Bengal* (reprint, Calcutta: Indian Studies, 1965), 25.

Regarding searches for water sources, see the remarks of David Ludden, "Agricultural Expansion, Diversification, and Commodity Production in Peninsular India, c. 1550–1800" (Paper delivered at the Association of Asian Studies Meeting, San Francisco, 25 March 1988).

Regarding migrations motivated by work opportunities, see Brian Murton, "Key People in the Countryside: Decisionmakers in Interior Tamilnadu in the Late Eighteenth Century," *Indian Economic and Social History Review* 10, no. 2 (June 1973): 177.

109. Ellis to BOR, 20 April 1817, MCR, vol. 1021, TNSA.

110. Ellis, Collector of Madras, to BOR, 25 June 1817, MCR, vol. 1022, TNSA.

111. Ibid.

112. Crole says that after the collapse of the Permanent Settlement, which began almost as soon as it was implemented in 1802 and continued until it was formally abolished in 1818, taxation in the area was "followed by the intermittent efforts of 15 or 20 officers [collectors] to make a survey and ryotwar settlement of the district which gradually reverted to Government, as one zemindar after another became insolvent." Crole, *Chingleput,* 273. Though the Permanent Settlement was introduced into the Chingleput district in 1802, the ryotwari system was introduced into two areas of the district, Kanchipuram and Madurantakam, in the very next year. In 1817, the ryotwari system was introduced into the Manimangalam casba in 1817 and 1818 and at the same time Ellis introduced the ryotwari system into the village of Vayalur (in the present-day Kanchipuram taluk).

113. Secretary of Revenue Dept. to the President and members of BOR, 2 August 1814, in C. P. Brown, ed., *Three treatises on Mirasi Right . . . with the remarks made by the Hon'ble the Court of Directors* (Madras: D.P.L.C. Connor, 1852), 1.

114. A. D. Campbell, secretary to the Chief Secretary, 17 April 1817, MCR, vol. 1021, TNSA. Campbell was already a Telugu scholar and one of a large

number of Campbell family members involved with India (including the governor of Madras in the 1780s), as well as the future author of a Telugu grammar and dictionary prepared for the use of students in Madras College. He also served as a secretary in the Revenue Department of government.

115. BOR to Ellis, 18 September 1817, MCR, vol. 1022, TNSA. Ellis's letter was dated 30 May 1816.

116. Extract of Revenue Letter to Fort St. George, 2 January 1822, in Brown, *Three treatises*, 155.

117. Minute by Sir Thomas Munro, Madras, 31 December 1824, in Brown, *Three treatises*.

118. Graham to Alexander Read, 22 October 1794, *Records of Fort St. George: The Baramahal Records, Management* (Section 1; Madras, 1907), 223, quoted in Murton, "Key People," 177.

119. Wilson, *Glossary*, 524.

120. B. H. Baden-Powell, *The Land Systems of British India* (Oxford: The Clarendon Press, 1892), 3:123–24n.

121. Ibid., 124.

122. Ibid., 122.

CHAPTER 3

1. Pres. and Council to Committee of Assigned Revenue, 26 July 1783, Abstract of the Jaghire Revenues by . . . time of Nabob Sadootoolala Cawn, JR, vol. 2, TNSA; Jaghire Committee to Govt., 3 January 1784, "Account of Collections of the Revenues of the Hon'ble Company's Jaghir for 9 years from Fasli 1181 to 1189, that is from 1771 to 1790 [sic 1780], CCR, vol. 440, 1784–86, TNSA.

2. The British in the Madras area abandoned the use of tax farmers or "Renters" in 1792 after the war with Tipu Sultan. In their earlier dependence, they needed tax farmers to revive the productive power of the Jagir. In this, they were in many ways following the example of the political systems of the subcontinent such as the Marathas and others, which used tax farmers to "restore areas which had fallen behind their normal productivity, yet were not totally ruined." See Wink, *Land and Sovereignty*, 354–55.

For a list of income figures for the Jagir between 1786–87 and 1792–93, see chap. 1 n. 39.

3. Irschick, "Peasant Survival Strategies," 226–27.

4. Place to Governor, 11 June 1799, BC, no. 2111, IOL.

5. BOR Minute, 5 June 1800, BC, no. 2112, IOL.

6. Ibid., Hodgson to BOR, 29 May 1800, BC, no. 2112, IOL. This income helped the Board of Revenue to convince itself that the collector had "successfully secured to the state their just demands without encroaching upon the rights of the Inhabitants."

7. Greenway to BOR, 20 May 1801, BC, no. 2113, IOL.

8. The remains of the Permanent Settlement at the end of the nineteenth century in the Chingleput district were "206 small proprietary estates; 29 are between R[s].1000–3000 [tax payment] and 177 under R[s].1000 each." Baden-Powell, *Land Systems,* 3:138.

9. Place's Minute, 7 October 1802, BC, F/14/150, IOL.

10. Ibid.

11. In the words of the Board of Revenue, the Permanent Settlement involved "almost a total reduction of the establishment of servants, by the annulment of the present division of the country, appointing an aumeen to each lot, and placing a certain number of estates under charges of a Tahseeldar to be withdrawn as the proprietors take possession. It would also cause an immediate reduction of the District Charges of 15 Per cent." BOR to GOM, 16 October 1802, BC, no. 2109, IOL.

12. Greenway to Special Commission, 20 July 1802, SCPSP, vol. 4, IOL.

13. Ellis, Collector of Madras, to BOR, 25 June 1817, MCR, vol. 1022, TNSA.

14. Ellis to BOR, 25 June 1817, MCR, vol. 1022, TNSA.

15. Place to BOR, 2 November 1796, BC, no. 36, IOL.

16. Petition from 118 individuals to the Madras Board of Revenue, 21 June 1796, Madras BOR, MB, vol. 46, IOL.

17. Translation of a Tamil petition from the inhabitants of Carangooly to Edward Saunders and members of the Board of Revenue, 27 Cittirai of Kachadev or 6 May 1796, Madras BOR, MB, vol. 46, IOL.

18. Place to BOR, 18 July 1796, BC, no. 36, IOL.

19. Ibid.

20. C. S. Crole Minute, Revenue, GO, no. 590, 13 April 1875, TNSA.

21. Christopher John Baker, *An Indian Rural Economy, 1880–1955, The Tamil Countryside* (Oxford: Clarendon Press, 1984), 66.

22. Smollett to BOR, 13 December 1854, CCR, vol. 5835, TNSA.

23. Ibid.

24. Smollett to BOR, 27 November 1854, CCR, vol. 5835, TNSA.

25. Smalley to BOR, 4 November 1820, CCR, vol. 468, TNSA.

26. Ibid.

27. J. Babbington, Collector of Chingleput to BOR, 13 December 1823, CCR, vol. 3842, TNSA.

28. Ibid.

29. Smalley to BOR, 31 October 1822, BORP, vol. 929, TNSA.

30. Ibid.

31. While he was collector of the Jagir, Place began to establish what can be conceived of as "government gardens" in Uttiramerur southwest of Madras. By mid-1796, however, he had decided to move these gardens from Uttiramerur to Perumbakkam (in the present-day Kanchipuram taluk). There, "the soil appears so peculiarly congenial to the growth of all kinds of large trees, that I have ventured to extend the number of gardens to 12, proposing to occupy with extensive plantations, a very considerable space of ground, which by the information of the natives I believe never has been cultivated, but is remarkably well

supplied with water." He ventured out during a severe cyclonic storm on 29 and 30 November 1795 in an attempt to prevent damage and decided later that the storm had denuded the Karankuli area south of Madras so much that it should be replanted, particularly with coconut trees. Place to BOR, 16 July 1796, BORP, vol. 161, TNSA. Place also reported that many springs had suffered greatly by flooding in this storm and that, although the cost to repair them would be heavy, they would be enormously valuable. Place to BOR, 4 June 1796, CCR, vol. 447, TNSA. See the Conclusion for further discussion of this issue.

32. "The soil is unfavorable for forming banks and the expense of bringing stones is so great that revetments have not been generally made and it has led to the more serious consequence of omitting to construct calingulahs [exit canals for the water from tanks] which on a sudden flow of water are the safeguards of artificial bodies of water." E. Smalley to BOR, 24 April 1821, CCR, vol. 3840, TNSA.

33. Ibid.

34. Ibid.

35. E. Smalley to BOR, 24 April 1821, CCR, vol. 3840, TNSA.

36. Ibid.

37. E. Smalley to BOR, 31 October 1822, BORP, vol. 929, TNSA.

38. Ibid.

39. Ibid.

40. Ibid.

41. Ibid.

42. Place to BOR, 27 March 1796, BORP, vol. 168, TNSA.

43. Ibid.

44. One such example comes from the 1830s following the loss of land by many of the Zamindars or Mutahdars. In 1833, Collector Maclean wrote about a longstanding power-struggle between the Seyur Mutahdars and the Mirasidars of Seyur itself. These Mirasidars had for many years abandoned the cultivation of their lands because of the "present and former Mutahdars and are most anxiously looking forward to reoccupation of them." Maclean to BOR, 6 October 1833, CCR, vol. 3856, TNSA.

45. Crole, *Chingleput,* 272.

46. Cooke to BOR, 1 November 1819, CCR, vol. 467, TNSA.

47. Smalley to BOR, 5 December 1821, CCR, vol. 3840, TNSA.

48. Cooke to BOR, 31 July 1819, CCR, vol. 467, TNSA.

49. Ibid.

50. C. J. Shubrick to BOR, 20 October 1857, CCR, vol. 5838, TNSA.

51. R. W. Barlow, Collector of Chingleput, to J. Grose, Sec. to the BOR, 11 November 1874, no. 630, in Revenue, GO, no. 590, 13 April 1875, TNSA.

52. Ibid.

53. The phrase "bought in by government for a trifle by probably the nearest relative of the last holder, to whom it soon passes by private arrangement and no one is the worse except the Poyakary [Payirkkari or tenant] who is kept out and the Government that has lost a year's revenue" was copied verbatim by a later district collector, Tremenheere, in an 1891 report on the paraiyars.

54. The percentages of total unpaid tax demand in the Chingleput district between 1841–42 and 1851–52 (fasli 1251–61) were as follows:

1841–42	35.38%
1842–43	19.50
1843–44	15.50
1844–45	11.25
1845–46	12.00
1846–47	10.50
1847–48	11.44
1848–49	15.88
1849–50	15.88
1850–51	20.75
1851–52	22.00

Source: Cochrane to BOR, 4 March 1853, CCR, vol. 5834, TNSA. Cochrane said that because of the way in which rice was brought to the market in the late spring, rice prices went up only very slowly at the end of the fasli or revenue year. "The balances," he said, "are subsequently realized with comparative facility and any ill consequences which might be considered to result from this tardiness of collection are more than counterbalanced by the benefits that must arise from a system which though not exactly sanctioned is under existing circumstances forced upon the executive authorities." Ibid.

55. BORP, 1 April 1874, no. 754, TNSA.

56. Ibid.

57. The number of cases instituted to extract the tax arrears in the Chingleput district between 1855 and 1873 rose from 2,692 to 394,693.

58. BORP, 1 April 1874, no. 754, TNSA.

59. Ibid.

60. Ibid.

61. Ibid.

62. BORP, 25 May 1875, no. 1415, TNSA.

63. Revenue, GO, nos. 1010, 1010A, 30 September 1892, TNSA.

64. R. W. Barlow, Collector of Chingleput, to J. Grose, Sec. to the BOR, 11 November 1874, no. 630, in Revenue, GO, no. 590, 13 April 1875, TNSA.

65. Ibid.

66. BORP, 1 April 1874, no. 754, TNSA.

67. R. S. Ellis Minute, Revenue, GO, no. 590, 13 April 1875 (dated 13 March 1875), TNSA. The final order on the subject noted that more than half of the whole revenue realized by the sale of lands in the entire presidency was recovered in the single district of Chingleput and amounted in the revenue year 1871–72 to rupees 108, 358.

68. Ibid.

69. These are the people whom Place brought in to cultivate lands left vacant by the mirasi desertion in 1795–96. Place said that it was mainly on account of the Payirkkaris that he was able to bring in such a large revenue in 1795–96.

70. Ibid. Place's account of this encounter is in Place, 1799 Report, para. 164.

71. Crole contended that all of these rights claimed by the Mirasidars derived from the government. Ibid.

72. Place, 1799 Report, para. 704, quoted in ibid.

73. Ibid. Crole's evidence illustrating that the mirasidars were "ghosts" related to the fact that the mirasidars could not tell which lands were part of their original share and which were not. "Almost every holding is now composed of odds and ends of Pungus acquired in some of these ways [buying or selling] and has no relation whatever to any pungu. The so-called mirassidars themselves would be the first to admit that their possessions have no reference to the old Pungumalai, and to express their inability to distinguish the lands in which they are mirasidars from those in which they are not. This fact, and not a large body of Sugavasis [tenants], groaning under supposed wrongs, is the cause of the great portion of samudayam puttas." If they could point to nothing in the distribution of the lands in the village, then the Mirasidars could not represent themselves as being anything except ordinary title holders. It is of some interest that in many ways this resembled the system of karaiyidu or periodic redistribution that had ensured that Mirasidars would take advantage of both the less fertile and the more fertile lands in any given village. The difference between this and the previous practice was that land was now divided into individual fields, which were all noted on a survey register.

74. Ibid.

75. Native Officer, *On Bribery*, 17.

76. Ibid.

77. Revenue, GO, no. 590, 13 April 1875, TNSA. Emphasis in original.

78. Crole, *Chingleput*, 65.

79. Ibid., 242.

80. Revenue, GO, no. 590, 13 April 1875, TNSA. He provided figures showing that he had eliminated the arrears in the Madurantakam taluk, in the southern part of the district, which amounted on the average to rupees 100,000 a year.

CHAPTER 4

1. Henry Mayhew, *London Labour and the London Poor; a Cyclopedia of the Condition and Earnings of Those that Will work, Those That Cannot Work, and Those that Will Not Work* (London: Griffen, Bohn, and Co., 1861), 1:2–3. Quoted in Catherine Gallagher, "The Body Versus the Social Body in the Works of Thomas Malthus and Henry Mayhew," in Thomas Laqueur and Catherine Gallagher, eds., *The Making of the Modern Body: Sexuality and Society in the Nineteenth Century* (Berkeley: University of California Press, 1987), 90.

2. Gallagher, "Body Versus the Social Body," 97.

3. Ibid, 99.

4. Cuniliffe to BOR, 30 July 1855, MCR, vol. 5514, TNSA.

5. Crole, *Chingleput*, 177.

6. A masula boat was a kind of "boat used for crossing the surf on the Madras coast; it is usually from 30 to 40 feet long by 6 broad and 8 deep, flat

bottomed, and having the planks sown together with writhes of straw between each plank; it has ten rowers, and can carry twenty passengers." Wilson, *Glossary,* 334.

7. Orme, *Transactions,* 3:406, 409–10, quoted in Crole, *Chingleput,* 117.

8. Crole, *Chingleput,* 117.

9. I have been aided in my thinking by Catherine Gallagher, *The Industrial Reformation of English Fiction: Social Discourse and the Narrative Form 1832–67* (Chicago: University of Chicago Press, 1985), 6–10. She argues that those who opposed the abolition of the slave system and those who sought to reform labor conditions in the factories of early nineteenth-century Britain came together over the common use of the word "emancipation." The anti-abolitionists argued that the condition of the slaves was better than the condition of British factory workers and that essentially the latter should be attended to first. Cobbett in particular criticized William Wilberforce for not concerning himself with the grant of freedom allowed to workers in British factories.

10. Reverend Andrew Mearns, *The Bitter Cry of Outcaste London: An Inquiry into the Condition of the Abject Poor* (London: James Clarke and Co., 1883). This pamphlet and the accompanying sensationalist writings by a journalist named W. T. Stead in the *Pall Mall Gazette* particularly on 16 October 1883 and 23 October 1883 "caused," in Stead's words, "the appointment of the Royal Commission on the Housing of the Poor, from which modern social legislation may almost be said to date." F. Whyte, *The Life of W. T. Stead* (London: 1925), 1:105, quoted in Anthony S. Wohl, "Introduction," *The Bitter Cry of Outcast London* (New York: Humanities Press, 1970), n. 70.

11. K. S. Inglis, *Churches and the Working Classes in Victorian England* (London: Routledge and Kegan Paul, 1963), 67.

12. *How the Poor Live* and *Horrible London* (London: Chatto and Windus, 1889). Inglis has also noted that the influence of *Bitter Cry* was a result of what he calls "its exploitation" by Stead in the *Pall Mall Gazette* as well as a result of its timing. Inglis says that *Bitter Cry* "expressed exactly that mood of corporate guilt and apprehension which stirred some members of the comfortable classes after 1880 to lend a hand to their poorer brothers." Stead, says Inglis, "knew exactly how to and when to strike his readers. He took up *Bitter Cry* at a moment when the condition of the poor, and especially their housing, was being discussed in the monthly reviews, and threw the subject to the middle-class public at large, among whom many were prepared to feel uneasy about the plight of the outcast." Inglis, *Churches,* 69.

13. Charles Kingsley, "Great Cities and their Influence for Good and Evil," in *Miscellanies* (London: 1860), 2:342, quoted in Wohl, *Bitter Cry,* n. 45.

14. *How the Poor Live,* 44, quoted in Wohl, *Bitter Cry,* n. 51.

15. "General" William Booth, *In Darkest England and the Way Out* (London: International Headquarters of the Salvation Army, 1890); Henry Morton Stanley, *In Darkest Africa; or, The quest, rescue and retreat of Emin, governor of Equatoria* (London: S. Low, Marston, Searle and Rivington, 1890).

16. Booth, *Darkest,* ii (unnumbered).

17. Ibid., 11–12.

18. Ibid., 13.

19. Ibid., 14.

20. "The Equatorial Forest was, after all, a mere corner of one quarter of the world. In the knowledge of the light outside, in the confidence begotten by past experience of successful endeavour, he pressed forward; and when the 160 days' struggle was over, he and his men came out into a pleasant place where the land smiled with peace and plenty, and their hardships and hunger were forgotten in the joy of a great deliverance." Ibid., 15.

21. These included Mayhew, *London Labour*; Bernard Bosanquet, *Aspects of the Social Problem* (New York: Macmillan and Co., 1895); C. F. G. Masterman, ed., *The Heart of the Empire: Discussions of Problems of Modern City Life in England* (1901; reprint, New York: Barnes and Noble, 1973).

22. Some of the earliest Victorian documents using this technique were by Edwin Chadwick, *Report on the Sanitary Conditions of the Labouring Population of Great Britain* (London: H. M. Stationery Office, 1843).

23. Charles Booth, ed., *Life and Labour of the People of London* (1889; reprint, New York: Augustus M. Kelley, 1969) 1:6.

24. Booth, *Darkest*, 17.

25. Ibid., 18.

26. Ibid., 18–19.

27. John R. McLane, *Indian Nationalism and the Early Congress* (Princeton: Princeton University Press, 1977), 52.

28. Dadabhai Naoroji, "Poverty of India" (1873), in *Poverty and Un-British Rule in India* (New Delhi: Publications Division, 1962). He quoted British statistics and opinions of British members of the Indian Civil Service to substantiate his argument. For instance, he quoted among others the opinion of George Campbell who, referring to the land system in Madras in 1869, said, "The bulk of the people are paupers. They can just pay their cesses in a good year and fail altogether when the season is bad" (p. 42).

29. Dadabhai Naoroji, *Essays, speeches, and writings*, ed. C. L. Parikh (Bombay, 1887), 134–35, quoted in Bipan Chandra, *The Rise and Growth of Economic Nationalism in India: Economic Policies of Indian National Leadership, 1880–1905* (New Delhi: People's Publishing House, 1966), 2.

30. Ibid., 16.

31. William Digby, *India for the Indians—and for England* (London: Talbot Brothers, 1885). For an account of the relations between Digby and the Indian National Congress, see McLane, *Indian Nationalism*, 125–27.

32. J. Seymour Keay, "The Spoliation of India," *The Nineteenth Century* 14 (July–December 1883), 1–22, and 15 (January–June 1884), 559–618.

33. Samuel Smith, MP, *My Life Work* (London: Hodder and Stoughton, 1902), 197. See Samuel Smith, "India Revisited," *Contemporary Review* 49 (January–June 1886): 794–819.

34. Smith, *Life Work*, 198.

35. Ibid., 199–200.

36. Smith, "India Revisited," 806.

37. Smith, *Life Work*, 206.

38. Smith, "India Revisited," 811–12.

39. Dadabhai Naoroji, "Sir M. E. Grant Duff's Views about India," *Contemporary Review* 52 (August 1887): 222.

40. Gauri Visvanathan, *Masks of Power: Literary Study and British Rule in India* (New York: Columbia University Press, 1989), 136–40.

41. McLane, *Indian Nationalism*, 29.

42. Speech of W. S. Caine, M.P., about the Indian Famine Commission Report, 3 February 1902. Quoted in Smith, *Life Work*, 200.

43. See the discussion about authoring in Fox, *Gandhian Utopia*, 84–90.

44. William Digby, *The Famine Campaign in Southern India (Madras and Bombay Presidencies and province of Mysore) 1876–1878* (London: Longmans, Green, 1878).

45. Digby, *Famine Campaign*, 2:2.

46. See Dadabhai Naoroji's lecture before the Plumstead Radical Club on 27 July 1900 in *Poverty and Un-British Rule*, 577, quoted in Chandra, *Economic Nationalism*, 8.

47. Quoted in Chandra, *Economic Nationalism*, 15.

48. See the table reproduced in Chandra, *Economic Nationalism*, 18n, which compares, among others, the annual per capita income of the population in England, Russia, Turkey, Ireland, the United States, and India.

49. In his last chapter of "The Wealth of India," Moreland concluded that "the lower classes, including very nearly all the productive elements, lived even more hardly [at the time of Akbar] than they live now." W. H. Moreland, *India at the Death of Akbar: An Economic Study* (1920; reprint, Delhi: Atma Ram and Sons, 1962), 274.

Srinivasa Raghavaiyangar said that "in July 1890, Lord Connemara entrusted to me the task of examining whether the economic condition of the Madras Presidency has, on the whole, improved or deteriorated during the last 40 or 50 years of British administration." S. Srinivasa Raghavaiyangar, *Memorandum on the Progress of the Madras Presidency during the Last Forty Years of British Administration* (Madras: Superintendent, Government Press, 1893), v. Raghavaiyangar was inspector-general of registration in Madras at the time he wrote his work. His biography, written by Kē. Cuntara Rākavan and Kē. Ranka Rākavan, is *Tivān Pahatūr Śrīnivāsarākavaiyāṅkār* (N.p., n.d.). Srinivasa Raghavaiyangar's work was also the basis of Barrington Moore's generalizations on Madras presidency in his *Social Origins of Dictatorship and Democracy: Lord and Peasant in the Making of the Modern World* (Boston: Beacon Press, 1966), 364–65.

50. M. E. Grant-Duff, "India: A Reply to Mr. Samuel Smith, M.P.," *Contemporary Review* 51 (January–June 1887), 8–31, 181–95.

51. They appeared in the *Contemporary Review* in 1887 as a rebuttal. Chandra, *Economic Nationalism*, 23.

52. Grant-Duff, "Reply to Samuel Smith," 11.

53. Grant-Duff, "Reply to Smith," 12.

54. Ibid. In another place, Grant-Duff said, "They want comfortable livelihoods out of a Government in which Englishmen shall have less and less part, but which shall be maintained by English soldiers to the great inconvenience to England, for their benefit." Ibid., p. 31.

55. Grant-Duff, "Reply to Smith," 14. When Grant-Duff was governor of Madras he deliberately encouraged the development of a movement against brahmans. See Irschick, *Politics and Social Conflict in South India* (Berkeley: University of California Press, 1969).

56. Grant-Duff, "India; Reply to Smith," p. 25.

57. Quoted in Naoroji, "Views about India," 211.

58. Quoted in Naoroji, "Views about India," 212.

59. Naoroji, "Views about India," reprinted in Naoroji, *Poverty and Un-British Rule*, 305–40.

60. Quoted in ibid.

61. Quoted in ibid., 213.

62. Ibid.

63. This was in Naoroji's paper called "The Poverty of India," which, Naoroji says, was "placed before the Select Committee on Indian Finance in 1873. They were taken, but not published with the *Report*, as . . . [it] did not suit the views of the Chairman (Mr. Ayrton), and I was led to suppose, also of Sir Grant Duff, who was then Under-Secretary of State for India." *Poverty and Un-British Rule*, 1n.

64. Quoted in ibid.

65. Ibid., 217.

66. Francis Henry Skrine, *Life of Sir William Wilson Hunter* (London: Longmans, Green and Co., 1901), 394–95.

67. Resolution of the Govt. of India, Circular No. 96 F/6–59 dated 19 October 1888 (Famine Proceedings, no. 19, December 1888), quoted in Chandra, *Economic Nationalism*, 14.

68. In his paper, Reverend Andrew said that the paraiyars as a class were in a "wretched condition and forced to labor by their masters under a system which may be termed as semi-slavery." Andrew wrote that the chief secretary of the Madras government, Price, said that he "knew well where the agitation started from—from Chingleput [town]—through a paper I submitted to the sub-collector in 1889 which eventually came before the Gov[ernmen]t." Andrew Note, 4 February 1892, UFCSM, MSS 7846, NLS.

69. The idea of the "poverty of the soil" of the Chingleput district being the main cause of its present decayed state was possibly introduced into this dialogic activity by Crole, when he wrote his account of the decline of the mirasi system. Crole had written in a note about the mirasi system that "the soil of the district is generally of inferior quality and easily exhausted." BORP, 25 May 1875, no. 1415, TNSA. The source from which the under secretary's staff probably got this idea was, however, Crole's *Chingleput Manual*, in which he had written that the soil of the district was too poor to be able to withstand the effects of bad farming. Crole, *Chingleput*, 65. Then it was used by the under secretary of India to counter questions of Samuel Smith. His information probably came from the Scottish Free Church missionaries in Chingleput, who had gotten their information, in turn, from Tremenheere, the collector. So, essentially, Smith, the Scottish missionaries, and Tremenheere were being fed Crole's argument. It was Crole's ideas about the infertility of the soil in Chingleput that appeared in "Condition of the People—Papers laid on the table on 21st June 1889," which

stated that "owing to its infertile soil and to certain accidents of tenure, [it] was among the most backward parts of Madras Presidency." Quoted in Revenue, GO, nos. 1010, 1010A, 30 September 1892, TNSA.

70. BORP, RSLRA, 27 February 1888, no. 49, TNSA.

71. This was important in the discussion of Maṟaimalaiyaṭikaḷ, Vēḷāḷar Nā-karikam [Vellala civilization] (Madras: Teṉintiya caivacittānta nūrpatipu ka-ḷakam, 1975), 24. The ideas for this book were formulated in the 1920s.

72. See the account of the attempts by South Indian missionaries and others to change the position of the paraiyars in *The Times* (London), 13 July 1891.

73. J. Lee Warner, Collector of Chingleput to Secretary to the Commissions of Land Revenue, 17 August 1889, included in BORP, LR, no. 617, 6 September 1889, TNSA.

74. C. Mullally, Sub-collector of Chingleput to Collector of Chingleput, no. 884, 25 July 1889, in no. 617, 6 September 1889, BORP, LR, TNSA. Naoroji wrote two articles in the *Contemporary Review* in response to an 1886 article written by M. E. Grant-Duff, former governor of Madras. Dadabhai Naoroji, *Speeches and Writings* (Madras, n.d.), 583.

75. Mullaly's superior, J. H. A. Tremenheere, collector of Chingleput, spoke of writers to the Madras press who signed their letters "Poor Ryot." This "Poor Ryot" was generally, he said, "a mirasidar or some other superior landholder who has sometimes never seen his land and does not even know the names of the different varieties of rice. He is perhaps an attorney, perhaps an official, often a school-boy whom Government is preparing at great expense to take a University degree; but he is very seldom a ryot in more than name. . . . Some-times indeed he has farm labourers of his own, who live in styles and know kindness neither from God or man, but he mounts a Madras platform and is eloquent on the subject of the Indian Nation, seeing no inconsistency in de-manding equal rights for all." J. H. A. Tremenheere, "Note on the Pariahs," Revenue, GO, nos. 1010, 1010A, 30 September 1892, TNSA.

76. A. K. Ramanujan, *The Interior Landscape* (Bloomington: Indiana Uni-versity Press, 1975), 107.

77. Yule and Burnell, *Hobson-Jobson*, 732.

78. Hugh Cleghorn, *The Forests and Gardens of South India* (London: W. H. Allen, 1861), 197, 205, quoted in Yule and Burnell, *Hobson-Jobson*, 732. Cleghorn had also written in another context that prickly pear "excludes the air, and harbours destructive vermin and venomous reptiles. Cultivators object to it, because it spreads, cannot be kept within bounds, and impoverishes the land." He also pointed out that, "The bandicoot rat . . . , a most destructive animal, is partial to hedges of the Opuntia [prickly pear] . . . , burrows under them to a great depth, and roots up the seeds of garden plants sown near its haunts." Hugh Cleghorn, "On the Hedge Plants of India, and conditions which adapt them for special purposes and particular localities," *The Annals and Mag-azine of Natural History*, 2d ser., no. 34 (October 1850): 239–40.

79. Madras Presidency, *The Manual of the Administration of Madras Pres-idency* (Madras: E. Keys, 1885–93), 3:720. This manual also gives specific in-structions on how to destroy prickly pear. "If left on the ground it very soon begins to grow again, and must therefore be destroyed by water or fire; for

destroying by water put it into a rather shallow pool and sink it to the bottom, with stones. In 24 hours the water will begin to get thick and muddy, in two days it smells sour, on the third day a scum rises and the whole substance of the prickly-pear is decomposed. It then makes good manure and will not grow or vegetate; for destroying by fire, cut a number of the shrubby plants that usually accompany it, spread these over the ground to the height of a foot or two, lay the prickly-pear on the top, and leave the pile to dry for some days, then set fire to the heap; if too much of the prickly-pear be piled up, it will require a second firing; potash may be prepared from the ashes." Ibid.

80. *Madras Times,* 31 January 1891.

81. J. H. A. Tremenheere, the acting collector, held a meeting at Chingleput with the subcollector and the Tahsildars in the middle of a scarcity in Chingleput. At that meeting, Tremenheere said that digging wells would be best but that other minor irrigation and clearing sites of prickly pear were also important. *Madras Times,* 4 February 1891.

82. This alternative was in accordance with his superior Collector Lee Warner's letter and with Stokes's views. BORP, no. 2377, 19 October 1881, TNSA.

83. BORP, no. 1547, 7 July 1886, TNSA. This was the case of the petition of Rangya Naidu and other Mirasidars of Nemalacheri village, in the Saidapet taluk, in 1886, the dismissal of which by Collector C. J. Galton was later upheld by the Board of Revenue on appeal. The Mirasidars in this context were angry about sixteen Christian paraiyar Padiyals. The biographer of William Goudie called this decision by Galton "the 'Magna Carta' for the lower castes of south India." J. Lewis, *William Goudie* (London: Wesleyan Methodist Missionary Society, 1923), 58.

84. C. Mullaly, Sub-collector of Chingleput to Collector of Chingleput, BORP, LR, no. 884, 25 July 1889, in no. 617, 6 September 1889, TNSA.

85. Ibid.

86. Ibid.

87. Ibid.

88. *Madras Times,* 24 December 1890.

89. *Madras Times,* 25 April 1891.

90. *Madras Times,* 5 August 1891.

91. *Madras Times,* 19 January 1891.

92. In 1891, Commissioner Booth-Tucker, heading a Salvation Army deputation to India, wrote that "in districts which are as the very Paradise of India, [there are] thousands of cases of chronic destitution (especially in certain parts of the year) such as ought to be sufficient to melt even a heart of stone." Booth-Tucker, *Darkest India* (Bombay: n.p., 1891), 2.

93. J. H. A. Tremenheere, Collector of Chingleput, to Sec. to the Commissioner of Revenue Settlement and Director of the Department of Land Records and Agriculture, 5 March 1891, BORP, 10 March 1891, no. 132, TNSA.

94. Tremenheere, "Note on the Pariahs," Revenue, GO, nos. 1010, 1010A, 30 September 1892, TNSA.

95. Revenue, GO, nos. 1010, 1010A, 30 September 1892, TNSA. It was written some time in August or early September 1891, to the secretary to the commissioner of revenue settlement and the director of the department of land

records and agriculture in Madras and bears the date 5 October 1891 and the number 1290.

96. Cited in Ibid. The following discussion is based upon that report unless otherwise noted.

97. Tremenheere, "Note on the Pariahs."

98. Ibid.

99. Ibid.

100. Ibid.

101. One of the cases to which Tremenheere obviously referred was that over the way in which mirasi holdings were sold in the area of Nungambakkam in 1801. In that case, despite a compact among Mirasidars to not sell any of their rights to non-Mirasidars, one of their number did decide to sell to a "well-to-do Tamil Brahmin, a retired head writer in the Paymaster's Department." The delinquent Mirasidar claimed that mirasi holdings had been sold to outsiders in the 1790s and that he was very much in debt. In opposition to this particular sale, the other Mirasidars of the village claimed that the new purchaser said that "he would spend some thousands of pagodas to purchase the whole village and ruin your petitioners utterly." In judging the case, the Board of Revenue decided to uphold the general right of the Mirasidars to "control as a body both the disposal of village land and mirasi rights and the entry of strangers into the village." In addition, the board ordered the defiant but poverty-struck Mirasidar to either keep his own share or to sell it to other Mirasidars in the village. At the same time, the board "opened the way for future sales of mirasi rights to outsiders by permitting this if the mirasidars of a village refused to buy at a fair price the shares offered by their fellow landowners." Finally, the board "resolved to uphold the usages of the country, and cannot sanction the purchases, but [have] determined the lands shall be first offered to the other meerasedars at a reasonable price, which if they do not purchase, he will then be at liberty to sell." Susan Neild-Basu, from whose work these excerpts have been taken, showed, however, that despite the fact that Mirasidars within the boundaries of Madras were afraid that their rights would be abrogated by purchasers, this never occurred. "Mirasi shares were not the most desirable form of landed property, at least at this time." Petition to Governor of Madras and Minute of the BOR, 19 March 1801, BORP, quoted in Neild-Basu, "Madras," 104–6. Another one of these cases occurred in the village of Tondiarpet, again within the boundaries of Madras. That case, heard in 1808, concerned a group of Mirasidars who complained that they had been "arbitrarily removed from their rights." In the mid-1790s, when Place was collector of the Jagir, Tondiarpet fell within his jurisdiction (Tondiarpet was only made part of Madras formally in 1798). The case itself concerned the respective rights of a group of Ulkkudi Payirkkaris or tenants who had fixity of tenure. These tenants were Shanars or Gramanis who tapped toddy as a profession. From the 1770s, when a substantial conflict had developed between the Shanars or Gramanis and the Mirasidars (who were nel vellalas) over whether the tenants had the right to sell their land without the consent of the Mirasidars. In 1793, the Court of Recorder—the Mayor's Court—sustained the right of the Shanars or Gramanis to sell the property, a decision later confirmed by the governor and his council. Place was then

forced to deal with the situation in 1794. But he "astounded the mirasidars and even other officials by expelling the mirasidars from Tondiarpet and recognizing the Shanars as the new mirasidars of the village." At that time, of course, Place had other goals in mind. Fourteen years later, the vellalas whose mirasi rights had been transferred by Place to the gramani Ulkkudi Payirkkaris, were able to get the case heard before the Supreme Court, the successor to the Mayor's Court. On several occasions during that time, the vellalas "attacked the Shanars and destroyed some of their houses in the village; with a mob of Paraiyars [Pannai-yals and Padiyals] in the Black Town, they accosted a notable Indian figure whom they suspected of recommending the Shanars as mirasdars to Place; they refused to obey orders coming from the Collector and threatened peons sent by Place." However, by the time this case came before the Supreme Court, Place had, of course, changed his mind and the whole movement of the government was, in fact, to support Mirasidars. It was therefore not surprising that they doubted the legality of Place's decisions and declared that the vellalas were the "rightful proprietors of the village." Though the vellalas won legal recognition for their rights as Mirasidars, their victory "was an empty one because all the property in the village had by 1808 been sold. Everything in the village is proved to have since changed hands. Its constitution appears to be changed; the Meer-assee privileges are all done away; and a new order of things, and a different set of proprietors must be taken to have succeeded." Thomas L. Strange, *Cases in the Court of Recorder and the Supreme Court at Madras* (Madras: Asylum Press, 1816), 1:319. Quoted in Neild-Basu, "Madras," 102.

102. Tremenheere, "Note on the Pariahs."

103. Ibid.

104. In an editorial of the *Madras Times* on 5 August 1891, the editor wrote, "Under the old system of agrestic slavery, they were the personal property of their masters . . . and Pariah slaves of that time received kindnesses from the higher castes. . . . By the bestowment of freedom the Pariahs were placed in a relation to their masters, which was more independent but also more distant than the old one, and on account of this it became possible for the mirasidars to become more pitiless, and this is precisely what has happened. Government has loosened the obligation of the Mirasidar to protect the Pariah, loosened the bond and relieved the mirasidar. . . . It [the government] has separated the Pa-riah and left him helpless, only it has told him that he is free."

105. Tremenheere, "Note on the Pariahs."

106. Ibid.

107. William Goudie, "The Pariahs and the Land," *Harvest Field* (15 July 1894): 493.

108. Ibid.

109. F. W. Ellis, Appendix.

110. According to a village study of a group of untouchables in the Chin-gleput taluk during the 1970s, Moffatt found that, at least in the village that he studied, several important changes in behavior had taken place over the previous half century. Moffatt showed that, by the 1960s in the Chingleput district gen-erally though 50 percent of the upper castes owned land, 30 percent of the untouchables also did so. This, he felt, has locked many of the rural untouch-

ables "into a modern peasant adaptation, tending to foster political conservatism." Moffatt, *An Untouchable Community*, 46, 49.

111. Margaret Trawick, "Spirits and Voices in Tamil Songs," *American Ethnologist* 15, no. 2 (May 1988): 203, 205, 207–8, 212.

112. Ellis, in 1816, had written that the paraiyars sometimes "claim miras or hereditary private property" and that "it is generally allowed to them and their descendants on proving their former residence in the village, however long they may have been absent." Quoted in the Minute of the Board of Revenue, 5 January 1818, BOR Misc., vol. 257A, TNSA.

113. Place, 1795 Report, para. 36, quoted in BOR Note, Revenue, GO, nos. 1010, 1010A, 30 September 1892, TNSA.

114. Ellis, Appendix, quoted in BOR Minute, Revenue, GO, nos. 1010, 1010A, 30 September 1892, TNSA.

115. Crole, *Chingleput*, 213–14, quoted by the board, Revenue, GO, nos. 1010, 1010A, 30 September 1892, TNSA.

116. Tremenheere, "Note on the Pariahs."

117. Ibid.

118. BOR Minute, Revenue, GO, nos. 1010, 1010A, 30 September 1892, TNSA.

119. Ibid.

120. Ibid.

121. Revenue, GO, nos. 1010, 1010A, 30 September 1892, TNSA.

122. Baden-Powell, *Land Systems*, 121–22.

123. Place, 1799 Report, paras. 62–63.

CONCLUSION

1. Native Officer, *On Bribery*, 15.

2. Perhaps the work that best epitomizes this activity, aside from that of Henry Sumner Maine, is Baden-Powell, *Land Systems*.

3. Baden-Powell, *Land Systems*, 3:121. He writes, "Brahman (and other) proprietors largely employed slaves to cultivate for them: and these slaves were looked upon as *glebae adscripti*. It is curious that these also called themselves 'mirasidar.' . . . 'The Vellala,' they said, 'sells his birthright to the Sunar (goldsmith and moneylender); the latter is cajoled.' "

4. The citation for Baden-Powell is Crole, *Chingleput*, 213.

5. P. B. Smollett to BOR, 27 January 1855, CCR, vol. 5836, TNSA. This proposition was sent to the House of Commons by the Madras Native Association in 1854 or 1855. Several members of the Madras Native Association were Mirasidars from the Chingleput district.

6. Ellis, Appendix, quoting Place, 1799 Report.

7. P. B. Smollett to BOR, 27 November 1854, CCR, vol. 5835, TNSA.

8. Crole said that it was "clear as noon-day, from these papers, that the mirassi system and a gross rental are inseparable parts of the system he [Place] exhumed and introduced." BORP, 25 May 1875, no. 1415, TNSA.

9. Tremenheere, "Note on the Pariahs."

10. Toṇṭa maṇṭala sataka urai (Commentary on the Tonda Mandala Sataka) in Citambaram Irāmaliṅka Suvāmikaḷ, Tiru Aruṭpā, 3 Viyakiyāṉam pakuti (Song of grace, part 3) (Madras: Arutpa Valakam, 1961), 154. It was originally published by the Ripon Press in Madras (p. 139).

11. Ibid.

12. Ibid.

13. Ibid., 156. The quality of sattuvam was goodness or purity, rajas was passion or activity, and tamas was darkness, dullness, or inactivity. See commentary in Franklin Edgerton, trans., The Bhagavad Gita (Harper and Row: New York, 1944), 141.

14. Toḷuvūr Vēlāyuta Mutaliyār, Vēlaṉ Marapiyal [Vellala customs] (Madras: Kudalur Kuppiyappillai, 1880). This was a translation into Tamil of an English petition presented to the Madras municipal commissioners.

15. Maṟaimalaiyaṭikaḷ, Velalar Nakarikam, 6–7.

16. The contemporary dictionary meaning of "velanmai" was agriculture.

17. Arjun Appadurai and Carol Breckenridge, "Public Culture," Items (Winter 1990), 79.

18. Velalar Nakarikam, 3.

19. Ibid., 5.

20. In 1905, Reverend Adam Andrew, a United Free Church of Scotland missionary in Chingleput, invoked the ideas of Kambar, the author of the Tamil Rāmāyaṇam in favor of agriculture. Andrew wrote: "Kambar, the Tamil poet has written beautifully in praise of agriculture. He has said, 'Even students of the Vedas and in other branches of knowledge must wait at the door of the husbandman. The prosperity of powerful kings depends on the plough share. So who can describe the importance of the agriculturist?' " Andrew invoked the writing of Tiruvalluvar, the author of the Tirukural, in favor of the importance of agriculture. Tiruvalluvar, said Andrew, had written:

> Howe'er they roam, the world must follow still the plougher's team;
> Though toilsome, culture of the ground as noblest toil esteem.

Adam Andrew, "Indian Problems," Indian Review (1905), 32; "Uḷavu" [Agriculture], Tirukural, no. 1035, quoted in ibid., 6.

21. Maraimalaiyatikal, Velalar Nakarikam, 12.

22. Baden-Powell, Land System, 3:111.

23. Ibid., 112–13.

24. Baker, Indian rural economy, 25–26.

25. Dirks, Hollow Crown, 248.

26. Ibid., 205.

27. Padre Manente had brought a group of 351 families from the northern Telugu "circar" of Guntur, where there was a famine in 1787, to the Jagir where those settlements, even in the late nineteenth century, were still intact. Crole, Chingleput, 237; President's Minute, 17 October, 1786, BORP, vol. 8, TNSA; Minute of the Board of Revenue and enclosures, 20 November 1786, BORP, vol. 5, TNSA.

Place forced many Mirasidars to sign an agreement to plant bamboo and other trees as a requirement for getting the right to rent their villages. That agreement or muchalka said, "We [the Mirasidars] will keep all our water-courses in good repair, attend to the planting of coconut, honey trees and bam-boo trees according to the Circar's [government's] orders or abide by such pun-ishment as may be inflicted." Place to BOR, 10 November 1796, BORP, vol. 168, TNSA.

28. In writing about the visit of some church deputies from Scotland to the area in February 1902, Reverend Andrew said that he had taken them to Mel-rosapuram. He wrote, "On Saturday they visited the Peasant Settlement of Melrosapuram and saw the land that was jungle in 1893 now converted into a neat and prosperous village inhabited by Christian converts of the mission, where daily services are held morning and evening to meet the spiritual wants of the people. They saw the fine garden that surrounds the prayer hall and walked up the village street which is lined on each side with beautiful coconut palms." Andrew to Smith, 22 February 1902, UFCSM, MS. 7845, NLS. Mel-rosapuram was a settlement that had seventy-two acres of land around it near the village of Senkunram, in the Chingleput taluk. It was called Melrosapuram after a certain Mrs. Melrose who had, along with other members of a congre-gation in Scotland, made a contribution of a hundred pounds for Andrew's work among the paraiyars in Chingleput.

29. Henry Sumner Maine, *Early History of Institutions,* new ed. (London: J. Murray, 1890), 70–72.

30. Ci. En. Aṇṇāturai, *Ellōrum in nāṭṭu maṉṉar* (Everybody is a king of the country), (Cennai: Tuyarmalar Patippakam, 1961).

Bibliography

ARCHIVAL SOURCES

Tamil Nad State Archives, Madras

Assigned Revenue Letterbooks. Vol. 13.
Board of Assigned Revenue Proceedings. Vols. 1, 4, 8.
Board of Revenue, Miscellaneous.
   Ellis, F. W. "Appendix [to the] replies to the questions respecting meerasi Right." 1814. Vol. 233.
   Place, Lionel. Report on the Jagir. 1799. Vol. 45.
Board of Revenue Proceedings.
   Land Revenue.
   Revenue Settlement, Local Records, and Agriculture.
Chingleput Collectorate Records.
Jaghire Books. Vols. 3, 8.
Jagir Records. Vols. 2, 3, 5, 6.
Madras Collectorate Records. Vols. 1021, 1022, 5514.
Private Letterbooks. Vol. 41.
Public Proceedings.
Revenue Proceedings.
   Tremenheere, J. H. A. "Notes on the Pariahs," Revenue, GO, nos. 1010, 1010A, 30 September 1892.

India Office Library and Records, London

Board of Revenue Proceedings.
   Miscellany Book.
Board's Collections.
Erskine Collection.

Ellis, F. W. "Lectures on Hindu Law." MS. Eur. D. 31.
Home Miscellaneous Series. Vols. 113, 223, 259.
Mackenzie Collection (General).
"Historical account of the government of Chingleput Rajah." Translated
    from the Marathi into English in the early nineteenth century. Vol. 9.
Police Committee Proceedings. Vol. 4.
Revenue, Government Orders.
Special Commission on the Permanent Settlement, Proceedings.

Archives d'outre mer, Aix-en-Provence

Feuilles Volantes no. 595, Fond Inde.

Madras Oriental Manuscripts Library, Madras

Kurumpar carittiram [History of the Kurumbar], Mackenzie MSS R. 8189.
Mayilapūr kantapparācan caritam [History of Kandapparajan of Mylapur],
    Mackenzie MSS R. 8141.
Nerumpūr kurumpar kōṭṭai kaipītu [Narrative account of the Kurumbar fort at
    Nerumbur], Mackenzie MSS R. 7754.
Toṇṭaimān cakkiravartti carittiram [History of Tondaiman Cakkiravartti],
    Mackenzie MSS R. 8350.

*United Free Church of Scotland Mission Archives, National
Library of Scotland, Edinburgh*

MSS vols. 7845, 7846.

NON-ARCHIVAL SOURCES

Exhibitions and Videos

"Tigers Round the Throne." Exhibition. Zamana Gallery, London. August
    1990.
Granada Television, *Empire!* Video, 1991.

Contemporary Published Works

Adam, William. *The Law and Custom of Slavery in British India*. Boston:
    Weeks, Jordan, and Company, 1840.
Andrew, Adam. "Indian Problems." *Indian Review*. 1905, 30–35.
Baden-Powell, B. H. *The Land Systems of British India*. 3 vols. Oxford: Clar-
    endon Press, 1892.
Booth, Charles, ed. *Life and Labour of the People of London*. 7 vols. 1889.
    Reprint. New York: Augustus M. Kelley, 1969.
Booth, "General" William. *In Darkest England and the Way Out*. London:
    International Headquarters of the Salvation Army, 1890.
Booth-Tucker, Commissioner. *Darkest India*. Bombay: n.p., 1891.
Bosanquet, Bernard. *Aspects of the Social Problem*. New York: Macmillan and
    Co., 1895.

"British Acquisitions in the Presidency of Fort St. George." *Madras Journal of Literature and Science.* 1879.

Brown, C. P., ed. *Three treatises on Mirasi Right . . . with the remarks made by the Hon'ble the Court of Directors.* Madras: D.P.L.C. Connor, 1852.

Chadwick, Edwin. *Report on the Sanitary Conditions of the Labouring Population of Great Britain.* London: H. M. Stationery Office, 1843.

Cleghorn, Hugh. *The Forests and Gardens of South India.* London: W. H. Allen, 1861.

———. "On the Hedge Plants of India, and conditions which adapt them for special purposes and particular localities." *The Annals and Magazine of Natural History,* 2d ser., no. 34 (October 1850): 239–40.

Crole, C. S. *The Chingleput, late Madras, District.* Madras: Lawrence Asylum Press, 1879.

Digby, William. *The Famine Campaign in Southern India (Madras and Bombay Presidencies and province of Mysore) 1876–1878.* London: Longmans, Green, 1878.

———. *India for the Indians—and for England.* London: Talbot Brothers, 1885.

Dubois, Abbe J. A. *Hindu Manners, Customs, and Ceremonies.* Translated by Henry K. Beauchamp. 3d ed. Oxford: Clarendon Press, 1906.

Edgerton, Franklin, trans. *The Bhagavad Gita.* Harper and Row: New York, 1944.

Ellis, Francis. "Account of a Discovery of a Modern Imitation of the Vedas, With Remarks on the Genuine Works." *Asiatic Researches or Transactions of the Society Instituted in Bengal for Enquiring into the History and Antiquities, the Arts, Sciences, and Literature, of Asia* 14 (1822): 1–59.

Ellis, F. W. *Replies to seventeen questions proposed by the Government of Fort St. George relative to Mirasi Right with two appendices elucidatory of the subject.* Madras: Government Gazette Office, 1818.

Gleig, G. R. *The Life of Major General Sir Thomas Munro, Bart.* London: Henry Colburn and Richard Bently, 1831.

Goudie, William. "The Pariahs and the Land." *Harvest Field* 15 (July 1894): 490–500.

Grant-Duff, M. E. "India: A Reply to Mr. Samuel Smith, M.P." *Contemporary Review* 51 (January–June 1887): 8–31, 181–195.

Horrible London (London: Chatto and Windus, 1889).

How the Poor Live (London: Chatto and Windus, 1889).

Hunter, W. W. *The Annals of Rural Bengal.* Reprint. Calcutta: Indian Studies, 1965.

Irāmalingaswāmi, Cuvāmikaḷ. *Toṇṭa maṇṭala sataka urai* (Commentary on the *Tonda Mandala Sataka*). In Citambaram Irāmalinka Cuvāmikaḷ, *Tiru Arutpā, 3 Viyakiyāṉam pakuti* (Song of grace, part 3). Madras: Ripon Press, 1855. Reprint. Madras: Arutpa valakam, 1961.

Kaye, John William. *Christianity in India: An historical narrative.* London: Smith, Elder and Co., 1859.

Keay, J. Seymour. "The Spoliation of India." *The Nineteenth Century* 14 (July–December 1883): 1–22.

Keay, J. Seymour. "The Spoliation of India." *The Nineteenth Century* 15 (January–June 1884): 559–618.

Der Königl. Dänischen Missionarien aus Ost-Indieneingesandter ausführlichen Berichten, Erster Theil, Vom ersten ausführlichen Bericht an bis zu dessen zwölfter *Continuation* mitgetheilet. Halle: Verlegung des Weysenhauses, 1735.

The Manual of the Administration of Madras Presidency. 3 vols. Madras: E. Keys, 1885–93.

Maraimalaiyaṭikaḷ. *Vēlāḷar Nākarikam* [Vellala civilization]. Madras: Tenintiya caivacittanta nurpatipu kalakam, 1975.

Masterman, C. F. G., ed. *The Heart of the Empire; Discussions of Problems of Modern City Life in England.* 1901. Reprint. New York: Barnes and Noble, 1973.

Mayhew, Henry. *London Labour and London Poor; a Cyclopedia of the Condition of those that Will Work, Those that Cannot, and Those that Will Not Work.* 2 vols. London: Griffen, Bohn, and Co., 1861.

Maine, Henry Sumner. *Early History of Institutions.* New ed. London: J. Murray, 1890.

Mearns, Reverend Andrew. *The Bitter Cry of Outcaste London: An Inquiry into the Condition of the Abject Poor.* London: James Clarke and Co., 1883.

Moreland, W. H. *India at the Death of Akbar: An Economic Study.* 1920. Reprint. Delhi: Atma Ram and Sons, 1962.

Naoroji, Dadabhai. "Poverty of India." *Poverty and Un-British Rule in India.* 1873. Reprint. New Delhi: Publications Division, 1962.

———. "Sir M. E. Grant Duff's Views about India." *Contemporary Review* 52 (August 1887): 221–35, 694–711.

———. *Essays, speeches, and writings.* Edited by C. L. Parikh. Bombay, 1887.

———. *Speeches and Writings.* Madras, n.d.

A Native Revenue Officer. *On Bribery as Practiced in the Revenue administration of the Madras Presidency.* Madras: Hindu Press, 1858.

Orme, Robert. *Transactions of the British Nation in Indostan.* 2d ed. 3 vols. London: John Nourse, 1775.

Ramaswami Naidoo, Bundla. *Memoir of the Internal Revenue system of the Madras Presidency, Selections from the Records of the South Arcot District.* No. 11. Madras: Superintendent, Government Press, 1908.

Skrine, Francis Henry. *Life of Sir William Wilson Hunter.* London: Longmans, Green and Co., 1901.

Smith, Samuel. "India Revisited." *Contemporary Review* 49 (January–June 1886): 794–819.

Smith, Samuel, MP. *My Life Work.* London: Hodder and Stoughton, 1902.

Srinivasa Raghavaiyangar, S. *Memorandum on the Progress of the Madras Presidency during the Last Forty Years of British Administration.* Madras: Superintendent, Government Press, 1893.

Stanley, Henry Morton. *In Darkest Africa; or, The quest, rescue and retreat of Emin, governor of Equatoria.* 2 vols. London: S. Low, Marston, Searle and Rivington, 1890.

Vēlāyuta Mutaliyār, Toluvūr. *Vēlan Marapiyal* [Vellala customs]. Madras: Kudalur Kuppiyappillai, 1880.

Vētanāyaka Piḷḷai, Mayūram. *Piratāpa Mutaliyār.* 1879. Reprint. Madras: Sakti kariyalayam, 1957.

Wilks, Mark. *Historical Sketches of the South of India in an Attempt to Trace the History of Mysoor.* Edited by Murray Hammick. 2 vols. Mysore: Government Branch Press, 1930.

Wilson, H. H. *Glossary of Judicial and Revenue Terms.* 1855. Reprint. Delhi: Munshiram Manoharlal, 1968.

Periodicals and Newspapers

The Hindu.
The Madras Times.
The Times (London).

Dissertations and Unpublished Papers

Barnett, Stephen Allen. "The structural position of a south Indian caste: the kondaikatti vellala-s in Tamil Nadu." Ph.D. diss., University of Chicago, 1970.

Blackburn, Stuart. "Inside the Drama-House: The Rama Story as Shadow Puppet Play in Kerala." Forthcoming.

Gurney, John. "The Debts of the Nawab of Arcot." Ph.D. diss., Oxford University, 1964.

Ludden, David. "Agricultural Expansion, Diversification, and Commodity Production in Peninsular India, c. 1550–1800." Presented at the Association of Asian Studies meeting, San Francisco, 25 March 1988.

Neild-Basu, Susan. "Madras: The Growth of a Colonial City, 1780–1840," Ph.D. diss., University of Chicago, 1977.

Van Hollen, Cecelia. "The Role of Civil Society in Orientalist and Anti-Colonial Discourses: Women as Model Citizens." Berkeley, 1991.

Printed Books and Articles

Amin, Shahid. "Gandhi as Mahatma." In *Selected Subaltern Studies.* Edited by Ranajit Guha and Gayatri Chakravorty Spivak. New York: Oxford University Press, 1988.

Aṇṇāturai, Ci. Eṉ. *Ellōrum innāṭṭu maṉṉar* (Everybody is a king of the country). Cennai: Tuyarmalar Patippakam, 1961.

Appadurai, Arjun. "Right and Left Hand Castes in South India." *Indian Economic and Social History Review* 11, nos. 2, 3 (June–September 1974): 216–59.

———. *Worship and Conflict under Colonial Rule: A South Indian Case.* Cambridge: Cambridge University Press, 1981.

Appadurai, Arjun, and Carol Breckenridge. "Public Culture." *Items* (Winter 1990): 78–79.

Arasaratnam, S. "Trade and Political Dominion in South India, 1750–1790: Changing British-Indian Relationships," *Modern Asian Studies* 13, no. 1 (February 1979): 19–40.

Arnold, David. *Police Power and Colonial Rule: Madras 1859–1947.* Delhi: Oxford University Press, 1986.

Bailey, F. G. *Stratagems and Spoils.* Oxford: Basil Blackwell, 1969.

Baker, Christopher John. *An Indian Rural Economy, 1880–1955, The Tamil Countryside.* Oxford: Clarendon Press, 1984.

Bakhtin, M. M. *The Dialogic Imagination: Four Essays.* Translated by Caryl Emerson and Michael Holquist, edited by Michael Holquist. Austin: University of Texas Press, 1981.

———. *Rabelais and His World.* Translated by Helene Iswolsky. Cambridge, Mass.: M. I. T. Press, 1968.

Basham, A. L. *The Wonder that was India.* London: Sidgwick and Jackson, 1954.

Bayly, C. A. *Rulers, Townsmen and Bazaars.* Cambridge: Cambridge University Press, 1983.

Breckenridge, Carol. "From protector to litigant—changing relations between Hindu temples and the Raja of Ramnad." In *South India Temples.* Edited by Burton Stein. New Delhi: Vikas Publishing House, 1978.

Brennig, Joseph J. "Chief Merchants and the European Enclaves of Seventeenth-century Coromandel." *Modern Asian Studies* 11 (1977): 321–40.

Brown, Judith M. *Gandhi: Prisoner of Hope.* New Haven: Yale University Press, 1989.

Chandra, Bipan. *The Rise and Growth of Economic Nationalism in India: Economic Policies of Indian National Leadership, 1880–1905.* New Delhi: People's Publishing House, 1966.

Chingleput: *A Statistical Atlas of the Madras Province, Statistical Atlas for the Decennium ending Fasli 1350 (1940–41).* Madras: Superintendent, Government Press, 1949.

Cohn, Bernard S. *An Anthropologist Among the Historians and Other Essays.* Delhi: Oxford University Press, 1990.

Cuntara Rākavaṉ, Kē., and Kē. Ranka Rākavaṉ. *Tivāṉ Pahatūr Śrīnivāsaṟākavaiyāṅkār.* N.p., n.d.

Dictionary of National Biography. Oxford: Clarendon University Press, 1917.

Dirks, Nicholas. *The Hollow Crown: Ethnohistory of an Indian Kingdom.* Cambridge: Cambridge University Press, 1987.

Elias, Norbert. *The History of Manners.* Vol. 1 of *The Civilizing Process.* Translated by Edmund Jephcott. New York: Pantheon Books, 1978.

———. *Power and Civility.* Vol. 2 of *The Civilizing Process.* Translated by Edmund Jephcott. New York: Pantheon Books, 1978.

Foster, George M. "Colonial Administration in Northern Rhodesia in 1962." *Human Organization* 46, no. 4 (Winter 1987): 359–68.

Fox, Richard. *Lions of the Punjab.* Berkeley: University of California Press, 1987.

———. *Gandhian Utopia: Experiments with Culture.* Boston: Beacon Press, 1989.

Fuller, C. J. *Servants of the Goddess: The Priests of a South Indian Temple.* Cambridge: Cambridge University Press, 1984.

Gallagher, Catherine. *The Industrial Reformation of English Fiction: Social Discourse and the Narrative Form, 1832–67.* Chicago: University of Chicago Press, 1985.

————. "The Body Versus the Social Body in the Works of Thomas Malthus and Henry Mayhew." In *The Making of the Modern Body: Sexuality and Society in the Nineteenth Century*. Edited by Thomas Laquer and Catherine Gallagher. Berkeley: University of California Press, 1987.

Ginzburg, Carlo. *The Cheese and the Worms*. Baltimore: Johns Hopkins University Press, 1980.

Goffman, Erving. "The Nature of Deference and Demeanor." In *Interaction Ritual*. New York: Pantheon Books, 1967.

Hay, Douglas. "Property, Authority and the Criminal Law." In *Albion's Fatal Tree: Crime and Society in Eighteenth century England*. Edited by Douglas Hay et al. Harmondsworth: Penguin Books, 1975.

Hill, S. C. *Yusuf Khan: The Rebel Commandant*. London: Longmans, Green and Co., 1914.

Historical Records of the Survey of India. 6 vols. Collected by R. H. Phillimore. Dehra Dun, 1945.

Hjejle, Benedicte. "Slavery and agricultural bondage in south India in the nineteenth century." *The Scandinavian Economic History Review* 15, nos. 1–2 (1967): 71–126.

Hobsbawm, Eric, and Terrence Ranger, eds. *The Invention of Tradition*. Cambridge: Cambridge University Press, 1983.

Inglis, K. S. *Churches and the Working Classes in Victorian England*. London: Routledge and Kegan Paul, 1963.

Irschick, Eugene F. *Politics and Social Conflict in South India*. Berkeley: University of California Press, 1969.

————. "Peasant Survival Strategies and Rehearsals for Rebellion in Eighteenth-Century South India." *Peasant Studies* 9, no. 4 (Summer 1982): 215–41.

Kolff, D. H. A. "Sannyasi Trader-Soldiers." *Indian Economic and Social History Review* 8, no. 2 (June 1971): 211–18.

Kumar, Dharma. *Land and Caste in South India: Agricultural Labour in the Madras Presidency During the Nineteenth Century*. Cambridge: Cambridge University Press, 1965.

Lewis, J. *William Goudie*. London: Wesleyan Methodist Missionary Society, 1923.

Love, H. Davidson. *Vestiges of Old Madras, 1640–1800*. 4 vols. London: John Murray, 1913.

Marshall, Peter. *The British Discovery of Hinduism in the Eighteenth Century*. Cambridge: Cambridge University Press, 1970.

McLane, John R. *Indian Nationalism and the Early Congress*. Princeton: Princeton University Press, 1977.

Mennell, Stephen. *Norbert Elias: Civilization and the Human Self-Image*. London: Basil Blackwell, 1989.

Mines, Mattison. *The Merchant-Warriors: Textiles, Trade and Territory in South India*. Cambridge: Cambridge University Press, 1984.

Mines, Mattison, and Vijayalakshmi Gourishankar. "Leadership and Individuality in South Asia: The Case of the South Indian Big Man." *Journal of Asian Studies* 49, no. 4 (November 1990): 761–86.

Moffatt, Michael. *An Untouchable Community in South India: Structure and Consensus.* Princeton: Princeton University Press, 1979.

Moore, Barrington. *Social Origins of Dictatorship and Democracy: Lord and Peasant in the Making of the Modern World.* Boston: Beacon Press, 1966.

Murton, Brian. "Key People in the Countryside: Decisionmakers in Interior Tamilnadu in the Late Eighteenth Century." *Indian Economic and Social History Review* 10, no. 2 (June 1973): 157–80.

Nandy, Ashis. *The Intimate Enemy: Loss and Recovery of Self Under Colonialism.* Delhi: Oxford University Press, 1983.

Neild-Basu, Susan. "The Dubashes of Madras." *Modern Asian Studies* 18, no. 1 (February 1984): 1–31.

Pandey, Gyanendra. " 'Encounters and Calamities': The History of a North Indian *Qasba* in the Nineteenth Century." In *Selected Subaltern Studies.* Edited by Ranajit Guha and Gayatri Spivak. New York: Oxford University Press, 1988.

Princep, Charles. *Record of Services of the Honourable East India Company's Civil Servants in the Madras Presidency from 1741 to 1858.* London: Trubners Co., 1885.

Ram, Ganga. *The Maharashta Purana: An Eighteenth-Century Bengali Historical Text.* Translated and edited by Edward Dimock and P. C. Gupta. Honolulu: East-West Center Press, 1965.

Ramanujan, A. K. *The Interior Landscape.* Bloomington: Indiana University Press, 1975.

Sahlins, Marshall. *Islands of History.* Chicago: University of Chicago Press, 1987.

Said, Edward. *Orientalism.* New York: Vintage Books, 1978.

Sarada Raju, A. *Economic Conditions in the Madras Presidency, 1800–1850.* Madras: University of Madras Press, 1941.

Select Committee on the East India Company: The Fifth Report on the Affairs of the East India Company. 3 vols. Madras: J. Higgenbotham, 1866.

Spodek, Howard. "On the origins of Gandhi's political methodology: The heritage of Kathiawad and Gujarat." *Journal of Asian Studies* 30, no. 1 (February 1971): 361–72.

Stokes, Eric. *The English Utilitarians and India.* Oxford: Clarendon Press, 1959.

Tambiah, Stanley. *World Conqueror and World Renouncer: A Study of Buddhism and Polity in Thailand Against a Historical Background.* Cambridge: Cambridge University Press, 1976.

Tamil Lexicon. 6 vols. Madras: University of Madras, 1982.

Thurston, Edgar. *The Tribes and Castes of South India.* 7 vols. Madras: Government Press, 1909.

Todorov, Tzvetan. *The Conquest of America: The Question of the Other.* New York: Harper and Row, 1982.

Trawick, Margaret. "Spirits and Voices in Tamil Songs." *American Ethnologist* 15, no. 2 (May 1988): 193–215.

Visvanathan, Gauri. *Masks of Power: Literary Study and British Rule in India.* New York: Columbia University Press, 1989.

Washbrook, David. "Progress and Problems: South Asian Economic and Social History c. 1720–1860." *Modern Asian Studies* 22, no. 1 (February 1988): 57–96.

Wheeler, J. Talboys. *Annals of the Madras Presidency*. Delhi: B. R. Publishing Corporation, 1985.

Wilson, W. J. *History of the Madras Army*. 2 vols. Madras: E. Keys at the Government Press, 1882.

Wink, André. *Land and Sovereignty in India*. Cambridge: Cambridge University Press, 1986.

Wohl, Anthony S. "Introduction." In *The Bitter Cry of Outcast London*. New York: Humanities Press, 1970.

Yang, Anand. *The Limited Raj: Agrarian Relations in Colonial India, Saran District, 1793–1920*. Berkeley: University of California Press, 1990.

Yeatts, M. W. M. Madras Report. Vol. 14 of *Census of India*. Madras: Superintendent, Government Press, 1932.

Yule, Henry, and A. C. Burnell. *Hobson-Jobson*. 2d ed. New Delhi: Munshiram Manoharlal, 1968.

Index

257